Praise for

An accessible guide to the confusing and fast-growing world of crypto scams. If you're thinking of investing in cryptocurrency, read this first! JAMIE BARTLETT, HOST OF BBC PODCAST *THE MISSING CRYPTOQUEEN*, AUTHOR OF *THE PEOPLE VS TECH*, *THE DARK NET*, *RADICALS* AND *THE MISSING CRYPTOQUEEN*, PRESENTER AND JOURNALIST

Crypto has proved the quickest get-rich scheme in all history. Unfortunately, the easiest people to rip off are those hoping to get rich quick, so scam after inevitable scam has preyed on the sector. Erica Stanford's page turner tells their bitter, but compelling stories. DOMINIC FRISBY, COMEDIAN, ACTOR, *MONEYWEEK* COLUMNIST AND AUTHOR OF *DAYLIGHT ROBBERY*

Erica Stanford covers everything that is oh so wrong and oh so right about the transformational world of cryptocurrencies. Prepare to laugh, cringe or be spooked. This book combines technology, business, mystery, fantasy and popular culture in a fascinating and enlightening way. And the best part: it's all true. ANTHONY DAY, BLOCKCHAIN PARTNER, IBM, AND HOST OF *BLOCKCHAIN WON'T SAVE THE WORLD* PODCAST

Fascinating read on the boom days of crypto's Initial Coin Offerings, analysing the hype that threatened to overshadow the technology. Erica Stanford captures the mood and energy of the time in this greatly entertaining and insightful work. CAROLINE CASEY, VICE PRESIDENT, INNOVATION AND CONSUMER EXPERIENCE, EUROPE, MASTERCARD

In what other book could you read about the biggest Ponzi schemes in the world, espionage, an $800 billion bubble, fake death, cryptoqueens, gambling and porn – literally 50 shades of the dodgiest grey with regulators and the FBI in hot pursuit? Erica Stanford brilliantly analyses the future of crypto in a world where the real future including security-backed tokens and CBDC's is only just beginning. BOB WIGLEY, CHAIR UK FINANCE, CO-CHAIR, CROSS MARKET OPERATIONAL RESILIENCE GROUP, BANK OF ENGLAND, BOARD MEMBER, DEPARTMENT OF INTERNATIONAL TRADE AND UK HOME OFFICE, NED, ADJUNCT PROFESSOR AND AUTHOR OF *BORN DIGITAL*

A marvellous romp through the crazy world of cryptocurrency and its wackier elements. But as well as the fun, we get a glimpse into what might one day give the global financial system a run for its money. MIKE BUTCHER MBE, EDITOR-AT-LARGE, TECHCRUNCH

*Crypto Wars* is a fascinating and gripping account of human nature and its demons emerging from the frontiers of the crypto economy. It is mandatory reading for investors, regulators and builders of our financial future. LEX SOKOLIN, FINTECH FUTURIST AND PHILOSOPHER, FOUNDER, THE FINTECH BLUEPRINT, AND HEAD ECONOMIST, CONSENSYS

This book is essential reading, especially for anyone thinking of dipping even their little toe into cryptocurrency. SARA VAUGHAN, INNOVATOR AND CREATOR OF GLOBAL BRANDS WITH PURPOSE, POSITIVE CHANGE MAKER

Erica Stanford takes readers through the complicated history of crypto hacks, scams and pump and dump schemes with such vivid detail and engaging narrative, you'll find it hard to put the book down. LESLIE LAMB, HEAD OF INSTITUTIONAL SALES, AMBER GROUP, AND HOST OF THE *CRYPTO UNSTACKED* PODCAST

As the market booms it's timely that someone has done justice to the extraordinary story of crypto – this unputdownable book captures the fun and the ups and the downs. It's a mesmeric read. CHARLIE KERRIGAN, PARTNER AND GLOBAL HEAD OF FINTECH, CMS

Erica Stanford's entertaining exploration of the world of scams, grifts, frauds and fantasies serves as a reminder that while on the one hand there is nothing new under the sun, on the other hand we have barely begun to understand the impact of cryptocurrency. DAVID BIRCH, AUTHOR OF *THE CURRENCY COLD WAR* AND INTERNATIONAL ADVISER AND COMMENTATOR ON DIGITAL FINANCIAL SERVICES

# Crypto Wars

## *Faked deaths, missing billions and industry disruption*

Erica Stanford

KoganPage

First published in Great Britain and the United States in 2021 by Kogan Page Limited

| 2nd Floor, 45 Gee Street | 122 W 27th St, 10th Floor | 4737/23 Ansari Road |
| London | New York, NY 10001 | Daryaganj |
| EC1V 3RS | USA | New Delhi 110002 |
| United Kingdom | | India |

www.koganpage.com

Kogan Page books are printed on paper from sustainable forests.

**ISBNs**

| Hardback | 978 1 3986 0069 0 |
| Paperback | 978 1 3986 0068 3 |
| Ebook | 978 1 3986 0070 6 |

**British Library Cataloguing-in-Publication Data**

A CIP record for this book is available from the British Library.

**Library of Congress Cataloging-in-Publication Data**

Names: Stanford, Erica, author.
Title: Crypto wars: faked deaths, missing billions and industry disruption / Erica Stanford.
Description: London; New York, NY: Kogan Page, 2021. | Includes bibliographical references and index.
Identifiers: LCCN 2021014955 (print) | LCCN 2021014956 (ebook) | ISBN 9781398600683 (paperback) | ISBN 9781398600690 (hardback) | ISBN 9781398600706 (ebook)
Subjects: LCSH: Commercial crimes. | Cryptocurrencies. | Swindlers and swindling.
Classification: LCC HV6768 .S727 2021 (print) | LCC HV6768 (ebook) | DDC 364.16/8–dc23
LC record available at https://lccn.loc.gov/2021014955
LC ebook record available at https://lccn.loc.gov/2021014956

Typeset by Integra Software Services Pondicherry
Print production managed by Jellyfish
Printed and bound by CPI Group (UK) Ltd, Croydon CR0 4YY

created cryptocurrencies not because having a cryptocurrency was an essential part of their project or necessary as a means of payment, but because, for a short while, launching one was an easy way to raise no-questions-asked money for their founders. The bubble surrounding the newest buzzword, initial coin offering, or ICO, was just taking off.

## The miracle technology

In early 2017, many people were starting to hear talk of blockchain technology for the first time. Blockchain – a decentralized and arguably more secure way of storing data and sending information and money – had been around since the invention of Bitcoin – and similar concepts since long before that – but by now companies were starting to use, or at least to investigate, how and if they should be using the technology.

Blockchain as a technology is game-changing for industries all around the world, providing transparency and accountability on a whole new level, but it's a new technology that is still rapidly evolving. In 2017 and 2018 it was hyped up just a little. It was highlighted not just as a technology but as the miracle technology to solve all problems. Blockchain, it was promised, would revolutionize every existing industry. Industries and markets that had existed for centuries and were worth trillions of dollars would be disrupted, collapsed and turned on their heads. Banks would collapse, and every industry from retail to religion, real estate to dentistry, porn to dating would be on blockchain. Big claims were made, and many literally believed that the existing players – giants such as eBay or Amazon or Google – would be replaced by the new wave of blockchain-based start-ups that promised to change the world just because they used – or claimed to use – blockchain.

This was the environment in which initial coin offerings became hyped and popularized beyond their founders' wildest dreams. ICOs made out that their start-ups – often little more than one-man bands – would change how these entire industries worked, that everything would need to go on blockchain, and that everything, regardless of whether it was already perfectly possible and easy to pay for by conventional means, would be paid for in cryptocurrency. People believed it, lapping up these claims and throwing billions upon billions of dollars into these projects – money that was mostly never to be seen again.

## The big bubble

In 2017, the crypto markets, already hugely volatile, erupted in a giant over-inflated bubble. Markets notorious for hacks, thefts and money laundering descended further into a Wild West known for scams, Ponzi schemes, corrupt infrastructure and thousands of joke projects which raised billions and dominated and distorted entire markets.

This bubble was largely spiked by initial coin offerings, which were a relatively new way of raising funds via cryptocurrency. ICOs allowed companies to create tokens out of thin air and sell those instead of issuing shares. This was great for companies; they could raise money without having to give away equity or go through a lot of red tape, all in the ease of an unregulated market where pretty much anything went. ICOs effectively offered a way for newly formed companies to raise vast amounts of funds without regulation, without having to do anything to first create a product or provide any accountability to anyone. Creating an ICO didn't require a company to do very much at all, except for paying someone on a freelancer site to build a website and list the token for sale on a handful of crypto-targeted platforms.

ICOs raised, by any definition of the word, silly money. Under normal circumstances a start-up might struggle to raise any money at all – thus sparing the market from another lost investment or inevitable insolvency down the line for projects that just weren't that good. Even the very best start-ups would traditionally look at their needs and at their running costs and would look to raise just as much money as they need to keep going for a year or so, maybe a few hundred thousand dollars, acutely aware that typically the more they raise, the more equity they have to give away. ICOs had none of these limitations. Projects raised millions of dollars. Then some raised tens, then hundreds, of millions. Some raised billions. The vast majority of the projects that raised these vast amounts of money have done very little to show for it since; many were outright scams.

## A new method of fundraising

Not all ICOs were scams; some have led to fantastic companies and innovations. In May 2017 a new (and very good!) internet browser launched their ICO. The Brave ICO sold out. In 30 seconds. They raised $35 million[3] and have gone on to do great things. By mid-2017, this amount raised for a new project wasn't unusual in crypto. New ICO projects were popping up in the thousands and raising millions or tens of millions of dollars in minutes or hours. The Brave example was merely faster than average. The month after, a new start-up appeared almost out of thin air and raised $153 million in three hours. The value of Bancor, the ICO in question, has since crashed and it's now facing some legal implications, but this amount wasn't unusual either.[4] Between June 2017 and June 2018, a then-unknown blockchain company raised $4 billion via ICO format, and it's still not entirely clear to many to this day quite what it has done with all this money.[5]

It was a time of easy money. ICOs brought to the world a new way of fundraising. Designed by early crypto enthusiasts as a way of raising funds without being dependent on or limited by third party institutions, what started out as an innocent funding mechanism quickly got out of hand. Unlike initial public offerings, or

IPOs, ICOs required no lawyers (or at least didn't know they did) and were, initially, not subject to any regulatory approval. More accurately, many ICOs chose to disregard this and instead tried to find ways to get around regulation, a fact that is now catching up with many.

To get funding, whether from banks, loans, start-up accelerators, friends and family, VCs or investors, takes not only a good idea but also a good and provable business case, a team, and the execution to see it through. In short, it requires convincing people who either know you or are experts in what they're doing to risk their money on you, and then, due to contracts or regulations, a certain amount of hard work to see the project through. ICOs bypassed all of this. They were more similar to crowdfunding but without any of the checks or red tape. Funds were raised in cryptocurrency, typically but not always Ethereum, the digital currency for the blockchain platform that most of them were built on top of. The crypto ICO era was a Wild West of thousands of opportunistic projects launching out of thin air into an unregulated space full of hope and hype and money being flung around wildly, where hacks and scams and unrealistic, wild promises were the norm rather than the exception.

ICOs were – in practice for some and in theory for many more – a chance to get rich quick, and offered their founders the chance to potentially get the same level of returns that early crypto investors had made. Some founders were really just in it for the money. One famously held on to 98 per cent of his ICO tokens, meaning he had an insane monopoly over the market he had created. Its investors, it seems, largely didn't question this. Veritaseum, the much-hyped ICO in question, nevertheless still managed to attract a remarkable amount of frenzied buying, from raising $15 million in its ICO to frantic trading taking its total market value to a peak of $381 million.[6] The founder has since settled with US law enforcement body the Securities and Exchange Commission (SEC) for its illegal ICO issuance.[7]

Under normal circumstances, more people might perhaps have wondered whether this was indeed a safe place to invest their money, but 2017 and 2018 really were the Wild West of crypto. Anything went, and for a while the money kept on flowing.

Initial coin offerings were the new big thing. They were the new and easy way of raising money, enabling start-ups to raise more money than they'd ever have been able to by other means, and the crypto space latched on. ICOs raised billions of dollars for their founders. From 2016 to early 2018 the market expanded at a record pace and pushed the nascent crypto market to a valuation of over $800 billion, until it all stopped and started to free-fall. The ensuing market crash wiped out around $600 billion, regulations were imposed, founders were arrested and scam after scam after scam was outed. Less than two years after the main ICO bubble began, 81 per cent were declared to be scams and 92 per cent had either lost all or the vast majority of their investors' money.[8]

## Creative hiring

The problem with ICOs was that they were very easy and cheap to create. Anyone could launch one without knowing anything about tech or business, or even without having anyone around them to provide basic common sense or assistance. To launch an ICO cost as little as a few hundred to a few thousand dollars, depending whether their founders used freelancers that lined up on fiverr.com and other gig-economy websites, or whether they paid the outrageous fees of the specialized ICO marketing agencies that popped up. All that was needed to launch an ICO were a few simple steps that could be copied or outsourced to almost anyone. To launch an ICO for the sake of launching an ICO was easy. With just a bit of tweaking outsourced to a freelancer or two, ICOs could decide how many tokens they would create, how much they would sell them for, get a simple template website and give their new cryptocurrency a name, list the tokens for sale on one of the many token listing platforms and in one go you have a money-printing machine that people would throw their money into.

LinkedIn, freelancer sites and gig-economy sites suddenly became full of ICO experts and ICO gig workers, people with no more expertise than anyone else but who were willing to make up ICO teams. Many of these new ICO 'experts' were even willing to be paid in the projects' tokens, rather than in government tender currency (known as fiat currency), in the either delusional or optimistic hope that the tokens would shoot up and stay up in value.

For a few tens or hundreds of dollars anyone could get an ICO website built, a logo done, a whitepaper written to explain what the project purported to do, the tokenomics (like its financial and technical model – what should be a rather crucial element) and its social media done to promote it. Some ICOs went a little further to promote their token sales, paying gig workers $5 or $10 to create videos or write (fake) reviews or testimonials about their projects, saying how good the projects were and pretending to be happy customers. Some went even more creative, paying gig workers to paint the ICO's name on their bodies[9] or source fake profiles for people to make up their teams, all in the name of marketing to sell their tokens.

In an ideal world, of course, it would be the ICO teams themselves who would work out their financial model, and write the technical whitepaper describing their projects, and even ideally write the content on their website. Ideally, the teams would comprise real people who were actually working on the project, not fake profiles comprising names, LinkedIn profiles and photos taken from unsuspecting people who often had no idea of what the ICO was or even that they were now suddenly supposedly a part of it! But many projects in the crypto ICO mania bypassed such lofty aspirations in the name of making a quick profit with minimal upfront time or financial investment.

ICO teams could be put together pretty quickly if the aim was just to delude naive and hopeful investors. The projects often really didn't care who they hired, or if the names or photos of their team were even real people, let alone real experts in their space. In 2017 an ICO reached out to me on LinkedIn asking if I would accept roughly $2,500 worth of their tokens in exchange for being their legal expert. When I replied that I knew a grand total of nothing about law, they didn't care – they just wanted some more LinkedIn profiles to add to their site. Presumably they were bulk messaging anyone who showed an interest in crypto on their profiles in the hope of getting a yes. I declined. At least I was a real person. Plenty of other ICOs resorted to more desperate measures yet. One Asian ICO showed a headshot of a very attractive team member, whose role in the project read 'Experienced graphic designer with a clear focus on identities and illustration'. Presumably the team behind the project weren't aware quite how famous the actor Ryan Gosling is, as they didn't seem to realize that using his photo for their ICO might raise a few eyebrows. And yet the ICO in question still raised $830,000 from 380 investors.[10] Others didn't go to such lengths of using celebrities' or strangers' photos; some ICOs just gave no details whatsoever of their teams, showing cartoon photos and first names that were just as likely to have been plucked out of a hat as they were to be the names of real team members.[11]

## The different types of scam offerings

Some ICOs were clear scams from the start. Some even said as much in the names of their projects. Some examples of ICOs that were blatant on that front were PonziCoin, which still raised $250,000, and ScamCoin,[12] which promised to be 'The only ICO you can be certain of! Get 0 per cent return from 100 per cent of your investments, guaranteed!' These rare, relatively honest ICOs spread warnings across their websites, going as far as to tell people that they had no value, or were a Ponzi, and that people shouldn't invest, and yet people still flung money at them.

One ICO called itself Useless Ethereum Token – named after Ethereum, the blockchain protocol it was built on, but making clear on its website that the developer would do nothing with the funds he raised other than buy himself some tech, primarily a flat screen TV. Useless Ethereum Token is quite possibly the first ICO to be fully accurate in its claim, claiming to be 'The world's first 100 per cent honest Ethereum ICO'. The developer states clearly that the project 'transparently offers investors no value', that it's definitely not audited and that its smart contract was copied from GitHub. The developer behind the Useless Ethereum Token made his point loud and clear: 'You're going to give some random person on the internet money, and they're going to take it and go buy stuff with it. Probably electronics, to be honest. Maybe even a big-screen television. Seriously, don't buy these tokens.'[13] And yet people parted with $40,000 of their money to the project.[14]

Some ICOs went the opposite route, aiming to separate their prospective investors from their funds by going for slightly more elusive names. ICOs came with names using words such as Real, Rich or Gold, perhaps hoping that investors would take their names at face value. Sure enough, people did, and these projects raised money too. Most ICO projects made very little effort to hide the fact that they offered no purpose or value.

Other ICOs made themselves sound amazing. Implausibly so. They promised they had partnerships with MasterCard or Visa, or with Amazon or Microsoft. Some of the ICO start-ups claimed to have huge pre-existing customer and user bases, bigger than those of many of the world's largest companies. They promised technical feats that haven't been possible for the largest corporations that have billions to spend on achieving them and have all the experience in the world to make it happen. Some ICOs claimed that they would bank the unbanked, bringing banking to the 2.5 billion people around the world that the world's largest banks have never brought their services to. Although this is more due to their lack of desire to spend the effort and money to do so, seeing it as economically unviable to do this act of service for the world's poorest, than due to the technical impossibility of the feat, it is no mean feat nonetheless and realistically probably not viable for any small, unknown start-up. They simply made claims that can only be seen as ludicrous, and yet people believed them. These projects cumulatively raised billions of dollars.

## Opportunities for opportunists

With a few really exciting business and technological exceptions, ICOs ran the gamut of opportunistically worthless to outright scams and touched on almost every industry on earth. One example of a relatively typical, equally worthless and scammy ICO was a niche Chinese project centred around tea. Pu'er Coins were created to sell ownership in Pu'er tea in exchange for ICO tokens. Of course, the Pu'er tea industry has been doing perfectly fine for centuries until now, selling the specialist tea for money. There is zero need to have a cryptocurrency to buy or sell Pu'er tea, or any other type of tea for that matter. But the hype surrounding the ICO bubble encouraged opportunists to come out of the woodwork and try their luck at scamming investors in every field, including niche, luxury tea. Six men held roadshows in posh hotels across China, promising investors high returns for buying tokens representing a fraction of the billions of dollars' worth they claimed to hold in Tibetan Pu'er tea. In a short amount of time, the six men raised $47 million from 3,000 Chinese investors. Only after they'd raised this money did it transpire that they didn't remotely own any billions worth of Pu'er tea, certainly not even $47 million worth, and had no knowledge about this market or any business selling Pu'er tokens whatsoever. The six ringleaders behind the fraudulent concoction were promptly arrested but the damage to their investors was done – they lost their money.[15]

One ICO, Benebit, which gave the pretence and appearance of not being a scam, amassed a large community thanks to its healthy marketing budget. The only thing missing from their scam was a team. Turns out they had taken the photos for what they claimed was their team from a British boys' school website. When people found out this was the case, the Benebit team were good enough to remove the photos from their site and social media feeds, but not before running away with about $4 million that they had just raised.[16]

More than one chancer tried their luck at creating an ICO using the name and brand of an existing company, presumably hoping that they'd actually get away with it. Followers of Turbulent Energy, a popular Belgian energy company, were delighted that the company had launched an ICO and now had its own coin that they could invest in. Turbulent's CEO was less delighted to find out about this. In their case, a lone Russian lady had used the company's name, lifted content from its website and created a new website, Facebook and Twitter page for the cryptocurrency she was now fraudulently trying to sell. Thankfully the woman in question only managed to rake in about $1,000 before the scam was shut down by law enforcement.[17]

Not all ICOs were scams from the start. Some were just as hopelessly opportunistic as they were hopeless. The vast majority of ICOs were just people or small, newly formed companies with ideas that they had somehow convinced themselves had some semblance of a business idea and potential behind them. This was 2017, when blockchain was still a buzzword and adding mention of blockchain to a company caused valuations to jump. One more example focused around tea, although this time iced tea. USA-based Long Island Ice Tea Corp famously changed their name to Long Blockchain Corp. Their stocks jumped 289 per cent overnight. The FBI are now investigating insider trading,[18] but this is a standard and all-too-common representation of the hype that the word blockchain added.

## Sex, dating, families, sand, wine and prayers

Lots of people started looking at what industries they could talk about putting on blockchain. The ICO sex space was popular and boomed. Of course, there was about as much need to put this industry on the blockchain as there was for Pu'er tea, but, nevertheless, projects materialized almost every week with the latest sex-related so-called revolutionary offering.

One, called SexCoin, launched its own literal sex coin – aimed at preventing scams in the sex industry – although how they intended to do this was never explained. The only place one could spend SexCoins was in their own virtual sex shop called SexCoin Maid, which never really took off. Slightly limiting.

Payment in the porn industry is a big and ongoing problem. People, for whatever unknown reasons, don't want porn purchases showing up on their bank statements – presumably some partners and family members would give them a hard time over the revelations. Camgirls and sex workers also struggle to get banked. Whilst some are happy to accept Amazon vouchers for payment, this isn't sustainable for micropayments for smaller deeds or for paying rent, and thus a whole flurry of ICOs sprung up to target the sex industry to take advantage of the failings of traditional finance for this particular space, without seeing that blockchain wasn't necessarily the answer.

SpankChain – founded by Spanktoshi Nakabooty – a play on the name of the pseudonymous Bitcoin founder Satoshi Nakamoto – came in to save the day with their micropayments for porn services currency SpankCoin. The SpankChain platform would allow its users to pay in SpankCoins for their live video content. Anyone would be able to do exactly what they wanted without having to provide their credit card information.

Unfortunately for those so inclined, the platform never launched. They managed to launch a so-called educational platform, presumably a course about female anatomy, called Crypto Titties, but the video platform never seemed to open and SpankCoins had no use. TittieCoin had perhaps the best offering of all to the crypto industry, allowing its owners to visit Tittie Island, a 'luxury resort style holiday destination with timeshare possibilities'.[19] Given the known amount of scams surrounding timeshares, one would have thought that people would see the combination of a crypto ICO, a sex island and timeshares as raising some red flags. Apparently not. For those wanting less clarity around what they would be getting for the investment, Dirty Coin offered a 'fast and discreet way to pleasure'.[20] Intimate offered a platform where one could buy anything one wanted, with its own crypto token, from vibrators to dates.[21] They just didn't really clarify how the dates would be served. These sex-related ICOs weren't alone; they were just some of the many creatively named projects piling in to join the ICO sex space.[22]

For those who fancied romance above sex, other far-fetched ICO attempts were based on dating. One of the well-known problems of online dating apps is that their users' data is hardly protected. Anyone can pretty much find anyone they want to, if they want to find out if they're on a dating app, to the point of quite easily being able to see when and where someone is online. Data on these apps, as with pretty much all apps, is open to exploitation, profiles and messages can be screenshotted and their users' whereabouts can be tracked if one so desires. Ashley Madison, a dating site for those wanting extra-marital liaisons, was famously hacked and its data exposed by people who thought they were doing the world a service by exposing cheats. It's a valid point, but not what the cheaters in question signed up for.[23] Bumble, a dating app popular amongst the tech-savvy youth, shows when someone logs on, and gives a pretty clear indication of how much they're using the app and how far they are away from you, for anyone who can be bothered to take the two minutes required to work out how the algorithms work. Some people may not like this level of exposure. It's well known that dating apps and sites aren't private or secure.

And so in 2017 and 2018 a string of dating apps on the block-chain were launched, claiming they wanted to make the data they held on their users more secure. In a way this would be true. Data held on a single centralized database, such as how Ashley Madison stored their data, is prone to being hacked, so it is in a way true that storing this data on a blockchain would make it more secure. But this is completely missing the point of how blockchain works. Blockchain holds a permanent record of information stored on it. Therefore, storing the data of profiles and dating messages as permanent data entry records – a rather pertinent feature of blockchain – would be the literal exact opposite of what anyone would want. There are technical ways to get around this using blockchain, such as storing information off-chain and encrypting access to it, but these ICOs were largely not looking at that. And yet these ICOs continued.

For those less inclined to invest in the sex or dating industries, there were more than a few religiously minded projects to restore faith in ICOs. Some cryptocurrencies claim to be backed by real-world assets. Much like the gold standard dollar that was backed by gold, Prayer Token made itself out to be backed by prayer. It doesn't seem clear whether its creator actually believes in God or prayer based on their words, that prayer tokens would be 'sent to God and stored on the blockchain'. As the creator claims, 'I don't know if prayer works, but if it does, then you're getting much more value out of a Prayer Token than almost every other token in existence… This is not a joke, scam, or grift. I will pray for you as honestly and sincerely as possible.'[24] Prayer Token didn't end up saving a vast amount of souls; the token didn't last long and has now ceased to be traded.

If people didn't want to invest in sex, dating or prayers, Family Points offered a way to disrupt the parenting industry. Quite how or why a cryptocurrency would be needed to do so was never explained. Sand Coin offered a way to buy sand. Wine Project's WINE tokens offered their investors a far more complicated way of buying wine than would be possible with a credit card or any other conventional payment method, but provided much reassurance to anyone looking at their site that they employ 'a lot more than 7 persons, we can count all the people who work with us in vines and in the production center, we will upload a picture with the whole team soon'.[25] Arguably, it's good that they can count their team, although typically proof of these individuals' identities or profiles or even a team photo does help to assure that the team does in fact exist. For those not wanting wine, Trash Coin offered to its investors 'the ultimate cryptocurrency to exchange all the garbage dumped in your wallet into a single token which can be traded in exchanges... now you can keep all the trash in one place'.[26] One could find an ICO for almost any niche.

## How to promote a scam

Roughly 99 per cent of ICOs had one thing in common. They had no need or use for a cryptocurrency or blockchain or any value to offer anyone else. And yet they managed to attract tens of billions of dollars in record time. How did they do this?

In part, ICOs didn't have to do very much at all. Much more was down to timing and a hyped-up market than individual projects. Projects that would have never otherwise been looked at twice by any other investor at another time raised millions in minutes. People saw ICOs as their chance to make money and wanted to invest, brushing aside and actively not wanting to hear warnings. Most investors really didn't look that deeply into the projects. If there were some glaring red flags, they were pretty much overlooked. People wanted to buy in to ICOs to get their chance at making big, quick money more than they wanted to take the time to assess the risks. Even when people who could recognize the scams for what they were shouted about them from the rooftops, ICO investors just didn't want to listen. Fear of missing out, or FOMO, and the resultant buying frenzy were well and truly kicking in.

Marketing ICOs, as a result of the hype and timing, was easy. All that was needed to promote their new cryptocurrency was a website, a whitepaper, some social media and some paid listings on ICO listing or rating platforms – all of which could be easily and cheaply outsourced. And as we will see with the uprising of 'bounty hunters' willing to do the work for the crypto tokens that had been newly created out of thin air, instead of working for cash, promoting ICOs often didn't even cost a lot of money.

## Bounty hunters

The concept of bug bounties has existed for a while in tech. Coders and techies will scan through the code of new projects and try – mostly ethically – to hack them. When they find bugs and flaws, the projects will typically reward them for their efforts. It's a standard and accepted payment for cyber security. Early ICOs started by offering bug bounties, paying out in their tokens for any security or coding flaws found. This wasn't enough; ICOs soon cottoned on that if they could get techies to accept their worthless tokens for this work, then they could get anyone else to do the same for other jobs, too.

ICOs started issuing bounties, out-competing each other to give out more tokens in more generous-seeming bounty rewards, in a bid to attract the most bounty hunters to work for them. A whole new job title appeared almost overnight on LinkedIn – bounty hunters! People, mostly from the developing world but far from exclusively, worked tirelessly doing social media, writing articles and producing content, creating videos, translating websites and whitepapers and doing all the tasks that ICOs suddenly didn't have to pay anyone to do. Of course, they paid in tokens, maybe 1–2 per cent of their token supply, but these were tokens that they had just produced out of thin air. The creators of ICOs could decide how many tokens they wanted to magic up when they launched their projects. These tokens, for the most part, really were worthless, only given value when some of them were bought or pumped up if they made it onto being traded on crypto exchanges. Most didn't.

Thousands upon thousands of people worked hours every day for these ICOs, for no money, in the hope of earning crypto tokens that would go up in value. Some of these projects' tokens did shoot up in value, and hopefully some of the bounty hunters managed to cash out before they crashed back down. Others never went up in value, crashing instantly the moment they hit the exchanges. For every ICO that released tokens and made it onto an exchange where they could be traded, at least one exit-scammed or crashed before it even got to the stage of being accepted onto an exchange where it could be exchanged or cashed out. Only 8 per cent of ICOs even hit exchanges,[27] meaning that 92 per cent of projects' token holders had no chance whatever of realizing money for their work. Holders of those tokens would never get their money or their time back. At least one ICO – including one run by a luxury titled British real estate developer based in Dubai – notoriously found ways to avoid paying the bounty hunters the full amount of the bounty rewards that they had worked hard to earn.[28] The ICOs that did the best had nothing really to do with the quality of the team or the usefulness of the product; so much came down to their ability to engage influencers to do their marketing.

## Marketing: The bad, the worse and the ugly

Some ICOs got so greedy, or so good at playing the game perhaps, that they didn't even pay in their tokens for their work to get done for them. Instead, they got their prospective investors to do their marketing. One ICO got its hopeful investors to do all its

26

marketing in exchange for the privileged right to invest in its token. Investors weren't too happy when the token crashed and burned and they found out the brothers behind the project never really did the work they had promised to do. Investors lost both time and money; some are now putting together a Class Action case against the ICO.[29] Anyone wanting to read up on exactly how unimpressed its investors are can Google 'GEMS ICO' and read the threads on Reddit for some sad but interesting reading. The irony about the GEMS ICO that got its investors to do all its dirty work: it aimed to be a 'decentralized mechanical turk', a 'protocol for contracting workers to perform micro tasks'.[30] The irony in crypto just doesn't stop.

Other ICOs just paid celebrities and influencers. More than a few of these celebrities subsequently got arrested or fined for not declaring that they were paid to promote projects, many of which turned out to be scams. Floyd Mayweather and DJ Khaled were amongst those fined[31] for failing to declare their paid role in promoting an ICO called Centra Tech,[32] which turned out to be one of the bigger scams going. John McAfee, cyber security mastermind who was behind many of the pump-and-dumps in the crypto space, and who we'll read more about later in this book, was recently arrested for allegedly pocketing $23.1 million for promoting ICOs whilst claiming to be impartial, causing thousands of investors to lose their money.[33]

## Sorry, but tough luck

The ICOs themselves weren't always entirely to blame. Sometimes good projects were scammed, their URLs and social media impersonated. Scammers would either take over their feeds or their chat channels, or redirect investors to different crypto addresses. This meant one thing: investors sent their crypto to the scammers instead of to the ICO it was intended for. In crypto, at least in the years leading up to 2018, there was no 'undo transaction' function.

If you sent your crypto to the wrong address, even if you were tricked into sending it to a scammer, you lost your crypto. The ICOs also never received it, so investors never got their tokens, and scammers ran off laughing. Sorry, but tough luck – that was pretty much all anyone could say by way of compensation. Crypto being crypto, this was a standard occurrence. With ICOs, you never quite knew if the crypto address you were sending your money to was the right one, or if you would get anything back for it. Sometimes you did, but depending on the projects you were hoping to invest in, often as not you lost your money and never heard of it again. Unless the ICOs were particularly decent and refunded investors or found some other work-around – which they were under no obligation to do – there was no chance of recovery in ICO-era crypto.

## ICOs: The big ecosystem mess

Despite many good projects and actors, and many who really wanted the best for crypto and for the crypto community, the ICO ecosystem, on the whole, was a dirty mess. Everyone and anyone who could took advantage of the hype and greed. ICO advisors appeared out of thin air and took advantage of ICO founders' ignorance; ICOs took advantage of their investors; crypto listing and ranking sites set up shop and charged what they wanted – some were good, some less good. Opportunists took advantage of ICOs and investors by organizing global road-shows for exorbitant prices, charging ICOs for private dinners and extravagant events to which they would invite investors. The only downside for the ICOs was money wastage: some attendees actually were investors, others, in many cases most, claimed to be or acted like investors but went along for their own networks or for the sake of a free dinner with zero intention of investing. These roadshows would still charge small fortunes for putting on a dinner and event in a different city every night.

Crypto exchanges got away with charging projects up to millions of dollars just to list on their exchanges. Exchanges knew that they were essential to the ICOs being traded and knew that the ICOs were raising millions, so charged accordingly. Exchanges didn't just charge high amounts, some were also guilty of everything from insider theft, coordinated hacks, closing down crypto wallets so that exchanges could trade away, profiting from any spikes or volatility at their users' expense[34] so that users sometimes lost access to their crypto, or even lost their crypto for good, or full-on market manipulation.

Unlike in other money raises, where investors hold companies to account and don't release funds until certain milestones are met, ICOs had none of these factors to hold their teams accountable. From the outset, they already had all their investors' money! This was a key factor about the ICO model of raising money that meant most teams had zero incentive to live up to all the ambitious claims they had made in their whitepapers. For many, it was far easier to just exit the scam – running off with the money and leaving their investors high and dry. Where traditionally companies at that stage might raise a few hundred thousand dollars, ICOs would raise millions or tens of millions, often overnight.

With many ICOs, their founders had gone from a worthless idea to sometimes suddenly raising millions or even tens of millions of dollars of what they saw as monopoly money – cryptocurrency that they could cash out into bitcoin or dollars or other government 'fiat' currency – with no accountability. For many, the temptation to leave and appropriate this money for themselves, and not carry through with any of the implausible ideas they had half-heartedly promised, was just too high.

Whilst 81 per cent of crypto ICO projects ended up being or turning into scams, 6 per cent failed and 5 per cent died,[35] 'only' around a third of all projects started off as such. The rest just couldn't cope or made hasty decisions once they'd made the money. The numbers are pretty grim: $9 million of investors' money was lost every day to crypto hacks and scams. Only 1.9 per cent of all ICOs have turned out to be successful.[36]

## Dead coins

In 2017, a website called Dead Coins started gaining traction. The project had quietly been keeping an eye on the crypto markets and reporting on some of the dead projects – cryptocurrencies that had lost all of their investors' money and stopped trading. The list of these dead coins just kept on growing. There are now several thousand cryptocurrency projects that once raised money – often tens of millions of dollars – then disappeared.

The reasons for these cryptocurrencies disappearing are listed as the projects being either dead, scams, hacks or parodies. Dead projects had no value or use-case from the start and no hope of making money or providing any return for their investors. In any other circumstance, outside of the Wild West of crypto, these projects wouldn't have been given the time of day and would have been politely – or perhaps not so politely – shown out of the room by anyone who knew what they were doing.

Reasons given for specific projects collapsing or scamming their investors were pretty wide-ranging and included everything from the project being abandoned by its team to the founder being a scammer; the team pulling a runner and disappearing; the project being an imitation of another from the start, the team having copied the exact source code and in some cases wording from another project; founders bleeding the money out; the team hiring a team of outsourced freelancers to replace themselves in a feigned attempt to carry on some of the work they did whilst they left and cashed out the money they had raised; the project being re-named in an attempt to defraud investors; or it simply being a failed project where the founders had so little clue that they blew the money up a wall and lost it in a sea of bad decisions and over-spending on other overpriced, dubious or scammy ICO practices.[37] I've paraphrased some, but the point is clear. The list of reasons goes on, and is freely available to see at deadcoins.com, making for what would be entertaining reading if it weren't sadly true.

Other projects got hacked, losing their investors' funds due to their own lack of any basic security measures. Given that crypto was one of the most risky and vulnerable environments and a prime target for regular hacks and theft, the number of crypto projects with grossly insufficient or non-existent cyber security was high. These projects really only had themselves to blame when their virtually non-existent security defences were breached and their funds stolen.

These were the boom years of the crypto Wild West. Thousands of scams started and stole billions of dollars from investors from around the world without any consequences, at the time. Little did they then know that law enforcement would catch on and would go back to investigate and arrest the founders of many of these.


## Instant legit bitcoin doubler

ICOs, their promoters and exchanges were only one part of the crypto Wild West of 2017–18. It seemed that if the words bitcoin, crypto or blockchain were involved, many hopeful investors' common sense went out of the window. Hope, or perhaps optimism, dominated, which led to an overwhelming prevalence of scams. There was so much promise of quick riches that people wanted to believe the claims made by crypto companies and offerings.

One of the most implausible crypto scams – and yet one that still exists today, still advertising all over search engines – is bitcoin doublers. The promise: send them your bitcoin, they would trade it for you, and within 24 or 48 hours they will send you back double. There are countless of these sites and they were, and sadly still are, promoted all over social media, on adverts on search engines and to anyone who would listen. No end of people sent their bitcoin. Rather less, if any, ever got their bitcoin back. And yet these sites and adverts still exist, still taking in people's money in hope of easy returns. One of the favourite words used by crypto scammers was, and still is, 'legit'. They genuinely seemed to think that putting the word 'legit' onto any site or any description would make people believe it wasn't a scam. Unfortunately they were right, and many people did indeed believe the claim of too many scams being 'legit'. Try putting 'double your bitcoin' or 'bitcoin doubler' or even 'legit bitcoin doubler' into Google or Facebook and see how many results are still live. The Wild West of crypto is far from being fully over.

## There is some hope!

It must be said, again, that not all ICOs were scams. There were some very good ones, projects with honest, hardworking founders who used an initial coin offering as an innovative funding method because they believed in cryptocurrency, or because the cryptocurrency was an inherent part of their business model, or simply because the concept is a great, independent way of fundraising. The Brave browser ICO, mentioned above, is one such example. The company is still going strong today, has launched a now very successful internet browser with its cryptocurrency a working feature, and has many happy investors. It's a shame that one has to highlight that, amongst the scams and the now defunct projects, there were some good ones. In an ideal world, it would be the other way round.

CHAPTER TWO

# Crypto exit scams

## The $50 million prank

In early 2018, a new ICO was launched promising to carry out the unrealistically large claim of democratizing cryptocurrency for everyone. They aimed to do so through what they said was a unique AI-fuelled ecosystem of crypto saving and investing for the masses. They raised $50 million, not a small amount of money. In gratitude, the team closed up shop and ran. The founder left a message on the company's Twitter saying just five words: 'Thanks guys! Over and out...'[1] with a selfie at an airport, and another of him with a bottle of beer at a beach. Their website was replaced with a full-screen meme from *South Park*: 'AANNND IT'S GONE'.[2] Not exactly an act of great taste for its panicking investors.

Theo Goodman, media and blockchain consultant and an active member of the crypto community in Frankfurt near where they were based, went to their premises. Their office was empty, monitors in place, some pizza and bottles left over. This didn't confirm anything, but looked as much like an exit scam as an exit scam could. Those who had been following the ICO or who had contributed to its $50 million raise took to Twitter; they wanted to know what was going on.

The founders of Savedroid, the ICO in question, had rented an office space in the main start-up hub of Wiesbaden, just outside Frankfurt in Germany. Once they had raised their money, they left, suddenly. Within 24 hours of leaving their office and posting their parting note on Twitter, they shut down their website and social media. Their admins left its subreddit forum and its Telegram chat group. The messages that took over their social media chat channels – 'Can't hide, fear for your life'[3] – were maybe posted by scammers or bots, a warning to the team, but who knows, it could have also been the team adding to the drama they were trying to create.

Savedroid's exit wasn't unusual for ICOs at this time. Exit scams were common and were almost to be expected. What was unusual about the Savedroid exit scam was that the CEO came back. CEO Yassin Hankir made out that this wasn't an exit scam, that this was all a hoax, designed to show how easily people fall for implausible claims in crypto and to point out how many scams there were. The whole hoax, he said, had been a PR stunt.[4]

Investors were initially relieved, hopeful that their $50 million wasn't entirely lost. But the hoax soon backfired. Investors were more angry at the team than anything, and lost any faith or confidence in the project. Savedroid wasn't a scam, and the project's aims in highlighting the problem of ICO exit scams might well have been in good faith, but, like many ICOs, Savedroid has far from fully lived up to its roadmap,[5] and for investors the end result sadly wasn't much different. The token price crashed;[6] any hope or confidence there had been in the project had evaporated completely. Within months the $50 million of raised value had disappeared anyhow. The token was now worth far less than it had been, around 98 per cent less, and trading had reduced to almost nothing. Today there's nothing really left of the Savedroid ICO except a template website, reminders of a tasteless PR stunt that badly backfired and a class action against them.[7]

In a subsequent interview to investigators, Savedroid's CEO said they'd been exposed and subject to so many scams during the process of their ICO, and it was such a frustrating experience for them, that they wanted to highlight the extent of the problem.[8] He has a point. As we saw in the previous chapter, the crypto ICO space in 2016 to 2018 was a hotbed of scams, with scams coming in every shape and size. But as the age-old adage goes, two wrongs don't make a right. Pulling an exit scam, even if it was a fake one, and in so doing costing their investors $50 million of their money in crashed value didn't help the crypto space in any way, shape or form. It just added to the fears surrounding the space.

For the Savedroid team, the prank was a poorly made, hasty decision. It seems they just didn't think about the consequences of their actions and carried out the whole thing in 24 hours. The sad reality for their investors is that the consequences were no different to any real exit scam – they still lost all their money.

## Run off with the money

In 2019, billions of dollars were lost in exit scams. The figure was far higher in 2017 and 2018 when the hype around crypto and the ICO bubble was booming. Exit scams have existed in other industries, but nowhere so predominantly as in the crypto space surrounding the 2017–18 ICO bubble. As we saw in the previous chapter, ICOs just made it too easy for almost anyone to raise money for projects that ranged from the awful to the truly bizarre. As it was so easy for these projects to suddenly raise money from ICO investors, without really having to invest any of their own time or money to do so, and crypto in those years wasn't quite subject to the same regulatory checks that it is now, the temptation to run off with this money was, for some, too high to resist.

## Aubergines and other vegetables

In Lithuania in early 2018 an ICO launched to sell vegetables on a blockchain. They did some typical ICO-style marketing, such as going onto gig economy website fiverr.com and paying gig workers $5 each to write the name of their company on their bodies, making out that it was loyal fans voluntarily writing their name in pen on themselves. It didn't take a BuzzFeed reporter long to work out that the girls photographed with 'Prodeum' written on their bodies were loyal to anyone who would hire them for the gig for a $5 fee.[9] Gigs where people are willing to write a company's message on their body for $5 are, it turns out, aplenty on Fiverr. Who knew.

The Prodeum ICO barely raised $100. It's good that they didn't raise a lot. Soon after the ICO, they took their website down and replaced it with one word written in small letters on an otherwise white, blank background: penis.[10]

## Maybe the most obvious exit scam of them all

It wasn't just ICOs that launched exit scams. From 2017 through to 2019, it was another month, another exchange pulling an exit scam. Many crypto exchanges were shady at best, and in those years very few checks were carried out, particularly on some of the smaller exchanges that went out of their way to stay anonymous.

Today, in debates about crypto, there is at least some general consensus that a degree of regulatory oversight to help prevent innocent people getting scammed isn't a bad thing. Just a few years ago, however, that wasn't so much the case.

One of the core concepts of blockchain technology on which cryptocurrencies are built is that it can be decentralized. Decentralization was the next biggest buzzword in crypto after ICO. If something was decentralized, it was seen as being more secure, as not being able to be hacked, as just 'better'. In some use cases, decentralized really is better. Some crypto exchanges promoted themselves as being decentralized – and in many ways this did and does offer perks. Centralized exchanges go through regulatory checks, but tend to share users' details with governments. Not everyone wants this, either from a money laundering perspective, or just from an ethical or data-privacy perspective. However, although decentralized exchanges offered many beneficial features, too much trust was placed in some of these exchanges that offered no security measures or checks.

In ICO-era crypto, generally 2016–18, people had, for the most part, no idea of the implications that would hit when the cracks started to show and regulation started to sink in. In the ICO era, some people who months prior hadn't known what cryptocurrency even was started talking about launching a crypto exchange as a viable get-rich-quick alternative to investing in crypto or launching an ICO. Exchanges started popping up all over the place with varying degrees of security. If a crypto exchange launched, there were often literally no checks into its security or team or anything about it. People would send their money to these new, unchecked, often anonymously run exchanges, store it there, and hope or trust blindly that it would be ok. Within the crypto community there was warning after warning to not store a lot of crypto on exchanges, to only keep there what you'd be actively trading with and store the rest offline, in a safer wallet. Not everyone listened, though. Storing crypto on exchanges meant greater potential for riches. It meant having more money available to trade or send straight to invest in the next ICO, or, in the case of those who invested in ICOs, having that particular cryptocurrency readily available for the off-chance that it would suddenly pump up in value on the exchange and they'd be ready to cash out. So these new crypto exchanges launched, run by people who didn't necessarily know what they were doing and who weren't necessarily aware of the legal implications that would soon catch up with them for doing so.

As the market perhaps inevitably came to see, crypto exchanges were possibly in the most obvious position to exit scam of them all. This was clearly highlighted by Canadian exchange Quadriga, which has just been ruled as being a scam from the start, and whose founder died leaving his users with no access to hundreds of millions of dollars of their money[11] – except that many have since been asking for his body to be exhumed. A lot of people don't believe he's dead. We'll see all about this story in Chapter 6, 'The faked death, missing millions and requests to exhume a body'. Much as with ICOs, crypto exchanges didn't even need to do so much promotion; they could just list their exchange and some people, given a willingness to trade in crypto, would just use them. White label exchange templates were easy to get hold of, and to a far lesser degree still are, for anyone wanting to Google it, for relatively little sums of money to enable you to have your own crypto exchange up and running in no time with almost no effort involved.

Crypto exchanges could hide behind being hacked and technical difficulties, and because both of these were so common in those days, it was often hard to know if they were telling the truth or not. In addition, some exchanges would store the crypto they held centrally in one wallet or account and keep a record of who had what. Had every user's crypto been stored separately, that would have been safer in the event of a hack. It's not like all their users would tend to withdraw all of their funds in one go, so if the funds were to slowly leak out, or if the exchange were victim to multiple small hacks, if the exchanges weren't keeping on top of it, they might never know until all of their money was gone. This sounds incredible, but is more or less what happened, as we will see with Japanese market-leading exchange Mt. Gox.

## Thank you and sorry

One South Korean exchange, Pure Bit, went down the unimaginative exit scam route favoured by many of the ICOs: launch an almost-finished crypto exchange, run an ICO over a period of a couple of months, raise a couple of million dollars, and during this whole time act as if everything is ok.

What was less ideal about the Pure Bit token raise was that they raised $2.8 million in an ICO in 2018 in what would be a fairly standard token raise except for the fact that ICOs had been made illegal in South Korea in 2017.[12] Whatever they did, they were going to end up in big trouble with the authorities. The team behind Pure Bit then sent that $2.8 million in crypto out to one single crypto wallet. This is the equivalent to storing that amount of money in cash in a physical wallet – it can be safe depending on what type of wallet you choose and where you store it. It can also, if one is so minded, make it easy to steal that one wallet and run off with the entire balance. Pure Bit then shut down their new exchange and website, kicked out every member of their chat group on south Korean messenger site Kakao, and posted one last message: thank you.[13]

Pure Bit, it is alleged, was a pure, clean exit scam, and one does have to wonder what investors were thinking given the illegality of any ICO in South Korea at its time of launch. Whatever happened, they were going to land in hot water.[14] Except, with Pure Bit, there was one twist to the tale. The day after closing the exchange and attempting to exit with his users' crypto holdings, the CEO of the exchange started to feel guilty.

The week after, a message appeared:

I negatively affected investors in the project psychologically and financially. I made an unforgivable mistake that cannot be turned around, blinded by money. It has been less than a day, and I have already started to suffer from guilt. Although it cannot be compared with the hardship faced by the investors, I also felt significant guilt. I sincerely apologize to all of the investors in the ICO who were affected by the operation.

Soon after, the exchange started to return some of the stolen crypto.[15]

## The art of hiding behind technical faults

Sadly for the crypto ecosystem and its investors, scammers feeling guilty, regretting their actions and refunding the money (at least some of it) was not the norm. Some crypto exchanges hid behind technical issues, citing technical faults as the reasons there were delays in processing withdrawals and why some people weren't able to access their money. One Polish exchange, Coinroom, allegedly didn't even bother to hide behind technical faults. They just sent users a message one day saying that they had until the next day to withdraw their funds before they were shutting it down. Some of its users were able to do so. If they failed to withdraw their funds in that sudden time frame, quite easy to do if not necessarily checking emails every minute, users would have to email the Coinroom team to request their withdrawals to be processed manually. Ironically, this was well within the exchange's rights, as they had put this clause into their user agreements that their users had – most likely unknowingly – accepted when they opened their accounts at the exchange.[16]

Where Coinroom stepped outside of its rights was when it suddenly stopped responding to withdrawal requests and stopped processing withdrawals altogether. They took down their website, closed the exchange, shut all their social media, and their phone stopped working. Even customers to whose withdrawal requests they had responded complained they'd only received part of their deposits back. The exchange, as far as anyone could see, had vanished.[17]

## The reinvention of the global financial system

PlexCoin started off as a rather ambitious-sounding ICO. The company told how it aimed to reinvent the global financial system, and in so doing has become one of the most infamous ICOs of all time. PlexCoin started by making some pretty impressive claims; impressive both for their magnitude and for their sheer impossibility, feats that no one in the entire global financial system has ever even come close to. For starters, PlexCoin said it would give out debit cards that would far surpass the feats achieved by every known bank to date. 'Revolutionary and unprecedented, PlexCard will be accepted everywhere in the world, regardless of your country's currency. Your card will adapt to the geographical area in which you are located.'[18]

No financial system in the entire world has ever been able to adapt money to geographical areas. Thus, we have the ongoing problem of forex and foreign transaction fees. Hence the EU created the euro, and the US has the US dollar instead of individual states all having their own currency. Adapting money to suit every geographical region regardless of the currency of that area has never been done, and there is no clear idea how this would be remotely possible. Unfortunately, we don't live in an age of magic money. If no country or financial institution in the world has ever managed to do this, it's not quite clear how PlexCoin thought they were going to, or how they thought they'd be able to convince enough people that they were going to. But this was a crypto ICO, aimed not at anyone who understood the financial markets, but, rather, specifically at those who didn't.

## The ability to predict the future and other red flags

On top of some other fairly impressively implausible claims[19], PlexCoin did raise enough red flags for anyone who wanted to see them. The thing was, as with other ICOs, not everyone wanted to see them. For everyone who wanted to see red flags, others were there to dismiss any negative talk as just greed spread by those who they thought just wanted to push the price down so they could buy in cheaper.[20]

PlexCoin were going to be issuing Visa cards. These Visa cards would be issued through another company, in their words 'a sister company that issues Visa cards and that meets our expectations'.[21] The fact that they didn't name the sister company in question should have raised some red flags.[22] There seems to be no evidence to suggest that Visa knew anything about this supposed partnership, and it can be assumed it's as fabricated as some of PlexCoin's other claims.

Another great claim: 'PlexCoin may be used just like traditional money to pay bills.'[23] Many in crypto hoped indeed to pay their bills one day with crypto. There are even some start-ups working on this. The problem is that PlexCoin claimed it would be possible to do so without addressing the reality of how they would work with all global energy suppliers, direct debit companies and bill issuers to make this an actual reality. A nice idea, but without global acceptance it is impossible and an arguably rather deceitful claim.

Typically, for anyone looking to invest their hard-earned money into a company, they would want to know what that company did and aimed to do. Most crypto companies would release that information in a whitepaper – a more or less technical paper detailing what they planned to do with the funds they hoped to raise. Now, many or most of these whitepapers were outsourced to freelancers or gig workers who weren't a part of the company, and who didn't care what the company did or didn't do so long as they got paid for churning out another ICO-template whitepaper, but at least there was some semblance of information about what the project purported to do. PlexCoin clearly didn't think this was necessary. Or more likely, they figured that if their whitepaper were released in advance of their ICO, it would be torn to shreds by people who would be able to spot the scam signs and red flags a mile off. PlexCoin released their whitepaper just a few hours before the ICO started. The reasons they gave made literally no sense:

> We wanted to avoid a tricky situation: a situation in which people could have read our white paper and develop our concept before we even launch it. We thus decided to make you linger a little bit! Here it is, and our pre-sale begins in a few hours.[24]

This is crazy. PlexCoin made such great claims that surely they would not be so easily copied. With this excuse for not releasing their whitepaper any earlier, they are in one go disregarding all of their claims, saying that if anyone just sees their ideas, they could copy them. It doesn't make sense, and it is just incredible that they would print this. But they did.

Just as incredible, and incredibly nonsensical, were PlexCoin's reasons for not showing the details of anyone working on the project:

> We know that eventually, we will have to display the names of some of our executives. However, we will try to remain discreet until all of our projects are launched. Nonetheless, we will never mention the names of our employees and subcontractors. This rule is paramount for our projects' security and for the people around us to remain safe... How do you want us to be able to guarantee you a total confidentiality if we reveal our identity? Any organization could then contact us, visit us and scrutinize our operations (and yours)! This is not what we want.[25]

To say they basically don't intend to show the identities of their teams is a red flag. To say they can't offer confidentiality without themselves being anonymous is, frankly, ludicrous.

In perhaps the ultimate irony, PlexCoin included a critique of other ICOs in their whitepaper. Quite how this was relevant or appropriate for a company claiming to change the global financial model isn't clear, but PlexCoin's whitepaper stated, accurately, that 'We noted that some ICOs have identical websites. We even noticed that some images and some team members presented were the same across different companies (we will not name them). We also remarked photographs of totally forged, misleading persons.'[26] The irony of this wasn't lost on many onlookers.

Perhaps PlexCoin's greatest claims were its supposed ability to predict the future. PlexCoin said, to the cent, what it estimated its tokens would be worth years into the future. This is quite the claim. PlexCoin was sold at 13 cents per token to its first ICO investors. There is a common marketing trick that if you tell people that the price will soon go up if you don't buy now, some people will buy now. So this is what PlexCoin did. They claimed that the initial value of their token was US$ 0.26, and that anyone buying in now would get it at half price, but that it would soon go up. If all tokens were sold in their pre-sale, the value of their token would suddenly be worth an estimated $1.76 per token. 'If this is the case', they said, token holders' purchase price 'will be multiplied by 1,354 per cent in 29 days or less.' By the end of 2018, they put into their promotional materials that they estimated that PlexCoin would be sold at $14.[27] This is crazy. There is literally no way of valuing a brand new and unknown stock or currency in advance, let alone almost guaranteeing its final value. And yet PlexCoin made it very clear to their prospective investors that the value of their cryptocurrency would always go up. Saying this is not just a red flag. It is illegal to make such claims, as well as impossible. Nothing always goes up. In the event, their guesses didn't turn out so accurately. Their token now, of course, is worth nothing. It stopped trading.

Despite these rather glaring red flags, PlexCoin still raised $15 million of the $249.5 million they hoped to. The SEC cottoned on rather quickly to the fact that PlexCoin was operating as a scam from day one.[28] After a two-month jail term and $100,000 fine, the founders – a couple – still weren't able to or perhaps weren't incentivized enough to give any of the details law enforcement were looking for. It isn't known if there was anyone else in the team besides the couple and some outsourced freelancers.

PlexCoin wasn't a typical exit scam, the founding couple didn't exit scam so much as law enforcement got to them first. Perhaps exit scamming was their intention. But the founders have been charged with having 'regularly transferred investor funds from the PlexCoin ICO... for the purpose of daily living expenses and home renovation products'.[29] Their assets are still frozen by law enforcement; many of their investors have lost hope of ever seeing their money again.[30]

## Shopping with investors' money

Unfortunately for their investors, the founders of ICOs relatively often siphoned off part or all of their investor funds for their personal gain. The thing is, they don't get fined so heavily for it; often fines were far less than they were able to siphon off, and in some cases, once settled, no further damages were pressed.

One ICO, Shopin, claimed it would build a personalised shopping platform and give shoppers personalised shopping profiles, all of course on blockchain.[31] The ICO launched with huge claims of partnerships that it never in fact had.[32] Despite this, it still raised $42 million, albeit fraudulently; its raise was based on lies and deception of its investors from the start. The founder allegedly went shopping – literally – with a good chunk of the proceeds, apparently spending at least $500,000 for his own gain on rent, shopping, entertainment expenses and a dating service.[33] Of course, the platform was never built, but at least the founder presumably got some good dates out of it. He was fined $450,000 for the privilege, at least $50,000 less than he is thought to have siphoned off.[34]

## Playing off people's hope

By far the largest pure crypto exit scam, so far, was a Vietnamese company called Modern Tech. Their ICO brought in $660 million from 32,000 people. This despite the fact that all transactions in crypto are illegal in Vietnam and so most of its investors would have been breaking the law by investing.[35] But PinCoin, the company's first ICO, appealed to people's greed.[36] In some ways, it's easy to see how Modern Tech raised this level of money despite it being illegal.

Just as with so many other scams, as we see with OneCoin, Bitconnect and Plus Token, promising or guaranteeing high returns appeals to those with hopes to better their life, a common and understandable human desire that can lead to some people overlooking some red flags. PinCoin promised monthly returns of 48 per cent. On top of that, they offered an 8 per cent bonus for every new person their investors brought in to invest.[37] The ICO had a good-looking website but other than a few buzzwords and pumped-up flowery words saying not very much, it had nothing on it.

In many ways, it was clear it was a scam from the start, but Modern Tech made sure to appeal to those people who weren't so financially aware, who wouldn't have been able to see that. Soon after its first ICO, Modern Tech launched its second ICO, Ifan, introduced as a way of payment between celebrities and their fans.[38] They said they aimed to invite Vietnamese singers into their network. Investors were told that both the new currencies' values would skyrocket once the platforms started being used. Of course this was a standard claim made by every ICO. It didn't happen.

PinCoin initially paid out to its investors, who got their monthly returns as promised. Then they switched, suddenly paying investors out in Ifan token instead. Then the payments stopped completely. The platform disappeared. Seven Vietnamese nationals fled the country[39] in what is thought to be the largest crypto exit scam in modern memory.

The problem with exit scams, in crypto, is that they are very easy to do. We've introduced some of the crazier parts of the world of crypto. Next up, some of the biggest and most infamous crypto scams. First of all, thanks to a viral BBC podcast series, we go into the story of the missing cryptoqueen.

## CHAPTER THREE

# OneCoin

## The missing cryptoqueen

### In the beginning

Bitcoin was a new kind of money. Separate from the banks and the governments that have been steadily losing trust following the 2008 financial crash, Bitcoin depends on algorithms that, unlike government-issued money, can't be manipulated. The worse governments act and the more they lead their economies into demise and ever-higher levels of inflation, the more people trust Bitcoin. This is a trend we see the world over.

Bitcoin had started out being valued at less than a cent in 2009 and reached its then peak in early 2014 at over $800. By then, people had started to take notice and want in on their own share of crypto riches.

That year, a new cryptocurrency started making waves. Its founder made big claims. OneCoin was to be the biggest crypto-currency, 'the Bitcoin killer',[1] and promised to do things never done before. It would be a new global currency that would democratize money, bring banking to the unbanked, change the financial markets, and bring its investors wealth beyond their wildest dreams. OneCoin offered people implausibly huge returns on their money, and – notably – even more generous compensation plans for its promoters.

Dr Ruja, its persuasive and domineering founder, was a confident speaker and good salesperson. From stages around the world she gave people what they wanted to hear. She told how the banking system was rotten and corrupt, how badly banks and governments treat people, how billions of the world's poorest were under-served, and mostly how her new cryptocurrency would address this, focusing on how rich OneCoin would make its investors.

## The end

OneCoin, tragically, did well. It seemed too good to be true. Unfortunately for its millions of people who cumulatively invested a hard to quantify but estimated $4 billion to $15 billion, it was.

The BBC carried out a year-long investigation into this clever and sophisticated Ponzi scheme, for their successful *The Missing Cryptoqueen* podcast series. They found that OneCoin offered nothing of value other than plagiarized so-called educational PDFs that were sold in packages for up to over a quarter of a million euros each.[2] OneCoin bore no relation to the rest of the cryptocurrency ecosystem. Unlike every other cryptocurrency, it wasn't exchangeable or tradable into bitcoin or any other currency. In short, OneCoin never was a cryptocurrency, but was simply numbers plucked out of thin air and continuously changed by its leader on a spreadsheet, designed to deceive and give false hope to its investors, who, between themselves, its founders unsympathetically described as 'idiots'.[3]

Law enforcement eventually got on top of the scam, and Ruja has been hunted by the FBI ever since. She has an estimated at least half a billion dollars to her name and a penchant for plastic surgery, so hiding, it seems, has been easy. Billions of dollars more are still unaccounted for. In a dramatic twist, Ruja's lover turned into an FBI informant and a hole she had drilled into his flat[4] to spy on his domestic allegiances led to her disappearance. It seems she had found out she was a wanted woman before this became public knowledge. That was 2017.

Ruja hasn't been seen since, sparking an international manhunt, years of court cases, many people facing life in prison and misery and financial devastation for millions of victims. To this day, no one knows what has happened to Ruja, where the missing billions are, and how some people are still getting away with selling what has been described by *The Times* as 'the biggest scam in history'.[5]

## The (missing) cryptoqueen

OneCoin centred around its founder. Ruja liked to show to the world she had money – she didn't go anywhere without her silk gowns, huge diamonds and red lipstick. She was the matriarchal queen and she wanted everyone to know it. Ruja was, to her credit, smart. She had a PhD in law, and made it known that she'd spoken at an *Economist* convention and had been on the front cover of *Forbes*. People were proud of her, for her big ideas, for bringing this dream into reality, for being a female leader and for giving hope and a purpose to people all around the world. Somehow she gained the title of 'cryptoqueen', and she knew how to play up to it.

## In the middle: Sell, sell, sell and get rich, rich, rich

Bitcoin is the first and dominant cryptocurrency that has, in many ways, changed how the world sends and perceives money.

OneCoin, Dr Ruja told a cheering, packed Wembley Arena, was 'the Bitcoin killer'. 'In two years, she shouted at her screaming fans, 'nobody will speak about Bitcoin anymore!'[6] OneCoin would make its investors' dreams come true.

It was an easy sell. People wanted to get into the new, fast moving world of crypto. Buying bitcoin and other cryptocurrencies was complicated. Stories abounded of how people had lost money by sending bitcoin to the wrong address or by storing bitcoin on a computer that they'd lost or by accident thrown away, but they still saw how much money early investors had made and wanted these same riches for themselves. People wanted to get rich with no effort, and this is what OneCoin offered.

Ruja told members to bring their friends, families and business partners to invest and share in the wealth that OneCoin would bring. And they did – people brought in everyone they knew. Many invested everything they had, giving Ruja their life savings, selling their homes, cars and livestock, re-mortgaging their houses, maxing out on credit cards and taking out loans they couldn't afford and might never be able to pay back, just to get their hands on the biggest OneCoin package they could.

Word about OneCoin spread like wildfire and the movement seemed unstoppable. The more word spread, the more followers they had, and the more confident Ruja became, making one thing clear: everybody needs to know OneCoin's name.

OneCoin attracted followers fast. The company and its affiliates held webinars and recruitment sessions in grand hotels every day, worldwide, day and night. The events hosted passionate members of the OneCoin network saying how their lives had changed, showing the world how it was a great family, and talking up Ruja. To anyone slightly more cynical it would have come across as well-rehearsed testimonials and sales pitches, but people flocked to these events in their thousands. Some didn't even know what they were there for, they'd been brought by friends and family. Their speakers could sell, and they sold the dream.

The more money they brought in, the more brazen OneCoin recruiters became. As the UK's *Mirror* newspaper found when they went to one of the seminars, recruiters told their audiences they were there to make them 'filthy rich'.[7] And their audiences believed it.

Soon, OneCoin was opening offices all around the world. It was an exciting time for its followers – they felt part of something that was really taking off, and believed that OneCoin was literally going to change the world and that they'd all become millionaires or billionaires.

## Don't trust Google

OneCoin was good at playing off the emotional needs of its followers. The company made out that they were offering more than 'just' a guaranteed get-rich-quick investment – they were a family, a community. Members had their own hand-sign – a circle and a one that they would make when they got together. Whatever its believers – of which there are still many – may say, OneCoin was, for all intents and purposes, a cult, with Ruja its leader.[8]

It was 'us against the world', investors were told. OneLife, the parent company behind OneCoin, told its followers that anyone who spoke against it were 'haters',[9] they were just jealous or didn't understand, or it was government propaganda trying to shut them down. Followers were even told not to trust Google![10] This is typical for cults and conspiracy theories. Anyone who questioned too much was bullied and kicked out. Simple.

The company played on people's desire to better their circumstances so successfully that one can understand why people might overlook some glaring red flags that stand between them and potential easy money. There were a few teething problems early on, but people believed these were just that.

## No way to get out

One of the most basic but crucial needs for a cryptocurrency is the ability to exchange in and out of real-world currency. Without this, it has no value. People bought into OneCoin under the sole premise that their OneCoins would go up in value and that they'd then be able to cash out into real-world, government-issued currency, known as fiat money. And yet, OneCoin was the only cryptocurrency not listed on any other crypto exchange; there was literally no way given to exchange it into bitcoin or into real-world government currency. OneCoin never gave any reasons why this was. It would take a few years for the real reasons to transpire.

Rather, OneLife was building its own exchange – xcoinx – a platform on which investors would be able to cash out their OneCoins into real money. When OneCoin launched, the exchange wasn't live yet, but OneLife always just said they were working on it. The excuses changed a bit too often to be ideal but it was always just around the corner. When the exchange did finally launch, it was almost immediately clear that something was wrong. It was easy to give euros in exchange for OneCoins, but OneLife seemed less willing to buy back OneCoins and give people back their euros. Already from early 2016, OneCoin was denying all but a very few withdrawal requests. Most people just couldn't cash out their money. This should perhaps have been more than slightly worrying to those holding their savings in it, given how big the company was aiming to grow and how much reserves they should in theory have had. Soon, the exchange would close altogether.

## Big, waving red flags

After its exchange closed, OneLife made a big noise about promoting what they said was set to be the largest global listing marketplace for cryptocurrency. This platform, DealShaker, was to be the only global marketplace for goods that could be bought in OneCoin. This was true; DealShaker was the only global marketplace for OneCoin mostly because no other site would accept OneCoin as valid currency. Just as having a way of cashing out of OneCoin was central to the ecosystem, there needed to be a way for people to spend their OneCoins for them to have any semblance of actual value.

In 2016, a man in London named Duncan Arthur was working in tech at a large American bank. He had a good job, but as he told the BBC for their *The Missing Cryptoqueen* series,[11] he was miserable. He describes his time there as sitting by the phone, waiting for the phone to ring. He wanted out and was desperate. The phone rang. A recruitment consultant had a job offer for him. Duncan Arthur was desperate enough to take it, red flags or no. That job was to build DealShaker for what was then the cryptocurrency start-up OneCoin.

Duncan Arthur has since left,[12] and regrets his time working for what he now sees is a scam, but he knows more than anyone about the inner workings of the platform. To the BBC, Duncan describes DealShaker as an online flea-market that lists nothing but rubbish. The number of users on the platform is also glaringly fabricated; the site claims to fluctuate between the unlikely range of 593,000–595,000 people being live on the platform at any one time, which would be a remarkable coincidence if true but is an implausible statistic that Duncan claims is as fictional as the value of the platform itself.[13]

In a world where Amazon, Alibaba and eBay are king, merchants have options when it comes to listing their goods, which they can list and sell quite easily on any other site for real-world currency. Any new online marketplace intending to attract merchants to list their goods needs to be cheap and easy to list on. DealShaker was neither. Merchants, not surprisingly, didn't line up to join the platform.

OneCoin's affiliates, who largely know nothing about online sales, were soon told they'd have to be the ones to source the merchants to list on the platform if they wanted to see any merchants there at all. This basically meant that they had no one that they could get to join of their own accord. That's like shopping malls telling prospective customers to find shops willing to pay overpriced rent to base in their centres, if they want to shop there. To list, merchants would have to take *at least* 50 per cent of payment in OneCoin. On top of this, OneLife would take a 50 per cent cut of whatever percentage of their listing they chose to list in real-world money, making it hard to see how listing on the platform was a viable option for any business listing any products that had real-world value.

Given their alleged belief in the platform and how much they claimed OneCoin would go up in value, it is interesting that OneLife choose to demand 50 per cent in euros instead of OneCoin for their own branded products and promotional T-shirts that they listed for sale on their platform. DealShaker crashed as badly as the xcoinx exchange soon would.

## Impossible, implausible economics

There was one glaring and pressing problem facing the OneLife team that it seems many eager investors missed in their excitement. The more that OneCoin rose in value against euros, the greater the reserves OneLife would need to come up with to cash these out, should anyone wish to convert back into real-world money. OneCoin, in practice, only had any real-world value if the coins could in fact be cashed out into euros when their owners requested. It was never made clear how OneLife would have the billions of euros worth of cash reserves it would need to back up the OneCoins. An economist would ask how that meant that the OneCoins had any real-world value at all, given that they couldn't actually be exchanged for euros or any other form of real-world currency, in any way.[14] But people didn't worry that they couldn't use or cash out their OneCoins straight away into their bank accounts; they saw the euro value of their coins on screen and that number just kept on getting bigger.

Despite these red flags and setbacks, people around the world continued to pour their money into OneCoin under the promise that the exchange would go live again, that DealShaker would indeed be the world's greatest cryptocurrency marketplace, but mostly in the hope and expectation that the coin would continue to surge in value. OneCoin kept on selling. Within two years, it had spread around the globe. By 2017 OneCoin had three million members worldwide. OneCoin was growing and spreading faster and faster.

How did a project that clearly posed so many red flags spread so fast and grow to become so out of control? Or, were the red flags so obvious at all?

## What dreams may come

In one of the most prestigious neighbourhoods in the Netherlands, in Naarden, an area full of millionaires and luxury estates, sits one particular mansion hidden behind garish black and red gates with the name of the house 'What Dreams May Come' sprawled prominently across the metal. Above that is a big, red metal sign with dragons on with the letters I and A on it – the emblem for its owners.

This house, says the owner, is the house of dreams. A young Igor Alberts, now its ostentatiously rich owner, was once broke and used to run past this house. In it, at the time, lived the richest man in the Netherlands. One day, Igor said, he would have a house just like this. Igor Alberts got his way. He made a vision board for his future. Foremost on it was a picture of Italian actress Monica Bellucci – that was how his future wife should look. On a trip to Italy, and with 10 kids already to his name,

Igor met a much younger Italian lady called Andrea who looked similar enough to his dream woman. Sure enough, Igor soon persuaded Andrea to marry him and the couple now live together in this mansion with their two kids.

Jamie Bartlett and his crew from the BBC went to pay Igor and Andrea a visit for their podcast series. The house is big. It might not be to everyone's exact taste, but it's clear that there has been no limit on the money spent on it. Black luxury cars fill the drive, and in the garden they have their own life-size fibreglass lit-up zoo. If anything equalled their house for ostentatiousness, it's Igor and Andrea's clothing collection. Igor boasts that Andrea's clothes alone are insured for a million euros. Everything is designer, and matching. Anyone interested can check out Igor and Andrea's Instagram @igoralberts.

This money didn't come from being an expert in cryptocurrency. Igor has for the last 31 years worked in multi-level marketing. In this time, he told the BBC, he estimates he made himself $100 million in profit.[15]

## A pyramid of money

Multi-level marketing, or MLM, is a form of marketing structure that is legal, on the caveat that there is a genuine product being sold. MLM works on a pyramid structure of affiliate payouts. Those who get in first, at the top of the pyramid, earn a generous percentage from those who buy from them. If their recruits then sell the product, those at the top also get a percentage cut from their sales. This goes on, all the way down the pyramid, which often has many levels.

MLM is one of those industries where, if you get in early and are good, you can become rich beyond your wildest imagination. Profits, as people like Igor demonstrate, can be obscene. Experienced network marketers who get in early and are at the top of the pyramid will always be able to find some people who will buy from them. The further down the pyramid you go, the more people there are trying to sell the same product to the same community of people, many of whom have been approached already. The vast majority, those who come in later and don't already have vast downline networks already built up, struggle and are almost guaranteed to lose money. They still have to pay the same product or affiliate fee that gives them the right to promote the product, but many will never make even this money back. Multi-level marketing rewards structures have been used to sell everything from vitamins to marketing courses, with more than one expensive supplement sold through MLM having been found to be little more than water, but more recently MLM has become popular to spread the growth of crypto scams. With MLM, you just always have to be that bit more cautious.

Igor Alberts knew how to find the newest and most lucrative opportunities in multi-level marketing. Experienced multi-level marketers know to get in early, moving from opportunity to opportunity, and get out when they know they have made all the money there is to make, or when they sense the project is about to collapse or close to being exposed as a scam. There are people around the world who have made careers out of it, those who have built up entire networks of people ready to sell through, who know all the tips and tricks and what it takes to sell every type of product to every type of person. These teams would thus move from product to product, some honest, others less so, not caring what it was but leveraging their existing networks and accumulated sales tricks to profit from every latest opportunity.

Sebastian Greenwood, one of the co-founders of OneCoin who now sits in a US jail awaiting fraud charges,[16] had built a career in multi-level marketing and knew how it worked. He had a downline of MLM marketers and knew how to get a new MLM concept off the ground. When Ruja met Sebastian, cryptocurrencies were booming and Ruja – the brains behind the operation – instantly saw the power, frantic hype and FOMO panic buying that multi-level marketing, if done well, could inspire. This was what she thought was needed to make her cryptocurrency go viral.

Ruja realized that the best way to make OneCoin – something that people could buy into that promised to generate huge amounts of wealth – spread across every corner of the earth was to have teams of multi-level marketers, with their salesmen and sales funnels and experience in place, primed and ready to make the world buy into her money-making products. All she needed to do was make the product easy enough to sell and make the commissions lucrative enough to attract the world's best and most aggressive teams of network marketers to work exclusively for her selling OneCoin. She saw that this could go viral. And it did.

Dr Ruja knew exactly what she was doing. In emails obtained later by the FBI, she described OneCoin as 'the b*tch of Wall Street meets MLM'.[17] Money printing meets multi-level marketing. Ruja just needed her team of multi-level marketers.

Igor Alberts was one of the world's best at multi-level marketing. Through his 31 years in MLM, he had built a downline team of thousands of the best professional MLM marketers the world had ever seen.[18] This giant, global team would quickly go into the latest opportunity, build sales funnels and affiliate sites, put on events and promotions with their perfected sales pitches, grow communities, and get out at the right time before it got ugly. As chance would have it, when OneCoin launched, Igor Alberts was looking for his next opportunity.

## The sweet smell of money

Igor was impressed by Ruja, He thought she looked like a queen. She was confident and had an academic track record he admired. And the sales potential of OneCoin was clear. He smelled money and was sold. Igor gathered all his teams and brought them all straight over to sell OneCoin.

In multi-level marketing, there are charts listing the biggest individual earners for different MLM products from around the world. When Igor and his team started selling OneCoin, out of the 10 biggest world earners in multi-level marketing across all companies, seven were from OneLife.[19] In no time at all they made OneCoin the biggest company in the world in network marketing.

He claimed that OneLife made more millionaires from selling its packages in network marketing in its first year than Amway, until then the biggest multi-level marketing company, had until then ever made in a 75-year history.[20]

Igor and Andrea Alberts knew how to make money and used all their efforts to push OneCoin. As they told the BBC, in their first month at OneCoin, 'We made in our first month almost €90,000 out of nothing. Bang!'[21] Then they made €120,000 in a month; within a few months they were making a million euros a month profit for themselves.[22]

OneLife had a series of names and titles that they gave to their sellers as praise and recognition for the amount of money they brought in – a leader board that acted as a further incentive to drive more sales. Right at the top was Igor Alberts, proud holder of the title 'Crown Diamond', the highest title they had, given to anyone who could generate €8 million worth of sales each month. When they left they were still making €2.4 million a month.[23] All from selling OneCoin.

OneCoin spread so far and so fast because it was being marketed by professional established MLM sellers who knew how to sell. They didn't know about crypto but they knew how to get people excited and buying. They were seasoned on-stage speakers, used to hyping up crowds and, crucially, wouldn't ask any questions about the product – people who in many cases would sell anything if the money was right. This is how OneCoin took billions of dollars from people all around the world, including many of the world's poorest.

## Faith in money

It wasn't just professional multi-level marketers who were guilty of bringing people's hard-earned money into OneCoin. Around the world, OneCoin investors themselves were incentivized to bring in new recruits, for which they would get 10 per cent or more of the money they invested, as well as up to 25 per cent of the money their recruits' recruits brought in, going down four levels, in a nice little pyramid scheme that the masterminds in charge had concocted. Forty per cent of these affiliate earnings would be paid mandatorily to them in OneCoin.[24]

In an ideal scenario, affiliate withdrawal requests would have been paid out by money that OneCoin had in the bank, or money that those affiliates had already brought in or invested. This, however, was Ponzi territory, so the pay-outs came from their new recruits. But by January 2017 affiliate withdrawal requests were higher than the new money coming in. There was only one thing for it. The xcoinx exchange, built to allow users to cash out from OneCoin, had to go. If affiliates, or any OneCoin holder, wanted a way to cash these earnings out into real-world money, these hopes were squashed flat at the start of 2017. The xcoinx exchange closed for good and didn't reopen, leaving no way to cash out of OneCoin tokens. But news of this travelled slowly. People still had faith in the setup, and not everyone yet wanted to cash out, so it took a while for people to realize that there was a problem. People kept on selling OneCoin in their hope of making affiliate riches; plus, 60 per cent was paid to them in government currency.

Not everyone had huge multi-level marketing downlines already built, but some OneCoin promoters had pre-made communities who by their nature trusted these people implicitly. Religious leaders around the world – innocently or out of personal greed – promoted OneCoin to their followers or brought in OneCoin salesmen to present to their congregations, taking a cut from every investment. Some were duped, perhaps thinking they were doing good for their communities. More than one religious leader in Africa suddenly started arriving at church in luxurious cars off the back of their OneCoin affiliate profits,[25] allegedly gloating as their communities lost their life savings.

## Fifty levels of grey

In the big, slightly underworld game of multi-level marketing, where there is a genuine product to sell, it's called network marketing. Where there isn't, it means the money coming in isn't coming from the sales of any product, but rather from the next set of investors. When this happens, it's a pyramid scheme – or a Ponzi. Ponzi schemes are illegal, but the difference between MLM schemes and Ponzi schemes is often grey at best. Both models are generally the same: high-pressure sales in industries known for making misleading promises and overstating their products.

In OneCoin, the particular product on sale just needed a bit of tweaking to give it a semblance of being legal enough to sell.

Unlike in other network marketing schemes, where teams would be trying to sell products, with OneCoin the product was selling packages of tokens that print money. It would be the easiest thing in the world to sell. Unfortunately for OneCoin, the opportunity to buy tokens that could be used to create more of an unregulated digital currency didn't quite count as a product. Authorities would have classified OneCoin as a Ponzi scheme early on and it might have been stopped from continuing a little earlier. But the people at OneLife knew how to get around this.

## An education: Plagiarized PDFs and some more miracle economics

OneLife needed a product that they could sell to make their MLM scheme look more legal than it was. As they couldn't promote packages containing only crypto tokens, they had to become a little more creative. So they became an education company.

OneLife sold packages that included educational courses. Their affiliate salespeople generally didn't really talk about this education, and many of the people who bought into OneCoin didn't mention it at all. Many didn't even seem to know about it.

Education was perhaps a fair cover for OneCoin's starter packages, which started at €100, but the biggest OneCoin packages went up to €228,000. It does seem hard to justify how the digital PDFs that OneCoin sent out were worth quite so much. Especially when, as the BBC's investigation quickly found out, their educational content was plagiarized almost word for word from a book called *Personal Finance For Dummies* by Eric Tyson.[26]

Unlike other cryptocurrencies, which anyone can buy on exchanges, you couldn't just buy OneCoin. To get OneCoins, you had to buy their educational packages, which would give you tokens, which would then, allegedly, mine or create more OneCoins. These packages, prospective investors were told, would give them so many OneCoins, which would go up in value so much, that just by buying one of the packages, prospective investors were led to believe they could become billionaires! Many OneCoin investors soon became billionaires – at least according to the numbers shown on the OneCoin website. They couldn't yet spend or access this money but that didn't matter, in their eyes, as it kept on going up and didn't crash.

In July 2016, a rare video of Ruja promoting one such OneCoin package was released to the public. This new package, the Ultimate Package, cost €118,000, not a small amount. In addition to the few digital sheets of plagiarized education that came with this package, its buyers would get 1,311,000 tokens, which would generate over two million OneCoins that at the time were said to be worth €7 each. The original OneCoin videos have been taken down by YouTube, but anyone interested to see the nonsense spouted in this video can still see this and other videos with a bit of Googling or via the link in the references. Anyone who follows crypto will know that some of the things mentioned, such as auto-mining meaning you mine coins at a better rate, are pure tech babble for something that doesn't make sense, and in crypto terms, for what OneCoin were describing, basically isn't possible.[27] This is economic mastery – or hyperinflation – at its best. Put €118,000 in, wait a couple of months for those OneCoins to be mined, and a few short months later you have €14 million. A high return indeed.

Effectively, OneCoin was a creation out of thin air that gave the best network marketing experts around the world high commissions for selling money-making machines that generate the hottest product around, a cryptocurrency hyped as being bigger and hotter than Bitcoin.

## The richest man on Earth

Igor saw the numbers on his OneCoin screen increasing and was hooked. As he told Jamie for the *The Missing Cryptoqueen* series, 'I did the calculation how many coins we needed to become the richest person on the planet... I said to Andrea, "We need to build it up to 100 million coins, because when this coin goes to €100 and we have 100 million, we are richer than Bill Gates." It's mathematic. It's easy as that.'[28] Igor and Andrea thought they would become the richest people on the planet with OneCoin. Igor and his wife weren't alone in calculating the riches of their newfound wealth. Other OneCoin affiliates, not even the most successful ones, had got into promoting OneCoin early enough to see the value of their coins to be worth more than €1 billion. Ordinary people believed they had become billionaires!

Unfortunately for the hopeful investors, the maths didn't quite stack up.

Blockchain enthusiast and founder of a crypto ATM firm, Tim Tayshun Curry, had been watching OneCoin from the sidelines, waiting for what he saw was its inevitable crash and trying his best to warn people before they invested and lost all their money. Tim started doing some calculations. Based on the numbers OneLife gave, every minute 50,000 new OneCoins were being 'mined'.[29] At the exchange rate at the time, roughly €30 per OneCoin, this meant that €1.5 million was being created every minute, or €2.15 billion per day was being created out of thin air by OneLife. By this time, 70 billion OneCoins had been created and more were being mined every minute. This made the value of OneCoins in circulation greater than the value of all the US dollars in circulation on earth. This was obviously neither possible nor vaguely plausible. No one else really seemed to notice, or to be bothered by this. People saw the numbers on their screens keep on going up and many, if not most, according to the thousands of comments left all over social media channels, didn't want to question.

## Hyperinflation

The benefit of a currency based on blockchain – a cryptocurrency – is that the quantity of tokens can't be manipulated. The number and inflation rate of tokens will be written into code on their creation.

As we will see in later chapters, crypto markets can be heavily manipulated but, in theory at least, blockchain provides a greater level of transparency over the creation of coins and transactions, and prevents a centralized entity being able to distort the token supply, as is frequently done by banks and governments. This gave some degree of reassurance to OneCoin investors, to whom Ruja had assured that OneCoin was the biggest and best cryptocurrency built on the most innovative blockchain technology.

Under normal circumstances, if a currency were to suddenly increase in supply overnight from 2.1 billion coins to 120 billion coins, it would be seen as hyperinflation. Inflation of over single digits is considered globally to be high. A sudden inflation of a currency of 5,714 per cent is extreme by any definition of the word. Generally speaking, increasing the supply of a currency makes the value decrease. This is basically true for every country and every currency in the world. Yet when OneLife suddenly decided overnight to increase the token supply of OneCoin by this amount, OneCoin investors mostly didn't panic; they were assured their coins were stored and recorded on blockchain and that this meant they were somehow safe.[30] Dr Ruja told investors that this increase (hyperinflation) of their coins would make the price of an individual OneCoin even more valuable, not less. It was yet another of OneCoin's many remarkable reinventions of the rules of basic economics.[31]

As Ruja explained to great fanfare, if OneCoin has more coins, the more people will know about OneCoin and the more it can expand and strengthen the brand.[32] It wasn't clear how this would work, or how this was even possible, but people believed her. To make up for the more than slight increase in token supply, Ruja doubled all their coins. For every OneCoin people had, they now had two. Instead of seeing the reality of the situation, that the value of their coins had in practice dropped by 30 times, leaving investors with 96.66 per cent less relative value than they had bought into, they clapped and cheered and praised their leader. All was good, because everything was recorded safely on blockchain.

## The missing cryptocurrency

Bjorn Bjorke was a technologist running his own IT company when in 2013 he took parental leave for the birth of his daughter. Bjorn took the time out to speak to me. He had heard about

Bitcoin, and spent most of the rest of that year of leave trying to hack it. He then used most of 2014 trying to hack it. By the end of this, he realized that he couldn't hack Bitcoin. But by now Bjorn was hooked. He started focusing on working in developing blockchain technologies and soon became seen as an expert in his field. In October 2016 Bjorn was approached by a Japanese recruitment agent specializing in MLM with a job offer for a role at a crypto start-up in Bulgaria, who wanted to hire him as their CTO. It was a good salary – around £250,000 a year. This was perhaps suspiciously high for the job on offer, but they wanted him to move to Bulgaria, for which they would rent him a nice apartment and pay for his car and other expenses. They wanted him to build their blockchain.

Now this is where Bjorn's ears pricked up. He knew how to build a blockchain; this is what he'd been working on. But the recruitment agent had said it was a crypto company that already had a cryptocurrency. A cryptocurrency, by definition, is built on blockchain. It isn't technically possible to have a cryptocurrency without a blockchain. Bjorn asked for more details. Finally, the recruitment agent revealed the name of the company: OneCoin. Bjorn had heard the name OneCoin mentioned before. To those in the crypto world, it was a little talked of but already known scam.

The timings here are interesting. On 1 October that year, Ruja was on stage 'switching on' their new blockchain.[33] This new blockchain would be bigger and better than the one they had before, she said. Six days after that, Bjorn was approached with the first phone call from the recruiter offering him the role of CTO to build a blockchain for this crypto company that already allegedly had a supposedly working cryptocurrency for years, but now needed a blockchain.

OneLife had the whole time been using an SQL database to store the data and values of OneCoin. An SQL database operates much like an Excel spreadsheet. Anyone can at any time go into the database and change the numbers in the boxes.

OneCoin wasn't on blockchain. This meant one thing – that the number in the box that recorded the value and the price of OneCoin could be, and was constantly being, updated by Ruja at the touch of a button. The fact that OneCoin was recorded on an SQL database, not on blockchain, meant that OneCoin could freeze accounts or coins at will and that they had full control over their users' holdings, whereas had OneCoin been on blockchain, only the coins' owners would have been able to move or use the coins. The numbers that people saw on their screens of what their OneCoin portfolios were worth had literally no value. Their value was being fabricated out of thin air based on whatever number Ruja wanted to enter into the box on that day. This was how the value kept on going up and why OneCoin couldn't be cashed out into real-world currency, and why even OneLife wouldn't accept these worthless OneCoins for their own branded merchandise. Ninety per cent of what OneCoin had been doing couldn't be done on a blockchain. As Bjorn put it: alarm bells were ringing.

## Plastic surgery to make it all ok

Investors eventually started to get wind that OneCoin perhaps wasn't all it had been made out to be. There were too many red flags, too many things not working. For some, Bjorn's comments confirming there was no blockchain, for which he has received multiple threats to his life, were the final straw. Panic started to hit. Many who had been loyally selling OneCoin until now and counting on the profits they thought it was making them realized they'd been promoting nothing but a scam to their communities and loved ones.

OneLife needed to reassure the world that OneCoin had some semblance of value to keep the scam afloat. The exchange was gone. DealShaker, by 2019, wasn't quite the global trading platform it was made out to be; faked numbers aside, it looked like it had virtually no users and by now Ruja had been on the run for two years. The team at OneLife did what any fake crypto Ponzi company would do in the circumstances: they launched a beauty pageant, in a back-street hotel in Romania. Jamie and his team from the BBC went, and did not feel comfortable there.

OneLife claimed their Miss OneLife beauty pageant would be the biggest event in the world, that it would be watched by millions of people, that L'Oréal were a sponsor and that it would be the first beauty pageant to be funded by cryptocurrency.[34] It probably wasn't quite the event organizers had hoped for. There were no hordes of TV cameras and no sign of L'Oréal, of whom there is no evidence that they were ever aware of any association with OneLife and whose logo was subsequently removed from the website,[35] but there were 30 stunning contestants, models who had flown in from around the world attracted by the generous prizes on offer. The prizes were probably the most bizarre to ever be offered to winners of a beauty pageant: €20,000 worth of the winner's choice of either the OneCoin cryptocurrency, or of plastic surgery vouchers.[36]

## Where did the money go?

No one is sure when exactly OneCoin began to run out of money, but already in early 2017 it's clear that they were having some major problems. Despite huge promised returns on investment, OneCoin had already been unable to meet their withdrawal requests since early in the year. Some affiliates claim they hadn't been paid or able to withdraw their money in months. Whilst some affiliates were more or less unaffected, before long the overwhelming majority were complaining that they couldn't get the money they thought they were owed.

This hit OneCoin's bottom line in a way the company really couldn't afford. Without happy affiliates, there was no one to bring new investment money in, and the complaints and bad press spiralled. OneCoin made sure to delete most complaints shortly after they were posted, but sentiment was clear – there was no money left in the OneCoin coffers to pay out investors and affiliates, and new investment money had dried up. Given the missing billions, it's still not known how much Ruja and the masterminds behind OneLife had siphoned out, or where exactly this money went.[37]

## Love spies

This wasn't the only worry for Ruja around this time. Ruja was married, with a young daughter. To add some more drama to her life, she had been having a long-standing affair with an American money launderer, Gilbert Armenta, who had been helping her move her money around. Ruja and Gilbert were talking of leaving their spouses and even spoke about what they would name their kids.

Gilbert was in trouble with the FBI. Ruja knew this, but this wasn't the problem. What troubled Ruja was that she didn't trust that Gilbert would leave his wife for her. In 2015, Ruja had apparently hired one of Luxemburg's top spies to be her personal problem-solver. Frank Schneider now ran a private intelligence firm called Sandstone and it was to him that Ruja allegedly went to get rid of all her problems. Konstantin, Ruja's brother, has said a few things in court, which Frank strongly denies. In 2017, however, the most pressing problem was her love life.[38]

In a move perhaps typical of two criminals carrying out an illicit though perhaps unrequited love affair, Ruja reportedly had one of Frank's men buy the flat beneath Gilbert's Florida home which he shared with his wife, and drill a hole in the ceiling, placing a microphone so that she could hear what was going on. Ruja planned to listen in to his private conversations with his wife. What Ruja didn't know was that Gilbert was already cooperating with the FBI, trying to win back some hope for himself by speaking out against her. The FBI had wiretapped his phones to record his conversations with her,[39] including one of her warning him about what 'these Russian guys' involved in OneCoin can do.[40]

By September 2017 Ruja knew they were in trouble. On a call that month to Gilbert, she threatened the involvement of organized crime, that there were Russians involved who were powerful enough to do anything they wanted. She sounded scared, but didn't yet seem to know the extent of OneCoin's troubles. Either way, by late September Ruja was in trouble. OneCoin couldn't pay out and wasn't bringing in the new investors it needed to keep up the facade, organized crime was closing in, and it seems her hopes of eloping with her lover and having his children had been shattered.

## The fake cryptoqueen

As OneCoin's troubles piled up, investigative researchers and angry investors started to close in. Many things about Ruja, they soon found out, were fake. The *Forbes* cover wasn't a cover. It was a paid advertisement OneCoin had taken out in *Forbes*' affiliate in Bulgaria that OneLife had designed to look like a front page of *Forbes International*.[41] When OneCoin used this page (extensively) in its promotions, they forgot to mention that it was just an advert. Speaking at the *Economist* convention was also bought – OneCoin was the Platinum sponsor.[42]

OneCoin was also far from being Ruja's only disappearance from a failed project. In 2009, Ruja, together with her metalworker father, bought a steelworks factory in Southern Germany, near where she had grown up. He knew the trade, Ruja was the brains and was to run the business. The factory had been thriving, employing 140 loyal workers who fed 140 local families. By 2012 the factory was bankrupt. Jamie Bartlett and his BBC investigation team spoke to them. As its longstanding employees all lost their jobs, Ruja was driving around in an expensive Porsche.[43] Her role in driving this once thriving factory to bankruptcy in such a short space of time led to Ruja being convicted of 24 counts of fraud. She pleaded guilty to charges including embezzling money from employees and suppliers, bank fraud, fraudulent accounting and even attempts to take the factory's machinery and ship it back to Bulgaria to sell. Ruja received a suspended jail sentence of 14 months.[44] The factory never heard from her again and, until OneCoin, for everyone not directly affected, the matter was all but regretful history.

## And she's gone. Take the money and run

It's not known whether it was just the problems facing OneCoin and knowing that she was wanted by the FBI, her shattered love life, or even pressure from organized crime that OneCoin was involved with that took Ruja into hiding. All that is known is that Ruja was last known to be on a last-minute Ryanair flight to Athens where she got into a car with some Russians and has never been seen again. Were these the same Russians she had warned about in the taped call with Gilbert? It's not (yet) known.

Ruja had discussed possible exit strategies with her co-founder in earlier times. Strategy number one: 'Take the money and run and blame someone else for this...'[45]

One man who perhaps knows more about Ruja and OneCoin than anyone else is Jamie Bartlett. The mastermind and presenter behind the hit BBC podcast series *The Missing Cryptoqueen* who gave one of the most exciting closed room talks we've ever had at our Crypto Curry Club events in London, he was kind enough to (virtually) sit down with me during the writing of the book and this is what he had to say:

## How did people not question or suspect that OneCoin isn't crypto?

Ninety-nine per cent of investors were MLM people or friends of MLM, so they'd heard about Bitcoin and the pizza guy (who infamously bought two Dominos pizzas for 10,000 bitcoin, at their 2021 (so far) peak worth a maximum of around $500 million), but didn't understand the technology surrounding cryptocurrency. MLM people tend to look at things like: does the founder have a PhD, did they work for a big company before, do the promoters drive nice cars? They generally have different ways of establishing trust, whereas crypto people would look at code or at GitHub.

A lot came down to people trusting friends. People were blinded by the great returns of Bitcoin and other cryptocurrencies, and so many really wanted to believe that OneCoin was also true. Psychologically, once you've decided something is true, you can find evidence to support it. Ruja gave enough evidence to those who wanted to believe it.

What needs to be noted is that OneCoin happened still relatively early in crypto. This was at a time when almost everyone was calling all of the different crypto projects a scam at points. Bitcoin people called Ethereum a scam, Ethereum people called Bitcoin a scam. Everyone was calling all of the smaller alt coins a scam. So OneCoin looked like just one of the many crypto projects that were accused of being fraudulent. The power of calling OneCoin a scam was lost. Also, OneCoin was started before all the information about it being a scam was all over the internet.

## Why did people keep believing OneCoin even when there were so many red flags?

Once you've invested your money into something, you have a psychological block, so it can be hard to believe that you've been ripped off. A lot of people just couldn't bear to see that, so kept up the hope.

Admitting you've been scammed, for many people who brought in their friends and family to also invest alongside them, means you've got to admit to your friends and family that you've also, albeit accidentally, scammed them.

There were a few levels of people:

- Those at the top who knew and didn't care that it was a scam.
- Those in the middle who suspected but didn't want to know the truth.
- Those at the bottom who really did believe in OneCoin and its claims, then found out it was a scam and kept on pretending because they didn't want to believe it.
- Some people who really didn't know it was a scam.

**Why did the multi-level marketing people get away with it? Why do you think it's possible for people to be repeat offenders in MLM scams?**

Those at the top of the MLM pyramids have made a lot of money; they have good lawyers now advising them what they can say to maintain their innocence. It's not necessarily fair.

Law enforcement in 2015 believed OneCoin was a cryptocurrency. They didn't do enough investigation into it, so they believed that it wasn't regulated, as cryptocurrencies then weren't.

There were also so many different crypto projects already, even in 2015, that I don't think law enforcement in different countries knew what to do, or which ones to focus on. In most countries they weren't regulated anyway and so no one knew which the responsible authority was.

**Do you think they will be punished?**

Law enforcement might step in and start investigating, but it's so hard to prove. It's so hard to prove whether people thought it was a real investment or a scam. Multi-level marketing itself is legal, so it's quite a grey area, and the multi-level marketing guys might argue their way out of any troubles.

**Do you think Ruja is alive?**

I think so, it's possible. I think it's 30–40 per cent likely she could be dead. There are people motivated to get rid of her. But then she has access to a lot of money, which brings power.

**Do you have any idea who really is behind OneCoin – is it mafia or organized crime? And if there was organized crime behind it, when did they get involved? Were they there from the beginning or only led it when it got big?**

It is possible that it was all a front from the start for laundering money for drug dealing or something else; there is the possibility that that's what happened. I personally believe it really was a joint idea between Ruja and Sebastian, that it started off as their idea, 50–50. Ruja brought the brains and the crypto side, and Sebastian brought the MLM – the multi-level marketing experience. Maybe organized crime then came into it.

**Do you think it was a scam from the start, or started out with good intent and got out of control?**

Maybe it was a scam, maybe it wasn't a scam from the start. It's so hard to know. But what Ruja did that was so terrible and that has had such a big impact on so many was to create this blend of crypto meets MLM that had never been done before. It was Ruja's idea to create an MLM-meets-crypto money-making product that would sell like wildfire. It got out of hand.

I think they initially tried to make it work if they could, then it spiralled out of their control. I think it got way bigger than they ever imagined it could possibly get. It's a bit like many of the other crypto initial coin offerings. ICOs in that sense, some were scams, some opportunistic that became like scams because their founders couldn't make them work and they got bigger than they expected.

I don't think it's as black-and-white as being a crypto scam. Some people initially really did believe it, and then got confused. That's why the MLM aspect was so important when it came to OneCoin. OneCoin offered all the big promises of getting rich quick and yet 99 per cent in MLM don't make any money, but people have the hope and want to believe.

## The scam goes on

Even if OneCoin does one day fully stop trading, the damage it caused lives on. At the end of 2016, some of the leaders of OneCoin left and allegedly are behind a new cryptocurrency, Dagcoin,[46] which more than a few onlookers would accuse of being a like-for-like copy of the OneCoin scam, judging by comments all over the internet and social media. People are led to invest real money under expectations of high returns, MLM affiliates get high returns for promoting it, and it offers educational packages through its affiliate network, Success Factory. Success Factory and Dagcoin have groups all over the internet, including an active Facebook group full of hopeful investors who either believe the hype or are too desperate to care. Dagcoin isn't proven to be anything yet, but according to many onlookers it is a blatant Ponzi scheme,[47] an almost exact copy of OneCoin, and is gaining investors fast who don't yet see that they're losing money to the scam.

Igor Alberts, the multimillionaire OneCoin promoter who made tens of millions of euros off the back of OneCoin's victims, says he and Andrea left OneCoin when they realized it was a scam. Igor has since taken his multi-level marketing teams to Dagcoin when he saw the law starting to catch up with OneCoin. They're now Dagcoin's biggest promoters, making $1.6 million per month from it.[48] Anyone wanting to check out the similarities between Dagcoin and OneCoin can check out Dagcoin's Facebook group for some mind-blowing insights into how these MLM schemes can grow.

Some of the ringleaders of OneCoin sit behind bars, others await trial, and Ruja is still on the run, her whereabouts unknown. Millions of people around the world, including many from the world's poorest countries who fell victim to good salesmen and to their religious leaders, will never see their money, often their life savings, again.

## CHAPTER FOUR

# Bitconnect

*The double Ponzi and the elusive,
unbeatable trading bot*

## Fluff and buzzwords, another new cryptocurrency

Another month, another ICO. The February 2016 ICO that would
go on to affect the most people was Bitconnect, then an unknown
name from yet another unknown start-up that appeared out of
nowhere. As with many other ICOs, Bitconnect didn't exactly give
much information on the company's website or marketing; the team
was anonymous, there was no information about who was behind
the project and it really wasn't clear what Bitconnect intended to do.
The website simply said:

> Bitconnect coin is an open source, peer-to-peer, community-driven
> decentralized cryptocurrency that allows people to store and
> invest their wealth in a non-government-controlled currency, and
> even earn a substantial interest on investment. This means anyone

holding Bitconnect coin in their wallet will receive interest on their balance in return for helping maintain the security of the network.[1]

That is a lot of buzzwords that basically don't say a lot. The whole paragraph, and in fact all of the information released about Bitconnect, was vastly more fluff than anything remotely substance-filled. It says that if one holds their coins, one will earn substantial interest. Why, or how, anyone would earn such interest for maintaining the network isn't clear and doesn't make technical sense. Nonetheless, Bitconnect raised $410,000 in bitcoin. This was before the big 2017 crypto bubble when people would throw millions at projects they knew very little about, but was still a notable sum given that people would have had no idea what they were putting their money into.

## 95,751.58 times richer than Jeff Bezos

By early 2017, the Bitconnect website had updated to say they had developed their own proprietary trading bot and volatility software, providing its users with a way to trade their money against Bitcoin. They also announced the launch of a lending platform. Bitconnect users wouldn't have to do any trading themselves. All they would need to do is lend their Bitconnect coin back to Bitconnect. Bitconnect would then use this to trade against Bitcoin where their trading bot would supposedly profit from Bitcoin's volatility and make money both for the lender and for the Bitconnect platform. To say that such a trade would be risky is an understatement. Quite how this worked, or how the bot could make guaranteed profits every day to pay Bitconnect coin holders the 'substantial interest' they were promised, was never explained.

Bitconnect holders could 'loan' any amount upwards of $100 to the Bitconnect platform, which would then supposedly trade these coins against Bitcoin and magically make guaranteed profit for all. Investors would have to lock up their coins for between

120 and 299 days.[2] Such a lock-up can be a standard part of an investment – some fund managers need money for a certain period of time to be able to have the best chance of generating the optimum returns for their clients, but investors should still be able to withdraw, even if for a fee. For a trading bot that works, supposedly, generating returns on a daily basis, it's hard to see why such a long lock-up would be strictly necessary. The forced lock-up of investors' tokens does give the impression that Bitconnect wanted to hold onto their investors' money without giving it back. A lock-up of money or tokens is a classic tool used by Ponzi schemes. Alarm bells should have, by now, started ringing.

Bitconnect's biggest selling point in their sales pitch was the extraordinarily high guaranteed daily returns they promised to anyone who bought Bitconnect coins and lent them back to their platform. In most industries, 5–10 per cent a year is generally considered a very good return on investment. Depending on how much one invested, Bitconnect would pay out interest of 47.5 per cent a month, or up to 570 per cent a year. Of this, 90 per cent a year was supposedly guaranteed.[3] This interest could then be compounded, meaning that Bitconnect's interest pay-outs would not only pay interest on the initial investment, but also on the daily interest pay-outs, if these were kept on the platform.[4] These numbers, with daily compounding, if users reinvested their daily interest paid out back into the platform, when put into one of the compound interest calculators freely available online,[5] soon started to get silly.

If someone invested $100 for one year and re-invested all their interest pay-outs, instead of cashing those out, by the end of one year they would have $11,776.75.

If someone invested $1,010 for one year and re-invested all their interest pay-outs, instead of cashing those out, by the end of one year they would have $169,663.50.

If someone invested $10,010 for one year and re-invested all their interest pay-outs, instead of cashing those out, by the end of one year they would have $2,862,743.59. That's over $2.8 million.

If someone invested $10,010 for five years and re-invested all their interest pay-outs, instead of cashing those out, by the end of five years they would have $19,150,316,162,940,756.00. That's over $19,150,316 billion. By contrast, Jeff Bezos, currently the richest man on earth, has a net worth of just over $200 billion,[6] crossing a global milestone after months of coronavirus lockdown added huge growth to Amazon's wealth and finances. According to these rates, someone who invested $10,010 in Bitconnect in five years' time would make Jeff Bezos look incredibly poor by comparison. They would in fact be roughly 95,751.58 times richer than Jeff Bezos.

## Reality check

There is a general saying that if something seems too good to be true, it probably is. Anyone taking the time to analyse these numbers might consider the long-term viability of these returns to be unlikely. Bitconnect didn't make it clear how they were able to make these incredible returns, other than with some vague comments about their trading bot.

Leading investment banks and hedge funds hire the world's best coders, traders and analysts and will pay whatever money it takes to acquire and use the best algorithms known for trading, no money spared. There is no fund or trader yet who has made guaranteed results, let alone in the hundreds of percent return per year, regardless of market conditions. There was very little known or said about how Bitconnect's elusive, unbeatable bot made by this anonymous team could generate such high guaranteed returns. If this bot were really making the guaranteed percentage returns that Bitconnect claimed, there would have been no incentive for the creators of this bot to share it with anyone. Sharing these results would have been detrimental to them, as had they just compounded their own returns and reinvested those into their own trading software, within a few years they would have been by far the richest people on earth.

Whilst some investors started to raise some doubts that this did indeed seem to be slightly unrealistic, most just didn't seem to question the process. Early Bitconnect investors seemed happy to be making money, or believed in the story of the bot, and chose not to question any of it.

## Literally no use or value

By now, Bitconnect had launched its own new exchange where one could trade bitcoin, a globally accepted digital currency, for Bitconnect's own coins, which they could then lend to its platform and profit from the guaranteed returns it offered. The vast majority of these bitcoin-to-Bitconnect trades were going through Bitconnect's own exchange, with high transaction fees imposed on anyone wanting to cash out of their Bitconnect coin profits. This made a healthy profit for Bitconnect from every transaction. Some people figured that it was in the transaction fees where Bitconnect made its real money instead of the trading bot, but still largely chose not to question further.

Other than using the Bitconnect token to supposedly trade against Bitcoin, Bitconnect had no use case or value. People would either just hold on to their Bitconnect coins in the hope of price appreciation, or would lend these coins out to the platform.

People heard about the returns that early investors were getting by lending their Bitconnect coins to the platform and, sure enough, all early investors were paid out in full, at least 1 per cent interest daily. Of course, this wasn't sustainable, but investors saw the wild swings that were making people rich in the crypto markets and saw this as an easy way to passively make these same returns.

Despite what should have been some pretty obvious red flags, people continued to flock to the platform, and once they had locked up their money they had a very good reason to tell everyone they knew about it – Bitconnect offered a very generous affiliate referral bonus structure.

## The great pyramid

There is a recurring theme in many of the crypto scams. These are not companies with long-term focus in mind; crypto scams wanted to get as much money as they possibly could in the shortest space of time, then close up shop and run in the hope they never got caught. To do this, just as with OneCoin, scam projects needed to get people falling over themselves to invest. To achieve this, particularly with a project with zero real-world use or legitimacy, sometimes traditional marketing wasn't enough. Many of the biggest crypto scams were in effect Ponzi schemes, where the money came in not from selling any product of value, but from the next set of investors. To get the new investors, the projects would offer high referral bonuses. This achieved one thing – the platform itself didn't have to do anywhere near as much of the work to promote itself – their investors did it all for them!

Bitconnect brought in professional scam promoters and also had more than its share of crypto-influencer YouTubers promoting the platform, bringing in thousands of victims who lost untold millions of dollars. Unfortunately for Bitconnect's victims, these YouTubers were uncannily good at separating people from their money. People saw the returns they promoted on their channels and believed them. Bitconnect promoters made a cut of the investment from everyone they brought in. Many of these influencers and YouTubers are still going free, with more than one having moved on to promote their next scam.

Again, just as with OneCoin, there is a trend in crypto Ponzi scheme promotion: hire known multi-level marketing scammers and influencers willing to sell any investment in exchange for money. Affiliates would take screenshots of their returns and profits, showing off to their many followers how much they were making. What these YouTubers omitted to mention was that most of their impressive profits from Bitconnect were their commissions from recruiting new investors. A strong referral incentive also drove thousands upon thousands of Bitconnect's investors to bring in their friends, families and communities in to invest. In many cases this was innocent; a lot of people really believed in the platform and saw it paying out as it had promised, a lot of those who promoted Bitconnect, at least in its earlier days, really weren't to know any better.

Just as we saw with OneCoin and will see with PlusToken, a common trend in crypto scams was bringing in money Ponzi style. Just as with these other crypto scams, Bitconnect's referral bonus structure was shaped like a pyramid. For every direct referral, the promoter or influencer would get 7 per cent of their referral's investment. If their referral then brought someone in to invest underneath them, the first referrer would also get 3 per cent of that investment. This went on, with investors getting a percentage cut of every person that invested who was referred by anyone they referred, down seven levels. Just as with OneCoin and the multi-level marketing structure, the problem with pyramid schemes is that those who carry the most influence and get in the earliest make a lot of money. Millions of dollars of commission pay-outs was not uncommon for Bitconnect.

It didn't take long for people to start commenting that the high returns and pyramid-shaped referral structure made Bitconnect look rather like a pyramid or Ponzi scheme. A lot of these pyramid-related comments were made by more seasoned crypto investors, who had seen this all before. Sadly, most of these concerns didn't quite reach the keen Bitconnect investors, many of whom were more focused on increasing their investments than on listening to advice.

## Advertising the scam

Bitconnect had a development fund for marketing totalling 10 per cent of investors' money and used this to invest heavily in promotions. On top of hosting glamorous investor-only events, these funds were used to reward promoters, and would pay for hundreds of thousands of dollars on advertising to YouTube, Facebook and Google. Leaked messaging chats show the lead USA promoter for Bitconnect was at one point bringing in around $7 million a week, leaving him with $700,000 per week to spend on advertising the scheme in the USA.[7]

Of course, this 10 per cent of investors' money that went on marketing wasn't mentioned to the investors. The team at Bitconnect had more tricks up their sleeve to bring new investors onto the platform. And, by late 2017, a few too many people had started to vocally doubt the platform. Bitconnect needed to do something pretty big to impress their investors and keep their most eager promoters motivated and loyal.

## Supercars, disco balls, awful music and bad singing. What could go wrong?

On 28 October 2017, a video went viral on YouTube and throughout the crypto world. For all the wrong reasons.

That day, there had been an awards ceremony at the Pattaya Exhibition and Convention Hall, an opulent events venue with a backdrop overlooking Pattaya beach in Thailand. The event was to celebrate Bitconnect's first year of public trading. No expense had been spared. There was a live entertainment show with dancers, singers, drummers and musicians, a symbolic sword fight, a gala dinner and awards ceremony. Even the winner of Thailand's Got Talent, Ku Ling, was brought on stage, dangling by his legs from a strip of red silk in a feat of aerial acrobatics.

The evening was an ostentatious celebration of Bitconnect's most vocal supporters. The platform's top affiliates and the top YouTubers who had brought in the most referrals were each given $10,000 in Bitconnect's token; seven top promoters and supporters each got $50,000 in the new currency. Glistening in centre stage in the spotlights were five supercars: a Porsche 911 Carrera S, a Mercedes GTS, an Aston Martin Vantage, a Ferrari California and a Lamborghini Hurricane, given with big show to the five most active promoters. They wanted the world to see how well their affiliates were doing. Basically, the platform needed more affiliates to keep the scam rolling, and soon. What better incentive than dishing out some nice new cars. The awards were presented by a man who went by the name of Michael Crypto. For anyone wanting to see the crass gifting of supercars, a video is easily findable by Googling 'Bitconnect's Pattaya supercar event'.[8]

People were brought on stage to share stories of how their investments in Bitconnect had changed their lives. One man in India who had bought into Bitconnect when it was 20 cents told how, thanks to a sharp gain in value and compounded interest, he now makes $20,000 a day, just a few months later. Carlos Matos, a New Yorker who had also bought into Bitconnect a few months prior, had a key role at the conference. Carlos was a showman and was good at getting the audience riled up. He told how his $26,000 investment was now worth $140,000,[9] that he now makes $1,400 day every day just 137 days since making his investment, how Bitconnect had changed his life and how the company was already changing the world.[10]

Giant-size models of credit cards were brought out, large enough and angled so that everyone there could read the word 'Visa' printed in large across them. People literally started dancing on stage alongside the Bitconnect team, holding the cards up high for everyone to see. One can assume that they were asked or paid to do so and that this wasn't some spontaneous gesture, but Bitconnect didn't publicize those details. A giant-size model of an ATM machine was then wheeled out, which one of the super-size 'smart cards' was duly inserted into, causing real bank notes to rain down on to the audience, who were told the new Bitconnect smart card would be able to pay for anything in the Bitconnect coins that were being so widely handed out. Registration for the card would begin that year on 1 December. We haven't found any evidence of Visa supporting the claims of their association with Bitconnect.

The team behind Bitconnect even launched a music album that night, headlined by a supposedly catchy but definitely cheesy hip-hop song, with teenagers dancing and singing about Bitconnect – 'We've got a good thing, and it's amazing.'[11] It wasn't made clear what relevance having its own music album had to a cryptocurrency, but with cars, money, dancing, disco balls and now their own songs, what could go wrong?

To get people to go, Bitconnect paid for their flights and accommodation. It was a good incentive to invest. Anyone who had invested – or would do so in the month following the announcement – a one-time deposit of $20,000 or more into the platform was sent a personalised invitation by post. If they came, Bitconnect would refund their flights and hotel costs to Thailand. Those coming from the UK would receive about £2,000 for their expenses. Two thousand people travelled there from around the world, most of those going not for the free holiday to a conference centre but genuinely excited by the honour of attending the event. All four hours of the event were screened live and are still on YouTube for anyone wanting an insight into the promotional events of a now closed-down scam. It's interesting viewing.

Carlos made himself known that night. A video of him singing over and over again in a high-pitched squeal of never-ending 'Bitconnecccccct' turned into an internet sensation in the crypto community, a never-dying internet meme of the embodiment of a multi-billion dollar crypto Ponzi scam in action. The video is freely available to anyone wanting to search for his name and 'Bitconnect annual ceremony' on YouTube.

As a promotional tool for Bitconnect, the event seemed to work. Clearly more people invested, as just a month later, at the North American Blockchain expo in Santa Clara, California in November 2017, Bitconnect chartered a private yacht, throwing a party on board for anyone who invested $1,000 in their platform. They offered a free yacht ride under the Golden Gate Bridge and a winery vineyard tour above Silicon Valley. A small price to pay to take in $1,000 per person, and some pretty smart marketing.[12]

## Some more warning signs

There were several other warning signs for anyone looking at Bitconnect who wanted to see them. Unlike other investment platforms that give some indication that capital might be at risk, a fairly standard legal requirement, Bitconnect had no such cautionary words on their website.

The website was full of spelling mistakes and poor grammar. Non-native English speakers can easily access online editors to quality check websites, or can hire native English-speakers to do some minor proofreading to correct the most basic of mistakes, for relatively low costs. The internet is literally full of sites or freelancers offering this service. This would be especially easy if the company behind the website had access to the world's best trading bot that could guarantee them high daily returns and had billions of dollars' worth of assets. That Bitconnect seemingly didn't even bother to spell check its website is inexplicable.

Bitconnect also never gave any proof as to the existence of their trading bot. Given this was what the company centred its entire investment offering around, one would have thought they'd have made a little more effort to convince outsiders of its existence. But, no.

It did seem, even early on to those who wanted to see the glaring red flag shaped clues, that Bitconnect was rather more intent on parting investors with their money than on informing them how they were doing so.

## The sound of warning bells

Thankfully, it didn't take too long before the warnings vocalized by the crypto community were picked up by international law enforcement. On 7 November 2017, just under a year after Bitconnect launched their ICO, they were issued with a strike-off notice by UK Companies House.[13] Bitconnect had two months to prove their legitimacy before being shut down in the UK, where they had registered an office for a 75 per cent shareholder by name of a Mr Ken Fitzsimmons.[14] There is no Ken Fitzsimmons listed anywhere on their site or anywhere else in connection with Bitconnect; it's presumed Ken is as fabricated as their trading bot.

For a while Bitconnect carried on as if nothing had happened. Some investors started to worry, but Bitconnect reassured people into continuing to buy their token, stating that any legal actions against a division of their company Bitconnect Ltd didn't affect the main company, Bitconnect International Plc.[15] They denied any wrongdoing and focused instead on pumping out search engine optimized content designed to rank higher on search engines and on social media than any negative press or legal mentions.[16] This strategy worked, for a while. Bitconnect investors continued their frenzied buying, pushing the token to its peak price of $463, up from 17 cents just a little over a year before.[17]

In early January 2018, the American states of Texas and North Carolina accused Bitconnect of illegally selling securities, a type of asset that is legal to sell, but only for companies that have gone through stringent checks with regulators and been given permission to do so, and then only to experienced or professional investors who know what they are doing and can afford to take the hit if they lose their money. To sell securities without the needed regulation is a big legal 'no', but is one that a lot of ICOs did anyhow, either because they didn't know or bother to find out more about the regulations, or because it was crypto and at the time unregulated so they thought they would get away with it. Bitconnect complied with a grand total of zero regulation and promoted their token to people who weren't experienced in crypto or investment, targeting those who they could most easily deceive.

Bitconnect was sent cease and desist letters from two US states, first the Texas Securities Board[18] and then the North Carolina Securities Division,[19] to force them to stop selling their token right away. Following these public legal actions, even some of the key YouTube influencers started to distance and disassociate themselves from the platform,[20] aiming to protect their own reputations. Bitconnect soon released a statement; they were closing their lending and exchange, leaving only their website open. The reasons they stated: bad press creating a lack of confidence in the platform, the two cease and desist letters, and DDoS attacks – otherwise known as distributed denial-of-service attacks – a relatively common type of cyber-attack caused by hackers wanting to disrupt websites. Bitconnect said that these issues had made 'the platform unstable and have created more panic inside the community'.[21] These reasons didn't make much sense. Given the supposedly unbeatable nature of their trading bot, bad press shouldn't have affected the platform. If everything was as they said it was, with guaranteed returns every day, the company would never have needed investors or public confidence; they could have happily carried on trading their own money and the results would have spoken for themselves. DDoS attacks can be prevented by having good cyber security and penetration testing. Buying enterprise-level security protection equal to any other billion dollar corporation would have been no problem for a company whose tokens at its peak had a market cap of $2.8 billion and that raised up to an expected $4 billion. Something didn't add up.

What ensued was what has become known as the biggest and most sudden bloodbath in crypto history.

## A big red bloodbath

It wasn't the team behind Bitconnect who lost their money in the crash. In December 2017 there were a few coordinated sell-offs of Bitconnect token, starting with a small sell-off of $300 million worth on 8 December, which crashed the value of the coin from around $450 to $365. Investors quickly bought the token back up to its original peak. On 17 December the price of Bitconnect started to crash again, from its almost peak of $457 per token to a low of $220 per token on 25 December, Christmas Day. That week, $900 million was wiped off the chart. Following this last market crash, which did rather spook their remaining investors, Bitconnect did a huge social media push, presumably spending some of their newly liquidated cash to bring in new investors. Investors bought the token back up, reviving some faith in the now-volatile token and in the project. But then the real sell-off started. From 30 December, when Bitconnect coin had reached its new peak of $463 per token, huge sell orders appeared, selling as yet unprecedented volumes of the token. For a week, investors kept buying the token back up, clearly thinking that, as the price had bounced back up twice, there was nothing that could stop Bitconnect coin.[22]

For a few days Bitconnect crashed slowly, from near its peak of around $450 to around $300 per token. Investors were desperate and panicking but most held on, either thinking or hoping that people would buy the coin back up at its new 'cheap' price. Most just didn't know what to do and anxiously watched the markets, hoping it would all go back up again and that the crash was just a temporary sell-off or glitch. Then on 15 January 2018 the token started its free-fall descent. Bitconnect crashed 87 per cent in a day. Investors would wake up on 16 January to their worst nightmare – the token many had plunged their life savings into, taken out business loans and re-mortgaged their houses for, maxed out their credit cards on and convinced all their friends and families to buy into was suddenly worth $11, down from highs of well over $400 when many had bought in, a loss of over 97 per cent from many people's initial investments. The market crashed from $2.8 billion to $12 million, with $1.5 billion wiped off its market cap in two hours alone.

By 17 January Bitconnect was by far the worst-performing cryptocurrency on CoinMarketCap, the popular crypto ratings site where prices and trading volumes are compared for thousands of cryptocurrencies. Many crypto old-timers, people who had been in crypto for years and had been warning everyone who would listen, long before its demise, that Bitconnect was a Ponzi and an unsustainable scam, were watching the charts and commenting about it all over Twitter. They expected this to be a sharp and sudden end to what had been the biggest Ponzi in crypto history.

It's quite possible, and perhaps the most likely possibility, that those early sell-offs were not investors who had bought Bitconnect tokens with their money or loans. Could it be those sell-offs were led by those who had started Bitconnect, cashing out their tokens into bitcoin, ready to run, in what is alleged to be a coordinated exit scam?[23]

Given that it seems the Bitconnect team had managed to cash out up to around $1.2 billion in their first sell-offs – not that it can be ascertained that this really was them – on top of any amount they sold out before then, and an unknown amount in the final sell-off that led to the freefall of Bitconnect, one might have thought the scam would stop there, that the orchestrators would have made enough to run, and that there would be no one left to trust the Bitconnect team or fall for the same scam.

Had Bitconnect ended then and there, at least that would have been an end to this particular scam. But crypto was unregulated, and the scammers behind Bitconnect hid behind anonymity and the arrogant belief that they'd never get caught. Bitconnect hadn't finished with their investors just yet.

## The double Ponzi: Two scams for the price of one

By late 2017 it had obviously become clear to the Bitconnect team that the Ponzi was running out of steam. They were getting fewer new investors; countries had started taking legal action against them and there was by now just enough noise in the crypto community warning people that Bitconnect was a scam to make some people start to listen. It's assumed the team had been cashing out their Bitconnect tokens into bitcoin, on top of the vast sums they would have accrued from transaction fees on their exchange. They must have pocketed billions. This wasn't enough; the team behind Bitconnect went for one final push. Just over a year after launching Bitconnect, it was time for the next. On 31 December 2017 a new domain was registered: Bitconnectx.co. Less than two weeks later, just before Bitconnect was about to start its free-fall descent with investors losing almost 100 per cent of their money, a second initial coin offering was launched, BitconnectX.[24]

After Bitconnect had plummeted from above $400 to fluctuating around $10 to $20 per token, the Bitconnect team released a statement to their frantic investors. They would honour a value of $150 per token, if they used their tokens to reinvest in the new ICO instead of cashing out and leaving with whatever little value they had left. The new Bitconnect ICO token was first marketed at a buy-in cost of $5 per token. Then $50.[25] Bitconnect suddenly changed their token price by a multiple of 10 overnight, without giving any reason why or making any changes whatsoever to the offering or website. Surprisingly, this didn't stop people crowding in.

Bitconnect limited how many of the new ICO tokens people could buy, and set daily purchasing limits, which were quickly reached. These limits sold out for the first days in a frenzy, giving the impression that the ICO was in high demand. This was despite the fact that early Bitconnect investors had bought in to the original Bitconnect at 17 cents, not $50, that by now, a year later, the crypto markets were at the peak of their bubble and were soon about to burst, that the company issuing this ICO had been subject to legal actions by the UK and two states in the USA, and that by the start of the BitconnectX ICO, hundreds of thousands of investors had already collectively lost billions of dollars in Bitconnect as it had crashed. Yet people still wanted in, even when they didn't know what the project was or what it would supposedly offer.

On top of the hundreds of thousands of desperate existing investors, who had collectively already lost billions, there were still new people who wanted in, in the hope of recreating the perceived wealth of early Bitconnect investors. People would still post on crypto chat groups, on Telegram or on Facebook asking for advice on how best to buy into the ICO. Incredibly, and sadly, the alarm bells from the failure of the first scam weren't enough to put everyone off, and as crypto wasn't at that time regulated, regulators didn't step in early enough.

The website for the BitconnectX ICO didn't really say much. All it really said was that investing 'allows you to earn interest for helping maintain security on the network by holding BCCX (the name for the token) in a Qt Desktop wallet that is attached to the network and allowing transactions to flow through it'.[26] As with their first ICO, this doesn't really mean anything, it's just a string of crypto-related buzzwords indicating that BitconnectX would be much the same as the original Bitconnect. The team at Bitconnect didn't even try to make it sound good, they just counted on people investing blindly. People were investing merely in the hope that tokens would go up as much as Bitconnect had in its early days and that they'd get rich quick. This second ICO managed to scam more money out of people before the website was closed, and nothing more ever became of it other than another huge loss of money for investors.

Given the coordinated sell-off by the team who created it, the lawsuits and cease and desist orders from law enforcement, the vocal noise about Bitconnect being a clear Ponzi scam almost from day one, and two ICO scams, one would have thought that the first Bitconnect would have ended there. After going from a dubious ICO to a $2.8 billion valuation, Bitconnect was delisted from almost all crypto exchanges, making the token literally worthless as nobody could cash it out or sell it. Yet the Bitconnect token continued to be traded for another eight months until 11 August 2018. When it was finally delisted from the last exchange, the last token sold for 68 cents, still giving the worthless, dead scam a market cap value of $6.69 million.[27]

Bitconnect had set up various legal and company structures around the world under what are still believed to be fake names. Some of the people believed to be behind the scam are in hiding. There have been a few arrests related to Bitconnect, including the project's alleged Asian head, Divyesh Darji, who was arrested as he travelled from Dubai to Delhi. Bitconnect isn't the first scam Darji's been accused of; he's also been associated with money laundering in India, where he's been accused of the theft of $12.6 billion of investors' money following the demonetization of rupee notes.[28] Darji is also allegedly behind another similar alleged crypto scam, Regal Coin, which seems to have taken some lessons from Bitconnect.[29]

## Bitconnect 3. Because two scams aren't enough

In September 2017, the next scam ICO launched. Regal Coin was an almost exact clone of Bitconnect and was founded by some of its promoters. It promised to let investors get in cheap to the new Bitconnect. Just as with Bitconnect, Regal Coin promised guaranteed returns of over 40 per cent a month, made, you guessed it, by a trading bot (which didn't exist), locked up investors' money, gave high affiliate rewards in a pyramid structure, incentivized YouTubers and influencers to promote it and gave no idea who was behind it. The promises weren't that different. The main differentiator was the awful quality of the English that appeared on its website, sentences that made a grand total of zero sense and to all appearances hadn't even been looked at by a native English speaker. Where Bitconnect could have done with an editor, Regal Coin's website and marketing were just plain bad. Just as with Bitconnect, some of its promoters knew it was a scam and a Ponzi scheme, but promoted it on the rationale that if you get in early enough, you have three months or so to make your money and run. Regal Coin crashed, from $70 per coin just after its launch in October 2017 to $0.0011 in 2020, its investors losing everything.[30]

## The last twist in the tale: The abducted abductors

There is one last twist in this tale. One person came forward to file a complaint against Bitconnect. Shailesh Bhatt, a property developer and businessman from India, charged into the Home Minister's office in his state of Gujarat, and said that eleven people, including eight policemen, had abducted him and extorted 200 bitcoin, then worth $1.8 million, from him.[31]

Bhatt had invested, it seems rather heavily, in Bitconnect, losing his money when the scam collapsed in January 2018. When India demonetized some of their main rupee notes in 2016, causing economic market turmoil, a lot of Indian money fled into crypto, causing a 25 per cent premium on the price of bitcoin in India in some cases. The country then effectively banned crypto transactions. So when Bitconnect collapsed, those who had invested, especially those who hadn't declared their investments to authorities, were in a bit of a quandary, and had to find alternative, more creative ways to try and get their money back.

Given the gravity of this case, the elite Gujurat Criminal Investigation Department was called in. Unfortunately for Bhatt, they found some inconsistencies in his account, and found evidence of fraud on an epic scale, all of which led to the unravelling, finally, of the masterminds behind Bitconnect.[32]

To compensate for his loss and his abduction, Bhatt allegedly in turn had several Indian Bitconnect employees abducted with the help of local policemen. From the former Bitconnect promoters, he extorted 1.55 billion rupees worth of cash and crypto at gunpoint,[33] including 2,256 bitcoin as ransom.[34] Bhatt has since gone on the run, and eight police officers face trial.[35] It seems the scam, at least in India, hasn't quite ended yet.

And the bot? It didn't exist. The incredible trading bot that guaranteed returns better than any fund has ever managed to achieve was as fabricated as everything else related to Bitconnect.

From one crypto Ponzi scam that scammed billions out of its investors to another. Our next chapter goes to China, and perhaps the highest grossing crypto Ponzi scam and one that is still shaking the crypto markets with its massive repercussions – PlusToken.

## CHAPTER FIVE

# Sorry we have run

## *The $17 billion exit scam*

## The formation of a scam

Just as some of the bigger crypto scams were coming to their demise in Europe, what may be the biggest Ponzi scheme in crypto was about ready to start spreading its tentacles across China and Asia. This scam would go on to take up to $6 billion directly from its investors and reach a final $17 billion valuation before its founders left, with just one message for their investors: 'Sorry we have run'.[1]

From 2 June 2018, subtle little mentions of a new crypto wallet and exchange started dropping into chat groups across social media in China.[2] Groups led by community leaders from a then-unknown crypto company quickly spread across China and soon across much of Asia on WeChat and other messaging apps. The groups seemed, all in all, innocent, at first. They gave free tips on the basics of cryptocurrency and on how to get started buying and trading, giving some pretty optimistic examples of how much money could be made. Groups were kept small, 100 to 200 people in a chat room, making it easier to maintain order should anyone start raising any questions organizers didn't want mentioned. Soon PlusToken, the company behind the groups, also started hosting conferences and meet-ups across China, South Korea and, before long, across much of South-East Asia and as far away as Russia, Ukraine, Germany and Canada.

There are more than a few uniting themes in the biggest crypto scams. Just as with OneCoin and Bitconnect, the organizers behind PlusToken knew how to draw crowds. They got packed rooms, full of people eager to learn more about the new big buzzwords of Bitcoin and cryptocurrency, and how they themselves could start owning little bits of these digital currencies. PlusToken went all-out. There were strobe lights, talks, lots of clapping and high-fives and the requisite loud, fashionable Korean K-pop music. Some of the attendees described them as shady, with high-pressure sales tactics. But, they worked. More and more people joined and filled their groups.[3]

Despite the crypto market crashing, there was still a lot of optimism from people who hadn't yet got into crypto and hoped for a repeat for themselves of the riches made in the preceding years. It was easy for PlusToken to appeal to these people. They released glamorous promotional videos with their members – or maybe, more realistically, paid actors, giving more-than-slightly rehearsed but clearly plausible enough testimonials to inspire enough faith to attract more and more people to their follower base and ever-growing list of chat groups. These people – it's not clear if they were paid or not – were presented as the face of the brand and appealed to PlusToken's Korean and Chinese audiences to join their groups.[4] No one seemed to notice or mind that no employees or anyone claiming to ever work for the company was really shown in full.

PlusToken chat leaders seemed to have a clear plan, though, and it seemed to work: get people to trust them, build up their hopes for high investment returns, and then drop the bomb of what they were really after. It wasn't long after forming the groups that PlusToken representatives started dropping in mentions of an investment platform that promised high monthly returns, 6 to 18 per cent per month, if they would only first invest $500.[5]

## It must be good because it's a buzzword

Decentralized was, and still is, a big buzzword in crypto. It's been heavily touted that if something is decentralized, and especially if it uses blockchain, then it must be good. In some cases this is true.

Centralized institutions are notoriously vulnerable to being hacked; countless companies who have stored their data on centralized servers have been compromised, with hackers sharing their users' private data for all to see. There have been so many examples of this hitting mainstream media. Too many cases have highlighted this recently: Experian, Adobe, LinkedIn and Yahoo! are just some of the companies to show to the world what happens when large companies holding lots of their users' highly sensitive (and valuable) data don't take adequate security measures or care to protect their customers' data. Sites frequently get breached, and the data for millions of their users is publicly exposed.

In the crypto space, as we will see with Quadriga and Mt. Gox, many crypto exchanges that hadn't taken adequate cyber security measures had also been hacked and millions of crypto investors had lost all their funds. Anything that mentioned the word decentralized was deemed – woefully optimistically in some cases – safe. So it made perfect sense that PlusToken would launch a decentralized crypto wallet and trading platform soon after its launch – it was all the talk in crypto and the perfect marketing ploy.

PlusToken gave a lot of assurances about the security of its platform. They said they used artificial intelligence and billion-dollar security technology, that their core team came from the original tech teams at Samsung and Google Pay,[6] and their development had taken place inside a research and development lab in Seoul, South Korea.[7] It's a shame, given how much money was lost to this platform, that the company didn't live up to any of these claims.

Buying, storing and spending crypto is generally considered to be difficult at best, and this was especially true in the years leading up to PlusToken's 2018 launch. Focus on user experience had been lacking; there were many crypto wallets, but none with a seamless or easy user experience. Crypto users were waiting for one thing: the first secure crypto wallet with the best and easiest user experience. The first company to make a wallet with a good user experience would be rich beyond their wildest dreams. For prospective crypto wallet creators, there was (and still is) a huge available user base and the ability to take a transaction fee every time money is sent. PlusToken wasn't the first company to realize this.

PlusToken, with their wallet and exchange, were keen to get more users and funds to maximize adoption of their new wallet. The community that PlusToken had built was not your typical crypto early adopter, investor or crypto users at all, but ordinary people who had heard about the easy money that was supposedly on offer and wanted some of this for themselves.[8] People trusted PlusToken, seeing it initially as a company that had built relationships with the community. Its team had, after all, taken it upon themselves to educate their community. Of course, this gave them the perfect chance to set the curriculum for what they would teach, and how their community would largely be misinformed and duped.

Enter the dog.

## Dogs in trading

In 2015 the PlusToken team had – supposedly – developed an artificial intelligence powered bot for arbitrage trading – a type of trading where one asset is bought and sold, often repeatedly, to take advantage of a price difference between different markets. In this case, the bot would allegedly focus on the price difference of bitcoin and other cryptocurrencies on different exchanges. By the time PlusToken was launched there were already numerous crypto exchanges selling bitcoin and other cryptocurrencies at a slight discrepancy of prices, depending on sales volume, liquidity, demand, trust in the exchange, and even regulation and ease of buying crypto in the country the exchange catered for. Usually the spread of price was nominal, but some traders would make a living sending bitcoin and other cryptocurrencies between exchanges, buying low and selling at a higher price on another exchange, and repeating the cycle. Some did this manually; others used algorithms to help find the best opportunities.

Arbitrage trading in crypto was (and still is) highly risky. Due to the fledging and unregulated crypto market, there was literally nothing safe about it: crypto exchanges could and often did shut down and disappear, victims either of hacks or of their founders exit scamming. Exchanges could also shut down certain wallets, blocking the ability to send or even access certain cryptocurrencies. Transactions could easily be lost, sometimes mid-transaction. Arbitrage trading was about as risky as trading got in crypto.

PlusToken didn't seem to pay much, if any, attention to these risks. They let everyone know that their bot – the inexplicably named AI Dog – would make money for everyone who touched it. AI Dog would capture the price and volume of each of the main cryptocurrencies on the different exchanges and would – according to PlusToken's website – automate arbitrage trading between them. All people needed to do was deposit anything from $500 of any of the major cryptocurrencies onto the PlusToken platform. The bot would then automatically – supposedly – find the best profit margins, trade your crypto, and return your crypto to your wallet with profit.[9]

Unlike a normal crypto wallet, where crypto would be stored without benefiting the owner in any other way financially except with the aim of keeping it secure, PlusToken touted one big benefit to attract users. Instead of just storing crypto in its wallet, PlusToken users would profit from any crypto held in their wallets.[10] To an onlooker, it might have looked a little confusing. PlusToken boasted of the security of their wallet, assuring their users that unlike other platforms where crypto may not be stored securely, their offering was truly decentralized, and that their crypto holdings would be stored securely in their decentralized wallet. There was one small factor in how the wallet maintained its users' crypto that PlusToken conveniently obscured.

The way PlusToken claimed to make their profits for their users – through arbitrage trading to take advantage of differences in the price of crypto on different exchanges – by definition took crypto out of these supposedly safe wallets. To allow the AI Dog to profit from arbitrage trading, the dog bot would have to send this crypto out of users' wallets and trade it between exchanges, one of the riskiest manoeuvres known in crypto and one where crypto can easily be lost. PlusToken never explained how they were both able to simultaneously store their users' crypto safely in their wallet and, at the same time, profit from arbitrage trading from the crypto they were holding in these wallets. To anyone experienced in dealing with crypto or sending crypto transactions, it would have been clear that something was a little amiss. To store crypto safely whilst sending it between exchanges for repeated trades isn't possible. Those behind PlusToken weren't targeting experienced crypto users. They were targeting those who they'd be able to lead to buy bitcoin to send into wallets on their platform.[11]

## High promises

The term synonymous with and popularized in the crypto bubble – FOMO, or fear of missing out – was just as applicable to PlusToken. More than one crypto project hoping to raise millions in minutes or hours took advantage of this concept and PlusToken was no exception. It was explained to investors that this chance to take advantage of the arbitrage trading opportunities in crypto would only be around for the short term, that soon crypto markets would stabilize as more money came in from investors, that soon the crypto markets would lose their volatility and that soon there'd be no more money left to be made. This was good high-pressure marketing – act now or miss out!

For PlusToken to attract high numbers of people to act now and invest their money into their platform, just as with OneCoin and Bitconnect and countless other crypto scams, they had to offer high returns for investing. For any money investors kept on their platform, they would get 6–18 per cent back every month.[12] Anyone keeping $1,000 worth of crypto on the platform would get between $60–$180 back every month,[13] or $720–$2,160 profit back in their first year, paid out in their native digital currency, the PlusToken. Just as with every other scam that offered such high returns, there was no realistic way these returns were sustainable or could be reliably guaranteed by any trading bot, no matter how good it was.

The numbers promised screamed 'scam'. But, whilst these returns may seem high, this was at a time when crypto markets had spiked. The crypto bubble from early 2017 to mid 2018, when PlusToken launched, had made some investors hundreds of times their investment, so, in this context, some might have seen 6–18 per cent a month as a safe and even modest guarantee. These promises also took place in the context of the multi-level marketing scam scene that had plagued China and Asia for the last years, creating a surge in fast wealth-gain. There had already been so many Ponzi schemes or high-yield investment programmes targeting these same investors that the returns offered by PlusToken wouldn't have seemed out of the norm to naive or hopeful investors eager to make their own riches, and a lifeline for those wanting to get into the seemingly hard-to-access crypto space.[14]

And so, within a year of its launch, PlusToken had gone from being an unknown entity to having millions of users each investing the minimum deposit of $500 onto the platform. By their exit in June 2019, it's estimated that PlusToken had three to four million investors with money on their platform, maybe more. PlusToken claimed to have 10 million investors.[15] Partly this fast growth was down to their slick marketing, targeting people through so-called educational WeChat groups and high-powered sales events, partly it was down to their promises and initial payouts of high returns, and partly down to its investors' hope, or greed. But, for its early days, PlusToken paid out, and for a while all seemed well.

## Juicy numbers and creative marketing

PlusToken had a very incentivizing rewards structure for anyone on their platform who brought in referrals. All people needed to do to access this was have invested at least $500 of their own money onto the platform. Then, in addition to their profits for their own investment, for every direct referral the referrer would also get 100 per cent of their referee's investment profit. That meant that if someone's friend joined and invested $1,000, not only would they get the profit from their own investment, they would also get an additional $60–$180 per month for every person they directly referred. If they referred 10 people who each also invested $1,000 onto the platform, they would get $600–$1,800 per month from their referrals, in addition to their own monthly profit from their investment.[16]

As we have seen with some of the other multi-level marketing based scams such as OneCoin and Bitconnect, referral commissions went on for several levels. PlusToken would pay out referral commissions down 10 levels of referrals. Not only were investors paid for their direct referrals, but anyone whose direct referrals brought in anyone else to invest would get 10 per cent of their investment for anyone their referrals brought, in a pyramid structure going 10 layers deep.[17] This meant that early investors and promoters could get very rich indeed. Even for those who just brought in their close friends and family, by referring just enough people, this could become a far more lucrative monthly income stream than one could ever get just by investing one's own money. Some did question whether this was a Ponzi scheme, but the general consensus seemed to be that so long as the money kept flowing in, all was fine.

The high referral rewards offered by PlusToken inspired some rather proactive marketing and lead generation from its investors. One placed a PlusToken sign amongst vegetables in supermarket stands,[18] filming this sign to tell his YouTube following that even supermarkets were now accepting the Plus currency. Presumably the supermarket in question never found out about its alleged acceptance of a scam currency.

Keen investors, motivated by the high affiliate commissions, also ran their own recruitment drives, masquerading as informational events, to get friends and family and everyone they knew to put in money.[19] Before long, an estimated four million people had been brought in to invest by their friends, family, followers and connections, bringing an estimated additional $4 billion onto the PlusToken platform. Some of these were people who thought they would just make a profit or get rich on the platform, without really knowing or worrying how. Many others thought they were really buying bitcoin and other cryptocurrencies and believed that they'd found a safe way of storing these in a decentralized wallet, without looking into how the platform worked or stopping to question the risk.

PlusToken maintained the illusion that any funds the platform gained were being used to develop their wallet and exchange, with the stated aim of being able to dominate the crypto markets when the next bubble hit. The more active that investors were in promoting PlusToken, the more PlusToken would reward them, increasing pay-outs based on their referral activity, as well as with high praise. Users would be upgraded to highly sought-after titles based on their promotional activity. 'Big Boy' and 'Great God'[20] were popular titles handed out to the most prominent recruiters – everyone wanted to reach these levels. So long as investors kept investing, the platform kept paying out. Until that stopped.

## Hidden, cryptic messages

From PlusToken's launch in June 2018, it only took a year until June 2019 when investors started reporting delays in being able to withdraw their funds.[21] Crypto withdrawal requests should normally be processed almost instantly. Some took to Chinese social media, posting complaints on chat app Weibo that they'd been submitting withdrawal requests for 35 hours, but with no luck.[22] Soon, still in the same month of June, investors could no longer withdraw their money at all. PlusToken's team initially tried to quiet these talks, saying that the withdrawal issues were due to a hacking attempt.[23] This was true, to an extent.

Crypto transactions, such as when sending bitcoin to another address, show up the details of the address it was sent to and from, and how much was sent. With Bitcoin and some other cryptocurrencies it's also possible to leave a message in the transaction data. In the first ever produced genesis block of Bitcoin, Satoshi Nakamoto, the unknown founder, left one note hidden in the transaction: 'The Times 03/Jan/2009 Chancellor on brink of second bailout for banks.'[24] The founder of Bitcoin wanted to make it clear to the world that the digital currency was created in response to the global failure and the manipulation that is the world's banking system.

When the founders of PlusToken ran, they were still actively stealing their users' crypto out of their exchange, sending these crypto funds to their own wallets on other exchanges. Mid their exit, PlusToken's unknown founder left a message hidden in one of their transactions in a similar style, but without any of the grace or good intent of Satoshi. The message the team at PlusToken left was clear: 'Sorry we have run'.[25] Users had lost around $4 billion of direct investment of their funds, the founders and PlusToken team had gone.

Until then, users had largely watched their funds accumulate on the app without cashing out. PlusToken had charged a 5 per cent transaction fee for any money moved out of the account.[26] This, and the prospect of more money to be made by the AI Dog, were seemingly enough to encourage its users to keep their crypto on the platform. The way that PlusToken had set up meant that investors didn't have control over the coins in their wallets. So when the founder made his exit, all users were suddenly locked out of their funds. All points of contact at PlusToken had gone. With no other options left, over 200 investors pressured Seoul authorities to launch an investigation into what was quickly being seen for what it was: a Ponzi scheme on an epic scale. Korean authorities duly acted, triggering an international manhunt.[27] For many people internationally, this was the first time they had heard about what had fast become one of the largest scams to hit Asia.

Had it just been people's direct investment into the platform, now thought to total up to $6 billion,[28] those billions would have been lost but no one else would have been directly impacted. However, the token had traded publicly on some Chinese exchanges. Frantic FOMO buying had pushed the token price up to $340 per token, giving the project a total market cap valuation of $17 billion.[29] This would have made PlusToken the third largest cryptocurrency in the world had it been listed on popular crypto listing site CoinMarketCap. Except it wasn't. They never listed it.

Despite PlusToken keeping their team's and founders' identities a secret, within days of the scam ending and unfolding Chinese plain-clothes police officers had touched down in Vanuatu, an idyllic South Pacific island country comprising 80 small islands with turquoise seas and white sand beaches. Less than a week later, together with Vanuatu police, they had captured six Chinese citizens and detained them at a Chinese-owned local property. The five Chinese men and one woman were promptly arrested and escorted on a chartered jet bound for China under an extradition order.[30]

Whilst those arrested were all Chinese, the scam had spread far outside of China. Investors from large parts of Asia as well as from Russia, Ukraine, Germany and even Canada were hit. PlusToken's investors lost it all.[31]

The people who were caught, however, don't seem to be the masterminds of the operation. The ringleaders of PlusToken have never been caught. Supposedly spearheaded by a young Korean man called Mr Leo who doesn't come with many more details other than the odd photo,[32] it's still unknown who was really behind the $17 billion PlusToken scam.

## Where's the money?

In every other crypto exit scam, it would appear that it's the founder who has taken the money. In PlusToken, it still isn't clear who made off with the funds. In many ways, this is where the PlusToken story starts to get interesting. The raid on the six suspects in Vanuatu should have given police some hardware or clues to work with. According to the police report, it didn't.[33]

Crypto analytics firm Chainalysis tracked down hundreds of millions of dollars worth of investors' crypto that investors could no longer access and that PlusToken had full control over. One notable feature about crypto is that, with the exception of some privacy-focused cryptocurrencies that hide transactions, with most cryptocurrencies, such as Bitcoin and Ethereum, all transactions can be publicly seen on the blockchain. This has made it easy for crypto analytics firms to track the coins associated with PlusToken wallets and notice if anyone has moved these coins.

What did become noticeable to those watching was the direct correlation between PlusToken sell-offs and the crash in the price of bitcoin and cryptocurrencies at various times since the scheme was stopped in June 2019.[34] They had accumulated so much crypto that it was enough to affect the global markets. The scam might have been stopped, but there's a lot of stolen crypto still unaccounted for, controlled by its ringleaders. They could still sell that crypto at any time, crashing the entire crypto markets further and affecting everyone.

## Take 2: The billion-dollar copy of the scam

Just one month after the start of PlusToken, a new multi-level marketing crypto scam hit China.

WoToken was promoted as a smart cryptocurrency wallet that would make high returns for its users without any work needed on their behalf; all they needed to do was invest some funds and the platform would magically make them rich. Returns were lower than PlusToken, but still would have screamed scam to anyone other than those most accustomed to watching the yields promised by the highest yielding multi-level marketing scams that had by now become commonplace across parts of Asia.

Those who invested $1,000 were promised a daily return of up to 0.5 per cent giving up to 182.5 per cent per year. Those who invested a minimum of $5,000 would get a daily return of up to 0.65 per cent or an annual return of 237.25 per cent.[35] Bearing in mind that an annual return in excess of single digits is considered high, these returns are basically impossible to guarantee. And yet, as we have seen, scam after scam did exactly that. Just as with PlusToken, WoToken claimed to make its returns for its users from algorithmic trading bots. Also just as with PlusToken, it never managed to prove the existence of these bots. There were other similarities, namely the generous referral commissions it offered to its affiliates, a trend common in crypto scams where affiliates are used to bring in maximum victims. WoToken also used some pretty creative marketing. The website claimed to have partnered with a MasterCard issuing company, Global Cash, which would allow their users to spend the crypto they had stored in their WoToken wallets. The proof they give for this: the word MasterCard written on their website, not even the logo.[36] Needless to say, it doesn't look like any such partnership with MasterCard ever existed. In short, it looked and acted exactly like PlusToken.

Thankfully, it only took the Chinese police a few months to become aware of the scam, and just over a year later, in late 2019, it was brought down after many investors complained they couldn't withdraw their money. By the time the WoToken app ceased its operations at the end of 2019, it had made over $1 billion from 715,000 individual investors using a 'super large MLM network' to part investors from their money.[37] Less than two years after PlusToken collapsed, Chinese police had cracked down on what was now the second ten-figure billion-dollar-plus crypto Ponzi scheme to hit Chinese investors based on an almost exact copy of the PlusToken model.[38] Six people were arrested and sentenced for this latest scam, its ringleaders seemingly coming straight from PlusToken.[39] It is, of course, slightly remarkable that anyone could have got away with one scam of this size, let alone two. But crypto was unregulated and so authorities were slow to catch on to closing down scams, largely leaving the crypto markets to their own devices, scams and all. It would be nice to say that authorities are now acting faster, and some are, but scam upon scam, exact replicas of past scams, are still ongoing.

In July 2020, after WoToken had been shut down, 109 people were arrested in connection with PlusToken, including 82 key members of the scam and what is thought to be its core team of 27, all deemed to be major criminal suspects.[40] Given the size and complexity of the scam, it is thought that there are many still out there. It's still unknown how many people were really behind PlusToken and how much exactly they did manage to scam out of people and keep. It's not unlikely that more coins will be sold off from an unknown wallet, and crash the crypto markets one more time.

Is it just a matter of time before China is hit by its third billion dollar-plus crypto Ponzi scam by a member of the same team, who are repeating the tricks they learnt at PlusToken?

## CHAPTER SIX

# The faked death, missing millions and requests to exhume a body

When the founder of a Canadian cryptocurrency exchange died suddenly on his honeymoon in India in December 2018,[1] the creditors of the $250 million stored on the exchange shouldn't have had cause to worry. Except what transpired was that Gerald Cotten, the founder, was the only one who had access to the wallets storing the quarter billion of investors' money it held.[2] It soon came out: most people don't believe he died. The crypto community and users at large think he faked his own death and have asked for his body to be exhumed for a post-mortem. The FBI have spent the subsequent years investigating, asking enough questions of at least one person close to the case to imply they themselves haven't ruled out that he's still alive,[3] and the whole case is now classed as a crime, a fraud from the start. The founder's supposed death came after months of problems and complaints about banking and withdrawals, and well-known and severe liquidity issues. The questions in most people's minds are: where is Gerald Cotten hiding with all his investors' money, and how did what seems to be an elaborate exit scam grow so large right under Canadian regulators' watchful gaze?

## A smiling man

A few years after graduating, a pale, blonde man known for his almost permanent smile moved to Vancouver and joined the then fledging Bitcoin community. Gerry went to local meet-ups, got to know some people in the early Bitcoin scene, and wanted to get more involved.

The Bitcoin community tends to be united by excitement at the idea of a digital currency set by algorithms and the benefits of a monetary system that isn't controlled or manipulated by the state or by a central banking system. Gerald Cotten had different interests. He was after the speculative investment potential of the volatile new currency.

There were several ways an early Bitcoin speculator could get involved in working in the space. Creating a crypto exchange was probably the most risk-filled and difficult to do, but these were early days where regulation didn't come into play and not everyone saw the law as applicable to them. Gerry Cotten, it seemed, was one of these. Buying bitcoin in those days was hard. Mt. Gox, the troubled crypto exchange we'll see in the next chapter, was at this time still going strong (to outside appearances at least), but it was based in Japan. Gerry wanted to create a Canadian-based exchange.

Gerry's exchange, QuadrigaCX, brought a glimmer of hope to Canada's Bitcoin community in its early days. Incorporated in November 2013, Quadriga was a new, local bitcoin exchange that soon developed a reputation as being cheap, fast and safe to use. Above all, they prided themselves on being Canadian and played this to their advantage in their marketing. What could go wrong?

## Everyone loves pizza

It wasn't hard for Quadriga to stand out in those early years. There wasn't really much competition for good user experience when it came to buying bitcoin. And it wasn't hard to gain early users. From his time attending local crypto meet-ups, Cotten had become a director at the Vancouver Bitcoin Co-op, which made it easy to get to know people.

Your average crypto event had hordes of students and people interested in the space descending greedily on the takeaway boxes full of pizza that would inevitably get brought in thanks to one or two local sponsors. Attendees would crowd around these, taking their slices to go hang over by the free beer.

The choice of potential sponsors to cover event costs in those early years was limited. Crypto was just too niche, and wasn't yet widely trusted or accepted as an asset class. Cotten bought himself almost instant loyalty for Quadriga by just sponsoring local crypto events. Giving people free beer and pizza must be one of the universally easiest ways to win over followers. Such sponsorships cost the exchange CA$500–1,000 per meet-up but bought goodwill, and almost a dependency from the event organizers and local community; there simply was, often, no other company that would sponsor crypto events in those days. Over time, sponsoring these events bought trust and a steady user base of investors depositing their money to buy and hold bitcoin on the new exchange.[4]

## Surrounded by hacks

In its early years, Quadriga got lucky – its competition, the other exchanges around it, all got hacked. In early 2014, just six weeks after Quadriga launched, Mt. Gox, then the world's largest exchange with 70 per cent of global bitcoin trade, which we'll see in the next chapter, was hacked and suspended its operations.

The world's second largest exchange, Vault of Satoshi, and Canada's then-largest exchange CaVirTex, also closed suddenly soon after, blaming hackers, both closing in the same week.

Quadriga became Canada's main bitcoin exchange virtually overnight, gaining a sudden, huge new influx of users. Gerald Cotten, who had never run a crypto exchange before and who was still relatively new to the world of crypto, basically couldn't cope. Quadriga had its share of issues – fines and losses amounting to tens of millions of Canadian dollars for partnering with unscrupulous payment processors who took or lost their money, for failing to file audits, and for not being able to determine the rightful owner of bitcoin – but the exchange had made money from the wild rise of Bitcoin and the user base kept on growing. Since Quadriga had been formed, the price of bitcoin had shot up from a few hundred dollars to over $20,000, netting the exchange a total of almost $2 billion in customers' bitcoin at the peak of the market.[5] The exchange got a cut of every transaction made.

## #luxurytravel

Quadriga had an office, but most saw this as largely a front. Gerry liked to run the exchange alone from his Macbook Pro. With the wild rise of Bitcoin and getting a cut of every trade for himself, he quickly made his riches and started to lead the indulgent lifestyle of an international jet-setter with money to burn.

Cotten and his then girlfriend, Jennifer, would travel around the world, taking private jets[6] and staying in some of the world's most luxurious accommodations. Jen's Instagram was full of photos of far-flung destinations, from Oman to the Maldives, Dubai and Myanmar, often using the hashtag #luxurytravel.

In Summer 2017, with the price of bitcoin rising, Cotten and Jennifer went to buy a boat. Sunnybrook Yacht Brokerage in Nova Scotia, Canada, near Cotten's Halifax home, typically tends to the well-dressed elite. Canada's *The Globe and Mail* did a deep dive investigation into the scam and spoke to the brokerage. Gerry, they said, stood out that day, turning up in a Tesla in a wrinkled shirt and shorts and worn-out Birkenstock. How much the yacht he would buy would cost didn't seem to be the issue, no price limit was ever set. He wanted a big boat, one big enough to be able to sail to the Caribbean without having to stop in Canada or the US for fuel. He chose a $600,000 Jeanneau 51 that had three cabins and a swim platform, and started taking sailing lessons around some local islands, him sailing whilst Jen and her two Chihuahuas sunbathed on the deck.[7]

That summer, he bought one of the islands, four acres of pine and beach on which he cleared trees and had a house built, but never seemed to move into or live in. He owned three other homes, scattered around their home province of Canada, and 14 rental properties. Cotten also had a Cessna plane, worth an estimated half a million dollars, but which he rarely flew, and a small collection of luxury cars in addition to the Tesla.[8] Not bad for one young man.

Either way, travels, boats, planes and a girlfriend all seemed far more exciting than the admin of running a crypto exchange.

## Did he actually die?

In November 2018 Gerry made a will and married Jen, then flew to Delhi for their honeymoon. The couple stayed in some of the most luxurious hotels in North India, posing at the main viewpoints including the Taj Mahal. Only the best, of course, was good enough. On 8 December they landed in Jaipur and were picked up at the airport in an Audi Q7 to stay at the Oberoi Rajvilas. The hotel is the best of the best, a luxury modern-day palace where rooms go for upwards of $1,000 a night. To anyone looking at the young couple, they lived the dream life, full of all the experiences that money can buy.

Shortly after checking into the Oberoi, Gerry complained of a stomach ache, was taken to a nearby private hospital and diagnosed with acute gastroenteritis. He had underlying conditions and had suffered from Crohn's disease. Within 24 hours of his complaint of a stomach ache, however, his condition had deteriorated, his heart stopped twice, and he died.[9] Except, ever since, rumours have been circulating. Many don't believe he is actually dead.[10]

A bit of a mess ensued surrounding the supposedly dead man's body.

The private hospital where Cotten had been treated sent his body back to the hotel where he'd been staying. The hotel sent the body out to be embalmed. The embalmer refused to accept a body from a hotel, on the grounds that no information about the cause of death was presented with the body. Quite why the hospital didn't send the body directly to be embalmed is as yet unknown. The body was taken to a local state medical college, where fewer questions were asked.[11] The next day his widow flew the body back to Canada where it was buried on 14 December 2018 in a closed-casket funeral in his home town of Halifax.

It took Jen over a month to announce his death via a Facebook post.[12] Why it took so long to announce, and why it seemed like his death was being kept quiet wasn't yet clear. During this whole time, Quadriga was accepting millions of dollars of new investor funds, but not returning any.[13] They didn't seem to think that it might be fair to stop accepting new money given that, internally, the exchange had pretty much ceased running.

## A major custody problem

Cryptocurrency can be stored securely in several ways. The first thing any crypto exchange would do, if it aimed to stay within the law, would be to set up secure back-up access in the eventuality of any founders' demise. It's such a standard, basic thing that it wouldn't even normally be questioned. No good crypto exchange would ever even think to be dependent solely on one person, it just simply wouldn't happen. The risks in crypto are just far too high.

One benefit of crypto exchanges is that they should in theory offer safe, albeit temporary, storage for your crypto assets. When sending crypto to Quadriga, you were signing away the control of your crypto. Unlike if you held your crypto yourself, on Quadriga, you had to submit to the exchange for withdrawals. If they didn't process your withdrawal, basically, as far as they saw it, that was tough luck.[14]

Crypto can be stored securely behind coded passwords, known as private keys. If you have the private keys, you can access your crypto. If you don't, crypto isn't a bank where you can call up or change your password online. Whilst some newer crypto storage devices and exchanges have customer service, early ones didn't. If you lost your private keys, particularly in the early days, you lost your crypto. There are hundreds of stories of people who lost the private key to their digital currency or accidentally threw away the device it was stored on, and in so doing lost their access to their fortune. There wasn't – and still isn't – anything anyone could do.

No good crypto exchange would ever store much of its own and its customers' assets online. Even in the early days of crypto when Quadriga was around, there were simply so many other methods of safer, backed-up storage for crypto that this would simply never be considered. Except for Quadriga. Gerald Cotten had stored Quadriga's entire CA$250 million of customer funds behind private keys, which only he had access to.[15]

The service that Quadriga offered on their exchange was touted as being a safe store for people's crypto; people trusted it to store their crypto securely. By holding their crypto on Quadriga, even for short-term trades, 76,000 people were giving Cotten a cut of their every transaction in exchange for their crypto's safe storage. Gerald Cotten, with his years of exposure to Bitcoin and running one of the largest crypto exchanges, storing up to billions worth of bitcoin, would have known the importance of and, more pertinently, the methods of safe and private crypto storage better than most. In 2014 he had stated in an interview that he wrote the keys on paper and kept them in a safety deposit box in a bank.[16] In the interview he warned of the consequences of losing passwords needed to access crypto: 'It's like burning cash in a way' – 'Even the US government, with the biggest computers in the world, could not retrieve those coins if you've lost the private key. It's impossible to retrieve those.'[17] This was not a man who would have underestimated the importance of good back-ups for such vast amounts of other people's crypto that he was being paid to keep safe.

The whole time it was trading, Quadriga had lied to its users about how it stored their crypto, assuring them that their assets were stored securely when in fact the assets were stored online in such a way that it made the hundreds of millions of customer funds easy to hack, and easy for Cotten to help himself to. There were no separate client accounts; all Quadriga funds went into one big centralized pool. Gerry seemed to act as if he had the right to treat these funds as if it were his own resources he was playing with.[18]

When he died, Gerald Cotten was the only person with the private keys to Quadriga's $250 million of funds.[19] There was no back-up. Without the private keys, no one could access the money. Unless anyone could find Cotten, this meant that investors' CA$250 million worth of crypto was suddenly lost into the ether.

## Law enforcement steps in – or tries to

Following Cotten's death and the revelation that only he had held the private keys, the Nova Scotia Supreme Court declared Quadriga bankrupt and appointed accounting firm Ernst & Young, tasking them with getting back Quadriga's creditors' hundreds of millions of lost funds. Traditional law enforcement, however, were utterly out of their depth. They just didn't understand cryptocurrency or what they were dealing with, needing the basics explained to them and shocking the crypto experts they spoke to with their lack of knowledge.

Ernst & Young, the appointed administrators, also made a series of impressive blunders. They simply did not know how to go about finding or recovering the missing crypto funds. Ernst & Young had been tasked with getting back some, ideally all, of the crypto that was held trapped in Quadriga's wallets, wallets now inaccessible due to only Cotten having the private keys. Perhaps their most derided mistake, which investors paid for on top of their million-dollar fee: Ernst & Young did manage to access some of Quadriga's remaining crypto funds that were still accessible, yet instead of transferring this to investors, they managed to send $1 million worth to one of Cotten's wallets, rendered inaccessible due to not having the private key.[20] It's not really clear how anyone, let alone an administrator, could make such a colossal but basic mistake.

The Royal Canadian Mounted Police, the FBI, and at least two other undisclosed law enforcement agencies were also appointed. Their findings, however, were slim compared to those found and shared by Quadriga's tech-savvy and angry investors on community groups and social media.

Cotten's death also came after months of problems, complaints and investors unable to withdraw their funds. When banks and law enforcement started to investigate after his death, it was clear that a lot more wasn't as it had seemed.

## The investors step in

Quadriga had around 76,000 account holders who all lost their investments when the exchange went down. Almost every crypto expert and enthusiast in Canada held some bitcoin on Quadriga, from hundreds of dollars going up to entire life savings. Many of these 76,000 were early crypto adopters, highly intelligent people who understand how cryptocurrency works, and are many of the most technically sophisticated people in Canada. These investors knew what they were doing when it came to deep-dive crypto research. These were, after all, many of the same people who had learnt about crypto and managed to buy bitcoin long before doing so was an easy feat.

These investors were angry, and were joined by many more in the crypto community who felt betrayed that an exchange claiming to be part of the community had lied to them, at a time when crypto as an asset class was just starting to grow and be accepted by the mainstream and reputation was everything.

From amongst these people, around 500 of Canada's tech elite formed a chat group on encrypted messaging app Telegram, favoured by many in crypto for the privacy it offered over other messaging platforms. They wanted to start their own private research investigations into what had actually happened at Quadriga. The questions on everyone's lips were: 'Where was Gerry?' and 'How did Canada's largest Bitcoin exchange get so bad, and lose so much of its investors' money, right under the eye of Canada's law enforcement?' This group served as a mastermind group on steroids. It was frequented not only by Quadriga's investors, but also by journalists and law enforcement officers. By getting these 500 brains together, many of whom knew the people behind Quadriga, researching, sharing information, and investigating, some very interesting details started to come to light.

## Suspicions mount. Where is Gerry?

The more investors dived deeper into the case, the more coordinated their fears became. Twitter and social media were soon hit by one joint message. One suspicion was voiced over and over again: the strong suspicion that Cotten wasn't dead.

Quadriga's creditors had started to get suspicious as information started to leak out about Cotten's death. One of the first facts to transpire was that the death certificate had misspelled his name. The death certificate issued two days after his death by the Rajasthan Directorate of Economics and Statistics spelled his name as Cottan.[21] On top of this, only two months beforehand, the former chairman and managing director of the company that ran Fortis Escorts Hospital, the private hospital where Cotten was treated, had been convicted of financial fraud,[22] causing some to suspect corruption. It all didn't look good. People started doubting the authenticity of the death certificate as well as other supporting documents from a country known for the ease with which you can procure fake or doctored certificates.

The circumstances surrounding Cotten's death were suspicious, to say the least.

Whilst the official cause of death was recorded as complications relating to Cotten's pre-existing Crohn's disease, the gastroenterologist who treated him, Dr Jayant Sharma, still thinks about that death. 'I revisited it many times in my mind. We did everything we could,' he said. 'We are not sure about the diagnosis,' Sharma told the UK's *Telegraph*, who tracked the doctor down. He continued by saying that he was surprised how quickly Cotten's condition deteriorated and confessed there was little medical follow-up. It is unclear whether he himself even saw the dead body. 'In retrospect, I would have ordered an autopsy or post-mortem,' he said.[23] Sharma told the *Telegraph* he spoke to a doctor who said he had seen the body, but there was no police investigation. It could be true; doctors deal with thousands of dead bodies, so probably don't over-think these things at the time. It's possible we'll never know.

Adding fuel to the already growing suspicions that Gerald Cotten is still very much alive, it soon came out that he had only written a will four days before leaving for India and 12 days before he died. The will stipulated $12 million worth of assets – his houses, rental properties, plane, cars and boat, and C$100,000 for caring for Jennifer's two pet Chihuahuas.[24]

Surprisingly, given that at the peak of the market Quadriga stored up to $2 billion worth of investors' funds, there was no mention of anything relating to the wallets or storage of these investors' funds in the will. To say investors weren't impressed by this is an understatement; they were shocked.[25]

Even more serious doubts started to be raised about the exchange when it leaked out that not only had Cotten not made any provisions for the Quadriga funds in his will, but he also had no backup access to the private keys only he knew.[26]

And so the investigations began in full. The FBI and Canadian law enforcement, and hundreds of Quadriga's angry and betrayed investors worked separately but in parallel, uncovering more findings and evidence than anyone would ever have imagined possible.

## The secret criminal founder

One of the facts that Quadriga had seemingly omitted to mention openly: Gerald Cotten wasn't its only founder.

Michael Patryn had sprung himself onto the Vancouver Bitcoin scene in the early days of the exchange, but wasn't liked or trusted even then. Unlike Cotten, who was known for generally being smiley, Patryn, who described himself as their advisor, only got himself any likes at all by association with Quadriga's pizza sponsorship of events. Joseph Weinberg, now the founder of several digital currency businesses, and then a student and attendee of the Vancouver Bitcoin Co-op meetings that Quadriga would sponsor, said of Patryn, 'It was quickly very clear that he wasn't who he said he was. Sometimes he'd introduce himself as Michael from India. Sometimes he'd say he was Michael from Pakistan. Or Michael from Italy. But it came from a place of organization – he knew what he was doing. It wasn't his first rodeo.'[27]

Patryn, since Cotten's death, had actively tried to distance himself from Quadriga. In the Telegram chat group formed by

Quadriga's investors, Patryn had tried to minimize what was perceived as his involvement in the exchange. He said he had met Cotten online, five years before.

Thanks to the dedicated sleuthing of some of the creditors who gave up their free time to track through encrypted messaging systems and deleted forum posts, as well as a detailed investigation by Canada's *The Globe and Mail*, something rather different and more sinister transpired.

In 2003, brothers Edward and Brian Krassenstein launched a shadow, underground website called TalkGold. TalkGold was a Ponzi and scam creators' heaven. On it were posts about all the latest scams, centred on a type of Ponzi called a HYIP, or high-yield investment programme, where investors are promised impossibly high returns that are in turn paid out from new investors' money. The site gave advice and tips on how to get in and out of these scams early enough to profit, how to start running scams, or even how to create your own Ponzi scheme.[28] TalkGold was active until 2016, when the Office of Homeland Security went to the brothers' homes in Fort Myers, Florida, seized assets and financial records as well as half a million dollars and, thankfully, closed it down.[29]

It was on TalkGold, and progressively on other similar sites, where Gerald Cotten's education began. Aged 15, Gerry discovered the site, logged on as username Sceptre and over the next ten years studied and learnt the art of deceiving others: how to raise hopes, how to attract investment, how and when to start a scam, how and when to exit, and, crucially, how to cover one's tracks when running one.[30]

Michael Patryn, then aged 21, had already joined the site in 2003, three months before Cotten. Both were regular contributors on TalkGold and soon also on other scam promotion websites. They were soon regularly responding to and commenting on each other's' posts, and before long, as is perhaps common on such sites, both had tried to scam the other, seemingly for fun as much as for putting what they had learnt into practice.[31]

They were clearly impressed enough by each other's attempts to scam them that they went into partnership.

## Scam practice time

Cotten was a quick learner. By December that year, at the grand age of 16, he had launched his own HYIP scam website, and on 1 January 2004 launched his very first pyramid scheme, S&S Investments, promising not very plausible sounding returns of 103–150 per cent within 1–48 hours. Within three months the scheme had run out of money from new clients to repay its 200 investors, leaving Cotten to make online threats in a bid to buy himself time.[32]

One of his posts would warn his investors 'If a threat of any kind is made... you are stating that you do not wish to receive a refund and you will not receive one'.[33] Even before his first scam closed, out of funds and taking most of its clients' funds with it, Cotten had started his next, Lucky Invest.

When Gerry's various scam ventures collapsed, it was Patryn who defended Cotten. Cotten launched several other scams, hidden behind fake names and hiding his location,[34] and more than once landing himself in trouble. Cotten and Patryn would go on to each run more sophisticated scams, defending each other in online chat rooms. They would even pose as satisfied clients of each other's platforms to trick others into investing.

In 2004 the US Secret Service arrested a man called Omar Dhanani for identity theft. Omar pled guilty of conspiring to transfer stolen identification documents and was sentenced to 18 months in federal prison. On his release in 2007 he was deported to Canada. Once in Canada, for reasons that remain unexplained, Omar Dhanani changed his name to the name he used in his online persona for his scams. First to Omar Patryn, then Michael Patryn.[35]

## Professional money laundering

In 2013 a platform and pseudo digital currency called Liberty Reserves was seized and shut down by US authorities. It was the biggest money-laundering case in US history. Liberty Reserves can be likened to a PayPal for criminals.[36] One of the third-party exchanges it worked with was called Midas Gold Exchange. Midas Gold and Liberty Reserve served one key purpose: they were used primarily by drug cartels and traffickers, human traffickers and Ponzi schemes to launder money.

Midas Gold listed one contact in its registration documents: gerald.cotten@gmail.com. The name attached to the account was Omar Patryn.[37] This was Cotten and Patryn's first real joint project – a large-scale money laundering operation that took a cut of every transaction.

By this time, at the end of Cotten and Patryn's involvement in Liberty Reserves and Midas Gold and after running a few more scams and attempts at money-laundering operations, a new venture with all the bearings of a HYIP Ponzi scam was already six months old. There was a Facebook page with a fake testimonial video from a supposedly happy customer who turned out to be an actor from a freelance site who made custom videos for $5.[38] This HYIP scam could be funded with both the Liberty Reserves illegal digital currency and bitcoin. Quadriga Fund used payment processors operated by Patryn, and was Cotten's newest venture. Less than three months after its launch, Quadriga Fund disappeared. In its place, QuadrigaCX, the crypto exchange, went live.

## How did Canada's largest crypto exchange go so wrong under the scrutiny of law enforcement?

By 2015, despite strong support from the Bitcoin community, some in law enforcement already had their eye on the exchange. Patryn hadn't helped their case by being arrogantly vocal, apparently bragging about his abilities to launder money.[39] But questions and complaints about Patryn with his criminal past and known connections to organized crime didn't get escalated.

A large part of Quadriga's success was down to Gerry. People liked him and trusted him. More importantly, they wanted to trust him, for the role he played in what they hoped was a local, Canadian-run exchange for the community.

Patryn clearly knew there were issues and tried to pass all the blame for the demise of the exchange onto Cotten, saying that 'Gerry stopped running the company legally and ethically from a filing standpoint after all of the employees, directors and officers left in January 2016'.[40] Just before then, Quadriga had raised nearly C$850,000 in private capital. Following a dispute with one of the investors, the entire board as well as co-founder Patryn had left, leaving Cotten without the investment and, as Quadriga's only full-time employee, alone in charge and with no accountability. Unfortunately, this didn't turn out so well for the exchange's investors.

## The money was already gone

When their public bid failed, Cotten stopped keeping up any pretence at internal records. It was around this time that Quadriga's users started to complain that they couldn't withdraw their funds. It soon become clear why. As blockchain experts and investigators started going through all of Quadriga's wallets after the announcement of Cotten's death, it didn't take them long to find out one thing: the wallets were empty. As summarized succinctly by *Vanity Fair*: 'We now know that Cotten began, no later than 2015, to steal his clients' funds.'[41]

Cotten had told his family that in the event of anything happening to him, he had set up a safeguard, known as a dead man's switch, for Quadriga. They would have received an email with details of access to the accounts and the ability to refund investors. That email never came.[42] Instead, a total of 76,319 people have come forward to claim they are owed $214.6 million from Quadriga.[43] Ernst & Young expect they will reclaim a maximum of $35–$40 million, mostly from its dollar holdings, including $9 million of assets that Jen, Cotten's widow, has agreed to hand over.[44] They haven't had much luck on the crypto.

## Where did the money go?

Before the exchange's demise, Cotten did pay out to some investors, mostly to those who were making the most noise in online forums.[45] Pay-outs were in cash, often sending paper bags or boxes of bank notes.[46] The cash element wasn't necessarily Cotten trying to get around the law. As a crypto company operating in Canada, Quadriga hadn't been able to get a bank account.[47]

Where did the rest of the money end up? It does look as if Cotten had several tricks up his sleeve to get as much of his investors' bitcoin off the exchange as possible and into his own private wallets on other exchanges. The Ontario Securities Commission calculated that $115 million of Quadriga's money was lost due to Cotten's fraudulent trading on his own exchange.[48] According to reports, he made 14 fake accounts on Quadriga for himself, using pseudonyms to do these numerous trades.[49] Not all of the money was lost to trading. Investigations indicate that Cotten basically just moved large client funds straight into his own wallets and then out to other exchanges.[50]

Many crypto exchanges make a habit of creating fake accounts to simulate enhanced trading volumes. That Quadriga was doing this was of no surprise to anyone, and was even disclosed by Cotten in their 2015 filings. However, unlike some of the other more dubious crypto exchanges that mostly fake volumes, Cotten took this one step further.

Evan Thomas, a litigator with Osler Hoskin & Harcourt in Canada, reported that Cotten had been creating fake accounts since at least 2016.[51] Not only was he creating fake accounts to trade genuine bitcoin between these accounts, but Cotten also created and traded counterfeit bitcoin – ie he traded bitcoin that didn't actually exist.[52] As has by now been widely reported, he was literally trading imaginary bitcoin to show increased volumes, creating the fake accounts on Quadriga to show bitcoin volumes that weren't there. When Quadriga's customers sold real dollars or cryptocurrency, Cotten would simulate trades to buy the real currency using his fake bitcoin,[53] accumulating more for himself for basically no cost. Cotten would take the real bitcoin and dollars, leaving his creditors' accounts with the fake bitcoin. Before his disappearance, Cotten had made around 300,000 such trades, siphoning off investors' bitcoin and money in every transaction, seemingly making hefty profits for himself and depleting Quadriga's reserves.[54]

## Gambling with others' money

On top of the counterfeit trades Cotten made on his own exchange to siphon off his clients' bitcoin, it appears he also made 67,000 highly risky and reckless trades using client funds on a margin trading account,[55] using other, competitors' crypto exchanges, betting huge amounts of bitcoin on volatile cryptocurrencies.[56] In a best-case scenario, this is a highly risky move. This bitcoin was lost amongst the incremental fees, trades and volatility. It looks like this is how he lost another $28 million of his customers' money,[57] money that was never his to play with. Were these trades a desperate attempt to recoup some of the investor funds that had been lost? Possibly. More likely, given that he had already siphoned off so much money to his own accounts, that these trades were his own greed playing out in attempts to make himself more money. Or, as per the theory that Jennifer Vander Veer, the lead investigator for the FBI's cybercrime division, posed to crypto experts: were these wild trades themselves an attempt at laundering away the money, hiding the bitcoin behind so many trades and different coins that he could have that cryptocurrency accessible to him, untraceable to investigators, at a later stage?[58]

Canada's *Globe and Mail* also found that Cotten at one time liquidated $80 million worth of bitcoin via an offshore exchange.[59] It's presumed that some of this money came from client funds from Quadriga.[60] It hasn't been recouped.

Cotten had previously mentioned having a safe bolted to the rafters in his attic. Here is where he is said to have stored the many private keys to the wallets holding Quadriga's creditors' funds. One of his contractors knew this, and after news of his death went to Cotten's house. The four holes were there in the rafters where the safe had been screwed, the safety deposit box, gone.[61] Someone, seemingly, had made off with the contents.

Eric Schletz, who had sold Cotten his Cessna plane and knew him from their small flying club in Nova Scotia, said, 'I've seen Gerry walk through an airport with $50,000 in cash.'[62] Other photos show wads of cash stored in Gerry's home. Cotten made many trips abroad, even boasting that he'd never been searched by customs. It seems fairly plausible that at least some of his investors' funds were carried away in physical cash, trip by trip, leaving Cotten with safe stashes of cash hidden away in foreign bank accounts around the world, ready for him to live off without ever revealing his original identity, should he, as many believe, still be alive.

It's unknown if in fact Cotten is still alive, and if so, where he is now, or what identity he is living under. If he is alive, he would have access to considerable funds, enough at least for anyone to buy a new identity. It is of course entirely possible that he is actually dead, although I have yet to meet anyone in the crypto ecosystem who believes that is the case. What is known is that it was only after the lawsuits and enquiries began after too many failed withdrawals, and the exchange was threatened with a formal investigation, that Cotten wrote a will, went to India, and a misspelled death certificate and a casket were sent back to Canada.

## We need to exhume the body!

On 13 December 2019 the law firm representing the exchange's users sent a letter to request the Royal Canadian Mounted Police exhume the body. An autopsy, they said, is necessary to 'confirm both its identity and the cause of death'.[63] Pressure on the RCMP remains high to exhume his body, with creditors worried that, if there indeed is a body, if yet another summer passes it will be too decomposed to provide evidence.

## An old-fashioned fraud wrapped in modern technology

A new investigation into Quadriga has come to one clear conclusion. Quadriga wasn't a series of mistakes or bad luck or poor accounting. As the Ontario Securities Commission has surmised: 'What happened at Quadriga was an old-fashioned fraud wrapped in modern technology.'[64] The report by the OSC sums it up as succinctly as anyone can:

> By the time of his death, the platform owed approximately $215 million to clients but had almost no assets to cover these liabilities. By November 2016, Cotten had injected so many fake assets into the platform that its eventual insolvency was all but assured. However, until it was ultimately shut down by the new directors, Quadriga never stopped accepting new clients and new deposits, even while teetering on the brink of collapse.[65]

As Cotten ran out of funds, investigations indicate he used new investors' deposits to fund the old. As Canada's regulator the

134

OSC summarized, sadly, 'In effect, this meant that Quadriga operated like a Ponzi scheme.'[66] A traditional, old-fashioned Ponzi scheme, a scam from the start. Had Gerry lived, Quadriga would most likely have come to an inevitable demise, only with more answers from the man behind the whole sorry affair.

## CHAPTER SEVEN

# Mt. Gox

*Hacks, leaking billions and an
unauthorized trading bot*

## And it was gone

The story of the rise and fall of the Mt. Gox crypto exchange isn't a scam. More, it is a series of hacks, mismanagement, a lot of bad luck and errors that caused the richest exchange in the early years of crypto's history to lose everything it had. Within three years, Mt. Gox had gone from controlling over 80 per cent of all crypto transactions to declaring bankruptcy, its wallets empty. Then in an even more bizarre twist of fate, due to the sharp increase in the price of bitcoin, it found it had so much more money left that, even after three-quarters of its bitcoin were lost to hacks, it would be able to repay its investors several times over but is still in a legal wrangle with the courts, unable to due to Japanese bankruptcy law. Mt. Gox was, at the time, the victim of the biggest theft in crypto and of a multi-billion-dollar money-laundering operation.

If you were in crypto before 2014, chances are you held at least some of your bitcoin in Mt. Gox, which means that almost every early bitcoin investor around the world is affected. It's still not quite clear quite how Mt. Gox managed to suffer so many hacks, leaks and misadministration without anyone noticing before it was too late and all the money was gone.

By February 2014, less than three years after it was founded, Mt. Gox had built up to over 80 per cent of all bitcoin trades passing through the exchange.[1] That month, they checked their bitcoin reserves. They should have had one million bitcoin. It had gone. Their coffers were dry and they hadn't seen the theft happening from underneath them. How did the world's biggest crypto exchange lose all its bitcoin worth hundreds of millions of dollars?

Today, all that is left of the Mt. Gox exchange is a flurry of lawsuits, thousands of frustrated investors, and a French-inspired café in Tokyo. This café has become a bit of an emblem for the remains of the once-dominant exchange. Near the main train hub and at the ground floor level of an office district, it was to be a hub for Tokyo's tech elite to talk crypto and innovation, and would accept bitcoin throughout. Over $1 million was spent on this café. Mark Karpeles, the CEO of Mt. Gox, had a thing about quiche – some would say he loved quiche more than he loved the exchange, so the café had its own pastry consultant and a $35,000 special pastry oven to make quiches.[2] The café was never finished; it's still in mid-construction, the name signs by the entrance now only just readable.

## Cards or coins

Many people assume that Mt. Gox is named after a mountain. The name Mt. Gox doesn't even come from crypto, but rather from a popular, albeit very niche card game – Magic: The Gathering. Mt. Gox stood for Magic: The Gathering Online

Exchange. The card game had a small but loyal market for trading these cards online amongst its players. Jed McCaleb, Mt. Gox's founder, who would go on to found two of the largest cryptocurrencies that are still around today, was a gamer and a self-declared geek. It took Jed a few years to realize that running a site trading niche playing cards wasn't getting much traction or worth his time, and he wasn't too interested in building it up. By 2010 he'd rewritten the source code and transformed the site, changing everything except the domain. Instead of a card game exchange, Mt. Gox was suddenly a crypto exchange.

Jed had got one thing right: timing. This was in the earliest days of crypto; Bitcoin had only been invented the year before in 2009, and there simply weren't many places where one could buy it. The few sites where one could buy or trade bitcoin at the time were difficult to use and untrustworthy at best. Mt. Gox wasn't easy to use by any definition of the word – there were simply too many barriers between regular government or central bank issued money, known as fiat currency, and crypto in those days, but Mt. Gox's user experience was just better enough than the alternative crypto exchanges that the orders to buy bitcoin for dollars kept pouring in, for larger and larger quantities. As the orders piled in from people wanting to buy tens of thousands of dollars' worth of bitcoin, Jed wanted out, this wasn't for him. The early crypto community was small. Word quickly got around that the exchange was up for sale, and a man he knew, Mark Karpeles, soon came in to take it over.

Karpeles, from the start, probably wasn't really cut out to run the world's largest crypto exchange and deal with all the complex regulation that came with it. He was a hacker and crypto enthusiast. To this day he still he goes by the name MagicalTux in online forums, and people close to him said he seemed to prefer mending servers or deliberating over quiche recipes to dealing with the important decisions and security infrastructure that would be needed to keep the exchange safe.[3] Karpeles had bought the exchange on the understanding that Jed wasn't sure of its legal status and that Jed wouldn't be liable for anything that came of it – an agreement that would come to haunt him later. Karpeles inherited Mt. Gox for free, Jed got 12 per cent of its profits for a term, but that was it, the responsibility was now fully Mark's.[4]

## Hack after hack after hack

On 20 June 2011, just as Karpeles was getting used to handling the reins of such a fast-growing crypto exchange, Mt. Gox had its first hack. The exchange would be hacked many more times in the following years, but this hack perhaps sealed the exchange's fate before its story had even really begun.

Mt. Gox's first hacker managed to get into Jed McCaleb's original administrator account. They used these stolen credentials to enter Mt. Gox's internal systems and manipulate the price of bitcoin, dropping the price from $17 to one cent. The hacker took their chance to buy 2,000 bitcoin at this new artificial valuation of one cent per coin, and then sell these bitcoin back to Mt. Gox users at its normal rate of $17 before making off with their profit. The hacker didn't make much, less than $34,000 in value at the time, and was never caught or seen from again. Some Mt. Gox customers also managed to take advantage of this hack – those who got lucky were on the exchange at the right time, buying 650 more bitcoin at this discounted rate. The new owners of these bitcoin decided it was better to take them off the exchange than return them to their former owners. Other customers lost their money, as did the exchange, but the main damage to the exchange came from the fear created by the news of the hack, which made headlines around the world.[5]

The crypto community went into panic mode. News of the hack and the headlines it attracted negatively affected the price of bitcoin, which affected all of their bottom lines. The main figures of the crypto community in 2011 largely all knew each other, or at least knew of each other, and were motivated enough to preserve the smooth running of the ecosystem to come and help out when there was a major problem. Mt. Gox engineers were working round the clock and crypto investors came in, some flying in from around the world, giving up their time, resources and money to buy the equipment and do what it would take to fix the problem so the exchange could resume running as normal again. After all, they almost all held bitcoin at the exchange.

Karpeles seemed less worried. Whilst his team and those volunteers who had rallied around worked through the weekend until the exchange was back online, Mark was nowhere to be seen from Friday evening until he came back to work on Monday, when he proceeded to get on with less important tasks totally unrelated to the hack. The volunteers who had all given up their free time were pretty unimpressed by his lack of apparent concern for or dedication to the cause.[6]

A series of other hacks followed this one, hacks that didn't make the same headlines but which caused more serious financial problems and had far greater security implications for the exchange. Mt. Gox was hit by a whole string of hacks in 2011 alone, hack after hack after hack, six in total. One of the hackers left such obvious clues to investigators that they returned the 300,000 bitcoin they had stolen, which would go on to be worth billions of dollars, for a 1 per cent (3,000 bitcoin) fee,[7] in exchange for not being threatened with legal action or investigation. Mt. Gox got lucky on that one. On other hacks they weren't as lucky, losing hundreds of thousands of bitcoin cumulatively.

In September that year, one group of hackers gave themselves administrative authority over the exchange's database, inflating their own balances from customers' bitcoin and then withdrawing these funds, making out with an estimated 77,500 bitcoin.[8] The next month, another hacker again managed to manipulate the exchange, tricking Mt. Gox into thinking it was making deposits to them instead of stealing from them, so that it wouldn't be immediately picked up when they stole the bitcoin.

For these hacks, in many ways Mt. Gox only really had themselves and their lack of security to blame. In those early years of crypto, Mt. Gox was the key target and arguably the most vulnerable institution in the whole crypto ecosystem – the exchange held more bitcoin than any other. In those years, there was no insurance or any of the institutional-grade crypto assets security we have in crypto today. The one thing they needed was cutting-edge cyber security. This level of security was expensive, and not easy to implement, but would have been possible and would have cost a tiny fraction of the money the exchange was losing due to its compromised security.

## Mistakes, bugs and losing bitcoin

Mt. Gox, despite being run by a quasi-hacker, was running off 'entirely untested code'.[9] This, coupled with mismanagement and some drastic accounting errors, led to the loss of yet more of the exchange's bitcoin. In October 2011, the same month as the latest hack, the exchange accidentally sent 44,300 of its bitcoin to 48 different users' accounts.[10] Some of those customers sent the bitcoin back, but most were grateful to pocket some free, unexpected money. This mistake lost the exchange another 30,000 bitcoin. The same month, Mark Karpeles changed to a new digital wallet software that was designed to store and protect the bitcoin under its possession. That software had a bug, which ended up sending 2,609 bitcoin to a broken address – which in bitcoin terms means it was lost forever.[11] These administrative mistakes followed the hacks one mistake and hack after the next, costing the exchange more and more of its Bitcoin at every turn.

The more that was going wrong internally at the exchange, and the more bitcoin it lost, the more successful the exchange was getting at attracting new users and storing more bitcoin under its roof. New customers kept on sending Mt. Gox their bitcoin, and the exchange was taking a cut of every transaction, so its accounts showed it as always making money. As the new money was coming in faster than it was being lost through mistakes and hacks, no one noticed the extent of the problems, or seemingly bothered to check its accounts to see how many bitcoin the exchange had at any one time.

## The law steps in

In 2013, Mt. Gox had made a deal with a US firm called Coinlab, which was headed up by some big names in crypto, for them to run the American operations of the exchange. Coinlab had fulfilled their share of the agreement, but then Mt. Gox, for reasons still not known, just didn't hand over this part of business. Coinlab sued for $75 million.[12] At the same time, the United States Department of Homeland Security issued a warrant against Mt. Gox. When Karpeles had taken over from McCaleb, he had agreed that he would be fully liable for the exchange's legal situation, or lack thereof, from before the handover. Karpeles had agreed to McCaleb's seller stipulation that he was uncertain whether Mt. Gox was compliant or not with US code or statute, or any other law for that matter. At the time, Karpeles had rather disregarded this. When it came to filling out some forms, Karpeles had been asked two crucial questions about Mt. Gox in relation to its dealings with crypto. 'Do you deal in or exchange currency for your customer?' and second, 'Does your business accept funds from customers and send the funds based on customers' instructions (Money Transmitter)?' The only possible legal answer to these two questions is 'yes'. Karpeles answered no, to both. It's not known quite how or why he came to that answer, but Karpeles had broken the law and $5 million worth of funds from their bank accounts were seized for their US operations.[13]

US law enforcement also set some bans on Mt. Gox. A month-long ban on accepting US dollars was imposed. As a result,

Mt. Gox lost access to the third-party e-commerce platform it used for American money exchanges. This caused the exchange some rather large problems, given how many of its customers were from the US. What this meant in practice was that Mt. Gox couldn't accept or cash out US dollars. This meant that Mt. Gox couldn't take in any new money, or cash out money to its existing users who held bitcoin in their exchange. Customers started experiencing delays lasting months on end in being able to withdraw their funds. Mt. Gox's Japanese bank also implemented a pretty heavy restriction limiting the exchange to processing only 10 transactions a day, down from 300,000. Customers now couldn't get hold of the money they thought they had stored securely in the exchange.

By now, Mark Karpeles was facing five years in prison[14] and Mt. Gox could barely process any of the transactions it needed to keep going. The exchange dropped from being the world's dominant exchange controlling 80 per cent of all transactions to third place, behind a Russian-based exchange, BTC-e, known more for its reputation for money laundering[15] than for processing genuine crypto transactions, and a Slovenian exchange called Bitstamp. At the end of 2013 Mt. Gox was still trading and had – or, as would soon be discovered, should have had – one million bitcoin under its control.

## And the money stopped

Mt. Gox kept processing what withdrawals it could until 7 February, when withdrawals suddenly stopped. They didn't give much of a reason to their customers, hiding behind the excuse of a software bug that had affected some other exchanges.

After a few days, customers started to worry about the status of their money that was locked in the exchange. A week later, their users were beyond worried – they were anxious and wanted answers. By this point, 21 per cent of their users had been waiting for over three months to withdraw their money.[16] Less than two weeks after withdrawals stopped, the price of bitcoin on Mt. Gox had plummeted. Mt. Gox bitcoin was now trading at less than half of what it had been, a clear indicator of how much trust in the exchange had been destroyed. By 24 February the exchange was gone, shut down for good. They didn't give any real explanation, but just hours later an internal document was leaked and went viral.[17] The exchange had been hacked, and somehow, despite being meant to have over one million bitcoin in its possession, had checked its accounts and found it now had precisely none. The company declared bankruptcy four days later.

## Leaking bitcoin

The leaked document that hit the internet shortly after the exchange went down revealed that the exchange had been losing its bitcoin not in one recent hack, but slowly, methodically, bitcoin by bitcoin, ever since it was first hacked in 2011. Mt. Gox had lost 850,000 bitcoin in total. At Bitcoin's current (and hugely fluctuating) all-time highest value of $48,000 per bitcoin in early 2021, this was worth over $40 billion. Some 740,000 of these bitcoin were stolen from Mt. Gox customers and the rest from the exchange itself. The exchange, in 2011, effectively had no security defences between its bitcoin and potential hackers. Had it encrypted its data, or performed any of a myriad of potential cybersecurity checks or protections that it could have, this attack might not have happened. It's still not known if the hack was enabled through insider information, or if the hacker cracked through the exchange themselves, but the hacker gained access to Mt. Gox's private key – like an encrypted digital password used to store crypto safely – and set up a series of automations which sent all of the bitcoin out of the exchange gradually over a period of three years until all the bitcoin were gone.

The hackers could, in theory, have taken all the bitcoin at once, had they wanted. The problem in crypto, and especially in its early days, was liquidity.[18] Unlike with government-produced fiat money, which can be printed infinitely, in total there will only ever be 21 million bitcoin in circulation, which are released gradually. At the time of the hack, only a fraction of these bitcoin were already mined and in circulation. Had the hacker stolen all 850,000 of the bitcoin held on Mt. Gox in one go, they would never have been able to cash them out. The liquidity simply wasn't there. The hack accounted for a huge percentage of all of the bitcoin in total circulation, and given that most bitcoin were owned and held in hard wallets by their owners and therefore didn't add to the liquidity pool on exchanges, cashing out in one go would have flooded the market. It would have completely crashed the price of bitcoin, and in so doing rendered their loot almost worthless. The large lump sum would have been much harder to cash out into fiat, perhaps even impossible without attracting suspicion. Such a large sum would have attracted the attention of both Mt. Gox and law enforcement, and might realistically have been seized. The way they played it showed that the hackers knew what they were doing and that Mt. Gox's accounting wasn't exactly as great as it could have been.

In three years, no one at Mt. Gox noticed that bitcoins were slowly but routinely leaking out of the exchange until they were all gone. The hacker had set the hack to drain the Mt. Gox coffers so slowly and so systematically that it looked internally like legitimate internal transactions, and no one at Mt. Gox thought to check.

It's speculated that when Karpeles acquired the exchange in 2011, up to 80,000 bitcoin were already missing. The exchange might have been bankrupt without him knowing it before he even started.[19] How no one at Mt. Gox noticed that its bitcoin were being leaked away and that the exchange had no bitcoin left until other problems hit and they had to look into it is inexplicable, only to say that almost anyone looking at the exchange from an informed external view point cited disorganization and mismanagement.[20]

To get the bitcoin, the hacker had copied Mt. Gox's private keys that guarded their crypto, so for the next three years nine out of ten of the bitcoin deposited into the exchange were stolen as soon as they came in. The money was just being drained right out. Karpeles said he just never noticed. As they were always getting more deposits, they never noticed almost all of it was being taken away. 'Bitcoin didn't exactly decrease,' he says. 'It's just that they didn't increase as much as they should.'[21]

## Where is our money?

When Mt. Gox shut down and froze customer withdrawals, people assumed the worst. Many stood to lose a lot of money. Protestors gathered outside the Mt. Gox building, some took to social media. One stood outside the offices for over two weeks with a sign asking 'MT GOX WHERE IS OUR MONEY?'[22]

With all this going on, Mark Karpeles took himself to his penthouse apartment in Tokyo and put himself under a self-imposed house arrest to avoid the protests outside. There, he started going through all of the old databases, records and now empty wallets and had one bit of good news: 200,000 of the 850,000 missing bitcoin were there, they'd been put away in an old wallet and hadn't been found since. This was solely down to poor accounting records; no credit can be given for good custody of their customers' funds. Not even the hackers had been able to get hold of them. In other times, this would have represented a gross case of poor accounting that would have otherwise rendered a lot of its users' funds unaccounted for, but under these circumstances this find was a rare stroke of good luck.[23] This left 650,000 missing bitcoin.

## The world's biggest puzzle

A Swedish software engineer called Kim Nilsson who held bitcoin at Mt. Gox took a different approach to the protesters standing outside the exchange's office. Kim hadn't worked on blockchain before, but got pleasure from solving puzzles and software bugs and had a reputation for getting to the bottom of a problem. To Kim, 'It was basically just the world's biggest puzzle at the time.'[24] Kim first taught himself blockchain analytics and then investigated every aspect of Mt. Gox's records and details of the hack. On the Bitcoin blockchain, all transactions can be permanently seen if you know where to look, so he tracked every aspect of this trail. Kim estimates he spent a year and a half of full-time work on this case over the next four years, investigating every aspect of the hack. It's not likely he'll vastly profit directly himself; his claim of 12.7 bitcoin makes him one of the smallest creditors if he does ever get repaid.[25] To Kim, this work is just what being part of the decentralized Bitcoin community is about.

Kim started off by investigating Karpeles, assuming he had some role in the loss of the bitcoin. However, as he got to know him, he quickly realized that that didn't seem to be the case and that Mark was just as keen to know where the bitcoin had gone as he was. Kim worked his way into Mark's apartment and confidence by bringing him the ingredients he needed to make his beloved quiche, in exchange for data that Karpeles fed him to help solve the case.[26]

Mt. Gox, Kim soon worked out, had technically been insolvent since 2012.[27]

It took him a few years of painstaking digging, but by early 2016 Kim had his suspect. Of the stolen funds, 630,000 bitcoin had gone to wallets controlled by the same person who had an account at Mt. Gox with the name WME. WME had one time given himself away on an online Bitcoin forum where he complained about another crypto exchange freezing his funds.[28] Here, he posted a letter from his lawyer showing his full name. Kim had been communicating with a special agent from the Internal Revenue Service in New York who specialized in catching cybercriminals, and showed him his findings.[29]

## Bye bye Mt. Gox money: Criminal mastermind money laundering

In July 2017, as he was on holiday in Greece with his wife and kids who were at that moment playing in the sea, police swarmed around a man who had stayed behind on the beach. Russian citizen Alexander Vinnik was a 38-year-old IT specialist. He was arrested for being the suspected mastermind and leader of a criminal organization who, according to the police report, had, since 2011 owned, operated and managed one of the world's leading e-crime websites.[30]

Vinnik was accused of stealing and laundering not only the 630,000 bitcoin stolen from Mt. Gox[31] in a $4 billion theft that is still the largest theft in the history of crypto, but also of hacking smaller volumes of bitcoin from other exchanges. Vinnik is thought to be the operator, or one of the operators, of the Russian BTC-e crypto exchange,[32] which was coincidentally founded at roughly the same time as the 2011 Mt. Gox hack. Some think that BTC-e's primary purpose was to launder the bitcoin stolen from Mt. Gox.[33] Several in law enforcement certainly seem to think so. The lack of basic security checks it implemented do nothing to disprove this line of thinking. Karpeles believes that it was Russian bitcoin exchange administrators behind a series of the hacks that hit his exchange.[34] BTC-e was taken down by law enforcement at the time of Vinnik's arrest, then in 2020 Vinnik was sentenced to a five-year prison term for money laundering.[35]

## A bot named Willy. And Markus the bot too

In 2014, when the exchange had collapsed, a database containing details of its trading, account balances, withdrawals and deposits was leaked onto the internet. It didn't have everything, but it gave investigators, watchful onlookers and investors enough data and ammunition to play with. It didn't take long for a very suspicious pattern of activity to show up that someone decided must have been a bot. The bot got named Willy, a name that has held throughout all the subsequent court hearings where Willy has come up again and again and again.

The aptly named Willy Report[36] – a WordPress blog dedicated to monitoring all actions on the subject and compiled by the author – soon came out, showing suspicious trends that went on until the leaked data stopped. Every 5–10 minutes, a different account bought 10–20 bitcoin. It always seemed to be a round number and was always for a very specific dollar amount. Each account only bought bitcoin with dollars, never selling any. Each trade was followed by a trade from a new account, designed to not raise eyebrows had anyone thought to check whilst the exchange was still active. And the accounts trading were able to make their trades even when the exchange was closed down and no one else was able to.

It was clear that Willy the bot had been programmed to make these trades, but on whose behalf?

The next patterns were different to Willy's, with odd or seemingly incorrect fiat amounts recorded for bitcoin purchases. The two bots seemed clearly to work alongside each other. The new bot was named Markus.[37]

By the time Willy and Markus came onto the scene, most of Mt. Gox' bitcoin were already lost and Willy can't be blamed for anywhere near the majority of the troubled exchange's problems. But, Willy bought a lot of bitcoin, a total of 250,000; enough, it is speculated, to affect the price of bitcoin. If so, this wasn't just exchange manipulation, this was market manipulation affecting the entire crypto markets.[38]

In the court cases that followed, Karpeles admitted to operating Willy as part of an 'obligation exchange' but said the bots were 'for the good of the company so not illegal'.[39] He pleaded not guilty to charges of embezzlement and data manipulation. The bots, it transpired, had been brought in to stave off the inevitable collapse of the exchange. After its 2011 hack, Mt. Gox already had a shortfall of bitcoin, and needed more bitcoin and volume to keep it going. The bots, by simulating volume and bitcoin traded and held on the exchange, helped this cause.[40]

## Arrests, money laundering, lawsuits, some more ongoing lawsuits and misspent funds

The trials surrounding Mt. Gox are ongoing, and results for the investors who are waiting on their money – whilst now closer than ever before to their hopes of getting some or all of their money back – keep getting delayed. There are several twists to this case and sad ironies for all investors involved.

Not all of the bitcoin held by Mt. Gox is available for recovery to investors. There are now so many claims on the remaining bitcoin, that the Mt. Gox estate only has 0.23 out of every bitcoin claimed to give out.[41] Coinlab, the creditor that sued for $75 million, has since upped their claim to $16 billion. Some funds have bought up investors' claims, and stand to do rather well out of it all.

Many Mt. Gox investors are worried that after years of waiting, they may never see the bitcoin they believe is rightfully theirs. Bitcoin has now risen hugely in value, so it's hopeful that investors might at least get all of their fiat equivalent back, if not the same amount of bitcoin that they originally entrusted to the exchange. A lot may depend on Bitcoin's value at the time this debacle is finally sorted.

The hackers didn't really do that well out of it, relatively speaking. Because they sold their stolen bitcoin into fiat straight away, they made an estimated $20 million. The irony is, that bitcoin would now be worth many billions of dollars. The Mt. Gox investors who had their bitcoin stolen have lost far more in dollar value than the hackers ever made.

Karpeles is hardly guilt-free, other than mismanaging the exchange. Kelman, a lawyer in the case, describes the last days of Mt. Gox as operating a bit like a Ponzi. 'When Mt. Gox didn't have any of the coins, he was getting new deposits from other customers to pay off other people – kind of like a Bernie Madoff.'[42] Despite his former wealth from running the exchange, Karpeles himself went bankrupt, and makes it clear he doesn't want to profit from the situation. But that doesn't explain reports that he spent suspected embezzled funds on 'sexual services',[43] a fact that disgruntled investors still waiting for their funds are understandably not happy about. In 2019, the Tokyo District Court found him 'guilty of falsifying financial records but acquitted him of all other charges, including embezzlement'.[44] He received a two-and-a-half year suspended sentence, so won't serve any more jail time unless he commits another violation within four years.[45]

One has to feel a little sorry for Karpeles. If his lack of security controls did cause investors to lose their bitcoin, this isn't the first and certainly won't be the last time people lose money through crypto exchanges. Almost every crypto exchange has been hacked at some point, with customers losing some or all of their crypto. Mark Karpeles has, rather unfairly, been accused by some of running a sophisticated Ponzi scheme, and 'of being a cybercriminal mastermind'.[46] He didn't have his eye on the ball, maybe and, by his own admission, he was in completely over his head,[47] but, unlike many of the other companies we're reading about in this book, whilst Karpeles appeared to be out of his depth, maybe even not competent for the role, it doesn't seem like his intention was to scam anyone.

## Last twist in the unfinished tale

The last ironically sad twist in the tale for all concerned: under Japanese bankruptcy law, the repayment to investors is at the dollar value of the asset at the time of bankruptcy. At the time of Mt. Gox's insolvency, bitcoin traded at $489.[48] One bitcoin is currently worth over $48,000 (although this fluctuates hugely). If the 200,000 remaining bitcoin were sold now and given to investors in dollars, all creditors would be happily repaid in full, in dollar value. Giving investors their bitcoin in dollar value today is a sensible solution, and looks closer than ever before to becoming a reality, but the courts and politics have been holding this up at investors' expense for years now and there is still, years on, no certainty for those who entrusted their bitcoin to the exchange.

## CHAPTER EIGHT

# Crypto mining

## *Creating nothing out of thin air*

Bitcoin, the first and most important cryptocurrency, is created by a process known as 'mining'. Satoshi Nakamoto, its pseudonymous and mysterious founder, created algorithms that had to be solved to win bitcoins. The first computers to solve the algorithms in each batch, known as a block, win bitcoin. In the early years of Bitcoin, following its invention in 2009, one bitcoin was worth very little and people mined the new digital currency either for curiosity, or for speculation. Now, a bitcoin is worth a lot of money, and in the last few years as demand has increased, bitcoin and crypto mining is now big business.

In its early years, when there were not many users and not much demand for the then relatively unknown digital currency, there was little competition, and solving these algorithms didn't require much computing energy. As bitcoin rose in value and popularity, more and more powerful machines were needed to outcompete each other to win the bitcoin from each block. For the last few years, only professional-size mining farms, basically large warehouses or factories full of the high-power computer machines used to mine bitcoin – known as mining rigs or GPUs – would be all pointing their energy towards solving the Bitcoin algorithms in the hope of winning bitcoin against competing operations.

Some early Bitcoin adopters had initially mined bitcoin from their own computers, but this took a lot of technical know-how, and, for many, cost more in energy than the bitcoins themselves were worth at the time. It wasn't really possible for an average, non-technical person to mine cryptocurrency – it was a complicated process! As bitcoin shot up in price and gained in popularity, more and more people wanted in. Trading in crypto is super high risk, the markets are so volatile that a lot of people lost money, but mining produced crypto for a steady cost and, if done right, was seen by some and heavily promoted by others as a stable form of income.

Companies started popping up offering remote or 'cloud' crypto mining as the next best thing in crypto. These companies would – in theory at least – buy and maintain the mining equipment and pay a passive income to their investors. They weren't without risks. Crypto mining equipment is expensive tech and hard to get hold of, and was prone to getting stolen. Perhaps needless to say, there is more than one story of great crypto mining equipment thefts.

## Easy money – watch the profits roll in

Cloud mining promised investors the chance to get cryptocurrencies mined for them, remotely, without them having to do any of the work or have to look after the machines themselves. It would be easy, passive money. In theory, at least, the cloud mining companies would put their investors' money towards the mining equipment and the energy costs needed to mine bitcoin or other cryptocurrencies. The bitcoin or the crypto they would mine would be worth more than the cost of mining it. Mining companies would then take their cut of the newly mined crypto to cover their costs and their profit, and send the rest to investors. Investors would, again in theory, get paid back out of the profits.

All investors had to do is pay their investment fee, and, as the many cloud mining companies that sprung up promised, sit back and watch the profits roll in.

It didn't take long for cloud mining to be touted as the next best way to profit from crypto. Cloud mining was promoted – with some very slick marketing in some cases – as effectively the same thing as printing money. Already in the early years of crypto mania, leading up to 2018 when the markets crashed and there was a bit of a reality check, there were some genuine companies offering cloud mining and crypto mining services to investors. But where there is money, especially in a field of new, emerging technologies, there are scams, hacks and some outright thefts.

## The $722 million money-printing machine

It wasn't long before the idea of cloud mining would meet and partner with another dominant trend in crypto scams that we see repeated over and over again in this book – multi-level marketing. Cloud mining was a way of printing money out of thin air, and MLM, as we see with several of the other largest scams in crypto, was the easiest way to get thousands of people to invest their money, for very little involvement from the companies themselves. It was a match made in crypto scam heaven.

One company in crypto cloud mining rose above all, ultimately making $722 million off the back of its sales.[1] BitClub

Network marketed itself as an easy and risk-free way for everyone to get into crypto investing. Why buy bitcoin, when you can invest effortlessly in the machines that make it?

BitClub Network had it all. All its investors had to do was sit back and watch their profits roll in. To attract these investors, it had a multi-level marketing set-up offering generous referral rewards, and employed the best salespeople who would jet-set around the world, showing off their glamorous lifestyles and making everyone want to be a little bit like them.

And Joby Weeks, its frontman and lead salesman, could sell.

An early Bitcoin investor, Joby, had bought Bitcoin when it was at $0.85 cents and watched the price ride up to thousands of dollars per bitcoin. He had done well out of his Bitcoin investments, buying enough when it was cheap to not have to worry about money anymore.[2]

Before he got into crypto, Joby had worked selling various multi-level-marketing or MLM schemes for products ranging from energy to supplements. Getting in early to these MLM schemes and being such a confident salesman put him at the top of the food chain in these companies. For anyone good at sales who gets into an MLM scheme early enough, it can be very lucrative.

There is a common recurring theme in crypto scams – if they can motivate good salespeople to promote your product, they do well. Multi-level marketing schemes can be the best form of motivation for salespeople who care less about what they're selling or who they're taking money from than they do about their own results. Just as with OneCoin and Bitconnect, not only do the top salespeople in MLM schemes get a commission from every person they recruit, they get a cut from every person their referrals recruit, typically going down multiple levels. This can mean ongoing revenue streams without having to do very much, if any, work past their first level of recruitment. These successes had given Joby a life of almost permanent travel, luxurious homes and a flexible schedule to go where he wanted.

## The dream life

When Joby met dental assistant Stephanie in their native Colorado as he went to her dentist surgery as a patient, they hit it off instantly. Three months later, they were off on their first adventure. The couple were almost non-stop on the go for 11 years, travelling around the world until five weeks before the birth of their daughter, when they finally went home to rest.

Joby had been a big fan of presidential candidate and Texas congressman Ron Paul, who had become popularized in the crypto community for his Libertarian views, and had previously made some donations to his presidential campaign. The couple wanted their daughter's birth to be attended by the 83-year-old. Ron Paul said he would, if the delivery were near his home, so Joby and Stephanie duly travelled to him, and the infamous Ron Paul was there for her birth. This was just the first of their celebrity encounters.

When Liberty was born, named after Ron Paul's movement, she hit a new record, becoming the youngest member of the All Fifty States Club, going to all fifty US states by the time she was 43 days old. Baby Liberty had her own Instagram feed showing her at landmarks across America and 'telling' the world, 'I'm the youngest person to visit all 50 states. I did it in 42 days at 43 days old! I've been to 45 countries & 4 continents. These are my adventures.'[3] Joby told the world that they were 'only just starting with her. We want her to go to every country in the world'.[4] And they did.

As a couple, Joby and Stephanie went around the world, posting photos of their adventures on his blog. They went to the South Pole and the Sahara Desert, to The Cook Islands, Machu Pichu, Tokyo and paid a visit to Liberland, the Libertarian state set up and favoured by many crypto investors. Along the way Joby met Richard Branson, even posing for a travel video with him. They visited 1,241 cities and 152 countries, not spending more than one week in any one place in their 11 years of travels.[5] Most of this travel was for Joby's work, but they made it fun and stopped for sightseeing wherever they went. To make travel with a baby easier, Joby bought a private plane. They were living the dream.

## The anarchists' resort

Following his early investment successes, Joby had become a vocal supporter of crypto, travelling globally to speak at conferences about it. His favourite crypto conference by a long way was Anarchapulco. Launched in Acapulco, Mexico in 2015 by popular crypto anarchist Jeff Berwick, the event has become popularized by the Libertarian crypto community and grown every year to now attract thousands of attendees and big-name speakers. Many of the earliest Bitcoin adopters, now big names in the industry, some who have made billions of dollars, gather there each year. Joby went to the first one along with a few hundred others. Weeks after the conference had ended, many were still there, staying on and soon forming a new and fast-growing community in Acapulco, with more than a few attendees moving permanently to the resort.

The resort town of Acapulco welcomed these crypto-friendly visitors with open arms. The once popular Mexican coastal town has had its share of danger, counting one of the highest murder rates in the West in recent years. The area is considered to be pretty lawless. US citizens are advised not to visit Guerrero, the state that Acapulco is in. US Government employees are banned from visiting it altogether, a fact welcomed by the attendees and which makes the resort the perfect place to host an anarchist conference.

Thousands now travel there each year from around the world. Attendees ranging from anarchists to successful business owners to conspiracy theorists and hippies rent out local homes and luxurious hotel suites and condos and pay in crypto almost everywhere they go. Local businesses, starved of tourist dollars, now accept payment in crypto for anything from juice and snacks to rides in Mexican horse-drawn carriages. When Joby Weeks first went to Anarchapulco in 2015, he was such a fan that he bought a 13 bedroom mansion complete with ocean view for $4 million, paid in bitcoin.[6] The same amount of bitcoin, at its early 2021 peak on news of Tesla buying into Bitcoin causing a price spike, would be worth almost $180 million.

Anarchapulco is where Joby Weeks came in contact with BitClub Network, a then relatively unknown crypto cloud-mining company promising to make crypto investment open to all, a year after it was founded in 2014.

## Printing money: The goose that lays the golden egg

BitClub Network was a tempting idea and an easy sales pitch. The company promised its investors a share in the crypto mining machines that, as far as its salesmen were concerned, printed money. In the following years Joby would go on to compare investing in BitClub Network to 'buying the goose that lays the golden egg'.[7] Given how hard it still was to buy bitcoin at the time, BitClub Network wanted to show off how easy it could be to hold crypto and to profit two ways, not only from its increase in value, but also from mining cryptocurrencies at less than their retail value. Who wouldn't want a way to create money out of thin air?

Joby was the perfect fit for BitClub Network. He was a jet-setting poster boy who liked talking about crypto. He'd made his money from crypto and that had fuelled his lifestyle, travelling in luxury around the world. People saw the life he led – which he went out of his way to show off with photos and videos on his blog and social media – and wanted what he had. He was confident and was good at talking, excelled at public speaking and he could sell. Joby quickly became the network's leading salesman. For Joby, BitClub Network was a chance to make money from two revenue streams that he knew a lot about – Bitcoin mining and a multi-level-marketing sales structure.

In his new role, Joby got paid to travel to the most luxurious and far-flung resorts around the world, much as he had done before. He would go to the richest, most exclusive resorts across North America wearing his trademark shorts, t-shirt and sandals, showing everyone how he lived the dream, travelling the world and staying in luxurious properties off the back of his Bitcoin riches and telling everyone they could too, if only they followed what he did.[8]

## Vague numbers, clueless leaders and fake testimonials

BitClub Network claimed to make getting started in crypto easy and accessible to all. For a $99 membership fee and starting from a $500 investment,[9] anyone could get their own slice of Bitcoin mining equipment which would (in theory) give them recurring income ever after. The returns might have been a little vague, and no details were given of where the mining equipment supposedly was, or who was behind the company, but early investors were happy, they got their money back, and so generally chose not to question the specifics.

Already, early on, it was clear to many onlookers that BitClub Network wasn't what it was made out to be. YouTube videos put out by the network indicated that the leaders didn't seem to have any knowledge about how mining pools worked or the associated risks of running one. Clueless is a strong word, but it's fair to say they were the opposite of industry experts. Testimonials on their website seemed to all appearances to be faked, names didn't correspond to the photos and it isn't known if any of the testimonials at all were real. Based on the track records of most crypto scams, it's fair to assume that testimonials and reviews were either faked or bought. A testimonial from one supposedly happy customer named Victor Diaz from Brazil turned to be using the photo taken of a convicted rapist in India.[10] They didn't say whether Victor in Brazil was in fact a real person. One hopes not, for his sake.

The leaders of BitClub Network became as known for their insulting comments about their investors as for the size of the scam they ran. They genuinely seemed to think that their investors would be too stupid to notice or question any discrepancies in the numbers and returns on their investments. They literally described their investors as 'dumb' and 'sheep'.[11] Not surprisingly, when the scheme eventually collapsed and the founders were arrested, some of the words they called their investors led to the people behind the giant $722 million scam not getting a vast amount of sympathy.

There were several aspects about the BitClub Network that quickly went from being vague to outright suspicious.

## The numbers game

To anyone looking closely at the numbers, it wasn't clear how investors were supposed to make their money back, and to trained eyes it didn't look likely that they would at all! Investors might have thought that all of their investment money went into mining expenses, such as paying for mining equipment and energy costs, and that they would be repaid from those profits. They were told that half of their profits, instead of being repaid directly to them, would go on a compulsory rebuy into more investment in BitClub Network, but otherwise, investors were led to think that the money marked as going to operating costs would actually be going for that. A fair assumption. Instead, profits paid out to investors only came after all BitClub Network's other costs had been paid from them. Other costs meant 60 per cent of investors' money going to pay the commissions for their salespeople and MLM promoters,[12] who brought in yet more investors.

When asked if the investors knew where their money was going to, Goettsche, the founder, was caught sharing in an internal discussion when asked by the developer, 'I guess most people do not know only 40 per cent is used for mining and the rest for commissions?' 'The leaders know,' Goettsche replied, 'It's the sheep that don't.'[13] It would be slightly annoying to find out that 60 per cent of your entire investment has gone on some salesperson's fat commission before you even start. This fact, amongst others, was kept rather hidden by the BitClub Network team.

It was important to BitClub Network to make sure that their earliest investors and promoters were well rewarded. Happy and well-paid early investors meant good reviews. Happy and well-paid early promoters meant people incentivized to bring more people into the network, which all meant lots more money for its team. Paying extra money to the early investors made it look like they were actually getting good returns from mining bitcoin, which served its purpose of encouraging more people to buy in.

Since its launch in 2014, BitClub Network had relied on tweaking its finances. Initially Goettsche had allegedly only posted about the need to fake the numbers 'just for the first 30 days while we get going', apparently instructing a co-founder to work some 'magic' on the company's revenue figures.[14] That wasn't enough. Goettsche allegedly soon suggested they 'bump up the daily mining earnings starting today by 60 per cent'.[15] The developer's less-than-reassuring response: 'That is not sustainable, that is Ponzi territory and fast cash-out Ponzi... but sure.'[16] It didn't exactly seem as if the masterminds behind BitClub Network thought they'd ever get found out.

BitClub Network obviously did what it could to conceal its real statistics. The extra profits used to pay the early investors and their promoters didn't come from mining. That money came from the next set of investor buy-ins.[17] Using money from new investors to pay out to old investors is typically known as a

Ponzi scheme. It didn't take long before this realization started to dawn on outsiders, and for them to publicly start crying 'Ponzi'.

## The magical missing mining machines

Next on the list of things that didn't stack up were the mining operations BitClub Network claimed to run. To one audience he presented to in 2017, Joby described BitClub Network as 'basically selling machines that print money'.[18] The company never went into any more specifics about these money-making machines, where they existed or how they were maintained.

One of Joby's biggest claims was that he had brokered sales of more than $60 million in mining equipment to BitClub Network.[19] Videos showed him leading tours of the data centre in Iceland where much of the mining was supposedly taking place. Some eagle-eyed followers, eager to see how BitClub Network would unfold noticed the exact, identical likeness between this video and another well-known crypto mining facility. A spokesperson for Verne Global, the owner of the facility in question, made it clear that they had never had a direct relationship with BitClub Network and couldn't comment on its mining capabilities.[20] Oops.

BitClub Network had told their investors that they had a choice of three different mining pools to invest in. In the subsequent 2020 trial, Balaci, a developer who had been with the company since its earliest days, admitted that at no point was he aware of the network actually operating three separate bitcoin mining pools. He also admitted to, at Goettsche's bidding, changing the numbers shown to investors to make it seem that BitClub Network was making more profit than what was actually being mined.[21] It isn't clear if they even operated any crypto mining equipment at all.

Maybe there's more to it, but Goettsche made exaggerated claims about mining capabilities, displayed clear contempt for investors and didn't hesitate to bump up payouts. One cannot therefore be entirely blamed for thinking that he was perhaps in it to make the maximum money in the shortest period of time, then retire, rich.

Internal emails and online chats obtained by federal investigators showed Goettsche telling Balaci to 'bump up the payout', and later to 'drop mining earnings significantly' to ensure one thing: that the ringleaders of BitClub Network could, in their words, 'retire RAF' or rich as f**k.[22] That was all revealed later, of course, after the scheme's collapse. But one thing was clear: the evidence of their mining capabilities seems as fake as the testimonials.

## Little more than water

The people behind BitClub Network didn't seem to really want people to know how their set-up worked, or what precisely happened with the money that investors put in. They wanted people to focus on the multi-level marketing element, where investors could earn commissions for anyone else they referred to the network, and on the high-potential returns.

Both Goettsche, the founder of BitClub Network, and Joby, its main salesman, came from a background of MLM sales, selling products masked as having nutritional or anti-aging benefits. The types of companies they'd worked for gave the impression they were more concerned about the money they took home than scruples around what they were selling or who they were taking money from. One of the companies Goettsche had worked for was accused by lawsuits of selling 'a mineral-enhanced anti-aging product that, in reality, contained little more than water'.[23] This is fairly common for multi-level marketing schemes, a concept that is legal but touches on the grey, dubious side of the law more often than their promoters would like their victims or users to know.

BitClub Network, to them, wasn't so different to the product containing little more than water. As long as enough people believed their claims of the network's money-making potential, that seemed to be all that mattered. Marketing materials made no mention of risk or of how the money would be made, but rather focused almost exclusively on the big dollar signs that people could make. One promotional video promised that a $3,599 investment could, if being 'very conservative', return the investor $250,000 over three years.[24] The video didn't go into detail about how they would make these great returns. The video also didn't touch on or answer the logical ensuing question, that if they could make such great returns on what is a very finite resource – Bitcoin mining – why the founders of this money-making masterstroke wouldn't just keep this secret to themselves and invest all their own money, ensuring their fortunes whilst the mining capabilities lasted?

As with any multi-level-marketing scheme, there comes a point where there aren't enough fresh people left to bring in, when the project has reached saturation point. That's the point at which they tend to unfold. If there's no substance behind a scheme, that's when it almost inevitably collapses, and is often only then revealed as being a Ponzi scheme. Several people had already long before called BitClub Network out as a Ponzi, and by now the scheme was close to collapse.

## The 'too big to fail' scam that failed

By 2019 investors had started to back out, worried about some comments that the whole thing was a scam and upset by reduced earnings. That same year, one of the defendants and ringleaders behind BitClub Network publicly broke off from the company. In a video showing off his new mining machines from his latest venture, from which he promised 'massive, massive rewards'[25] (a promise one should always be careful of), Joseph Frank Abel issued a rather delayed warning: 'I think BitClub is in very big trouble,' Abel said. 'If you're promoting BitClub Network today, you're promoting a Ponzi... They should have hundreds of millions in equipment, which they don't... All big lies.'[26]

The picture of the dream collapsed for many at the start of 2020, when three of the ringleaders behind BitClub Network were arrested. Goettsche, the founder, was arrested in his $1.5 million home. His passport and more than $9 million in assets he had acquired using investors' money were seized. It was later shown that over $233 million had moved through his accounts alone, of which $70 million was just in a two-month period.[27] That's a lot of money, made worse by the fact that by that point many investors had stopped receiving their pay-outs. Balaci, the developer, pleaded guilty to wire fraud and selling unregistered securities and got a maximum of five years in prison and a fine of $250,000. Joby Weeks was also arrested, and after a denied plea to President Trump now faces 15 to 25 years in prison.[28]

The company that had promoted itself in its videos as being 'the most transparent company in the history of the world'[29] and 'too big to fail'[30] had failed. They had created the largest crypto mining scam known, as well as one of the biggest all-time crypto scams, in total scamming $722 million out of their investors.[31] To this day, it's still unclear whether BitClub Network ever actually held any Bitcoin mining equipment.

## CHAPTER NINE

# Market manipulation

*Crypto pump and dump schemes*

## Needles and haystacks

If you look at the price charts for many cryptocurrencies, there is often a very sharp, sudden spike in their earlier days.

Most cryptocurrencies' charts either have a more or less gradual decline or increase in price, or display a virtually straight horizontal line, indicating not so much a lack of volatility as a lack of trading or interest altogether in the project. You can also sometimes see big waves where the cryptocurrency was gradually manipulated or affected by markets. But, in many cryptocurrencies, particularly the smaller, lesser known ones, at one or more times in their history there is a sudden vertical needle in the charts, an almost instantaneous increase in its price by hundreds of percent, and then, shortly, or often even almost instantly, after, just as rapid a decline in its price, back to where it started. If it didn't happen so frequently, one might be forgiven for thinking it's a blip in the charts, a mistake or a problem with the exchange. Except these needles happened all too frequently on charts of many of the smaller cryptocurrencies. These needles – sudden price increases in the hundreds of percent followed by a sharp collapse, were caused by a particular type of very legally grey trade known as the pump and dump.

In the world of crypto pump and dumps, some made money, often a lot, and most lost it all, often within seconds and often without really knowing what had hit them.

Manipulation of markets has gone on since trading began. Unfortunately for those wanting to profit from manipulating stocks and traditional assets, doing so is highly illegal, and tends to result in high fines and jail time. However, greed, money, and success can be big motivators and there are always some who will keep pushing the grey areas of the law until they either get their way or get caught. In crypto, there have been a lot of grey areas and the markets were volatile enough for individuals to manipulate to part hundreds of thousands of people, if not more, from their money in a whole series of promotions designed to pump and dump, project after project.

Stock exchanges that don't take adequate measures to prevent stock manipulations can face heavy legal penalties, so for the most part they play above the law. Unlike traditional stocks where markets are heavily monitored and regulated, cryptocurrency, as we have already seen, has been a bit of a Wild West. Regulation is starting to come, but until then, crypto markets have been treated as a free-for-all adventure ground where anything goes.

As we saw in the first chapter, thousands of ICOs led to the creation of thousands of small cryptocurrencies, most without any use case or value. These smaller cryptocurrencies didn't tend to make it onto the larger crypto exchanges which provided greater liquidity. Larger exchanges tended to charge higher listing fees and had slightly tougher criteria for accepting cryptocurrencies, meaning that the smaller cryptocurrencies tended to dominate the smaller, more decentralized crypto exchanges. These smaller exchanges were mostly a Wild West on a whole other level within the Wild West that was crypto in the bubble years leading up to 2018.

These cryptocurrencies, with their smaller total market values and their lower liquidity on the smaller exchanges, were easy to manipulate. Some individual investors holding as little as $10,000 or so would often single-handedly be able to distort the market of one of the smaller cryptocurrencies on one of the smaller exchanges.

To manipulate the markets of smaller cryptocurrencies was easy. Just placing large enough buy or sell orders could pump up prices or crash prices down. Anyone looking to manipulate these smaller cryptocurrencies didn't even need to buy or sell their holdings, just placing large 'fake' buy or sell orders was often enough to scare other traders. Just the presence of a large enough sell order would make enough traders think that there may be a problem with that cryptocurrency, or that the person placing the large sell order knew something that they didn't. Other traders would often then panic sell, or lower their sell price, offering lower and lower than the large order in the fear that otherwise they wouldn't be able to sell their holding and would be stuck with a worthless cryptocurrency in a market crash. Just the presence of large sell orders could result in the entire market for that coin crashing significantly down. Likewise, large buy orders could push the market on smaller exchanges right up for cryptocurrencies with lower trading volumes. Those placing the large buy or sell orders could watch, waiting until the last minute, and cancel their orders. If they had been intending to crash the market down, they would have had their bitcoin ready to buy the same cryptocurrency at its new lower price. And vice versa. Market manipulation at its unregulated best.

Individual crypto traders did their own such trades on smaller or larger scales every day. In a market so volatile that even individual traders could manipulate cryptocurrencies, organized, orchestrated group manipulations run by experts caused chaos.

## The art of social scamming

The 2017–18 crypto boom attracted a lot of people who had never traded or invested before. It's easier to get into crypto than penny stocks, and the rise of Bitcoin and some of the ICOs had made enough people publicly rich to make others want to risk, often, everything they had to replicate the same wealth for themselves.

Crypto and social media chat rooms went hand-in-hand. Investors flocked to new social platforms that offered varying levels of privacy and encryption. There were thousands of crypto chat rooms on Discord, Slack and Telegram where crypto investors would flock to talk about trading, investment or the different cryptocurrencies. Many of these groups and chat rooms offered genuine advice and useful tips in a great learning environment. Other groups had darker intentions and were created purely to take advantage of what their often-anonymous leaders saw as easy prey. Many of the new crypto investors were impressionable and easy prey for a practice that would be illegal in every other market outside of unregulated crypto – the pump-and-dump groups that became prevalent across these social crypto forums.

## Pump and dump groups

Pump and dump groups were a whole world of their own within the crypto ecosystem. Entry into the groups could be quite a lucrative revenue stream for their organizers. They charged high amounts, into the hundreds or thousands of dollars per person each month, all paid in crypto. Needless to say, many group organizers made more from running these groups than they ever did off the back of their crypto knowledge or trading. Pump organizers, being the first to buy in and the first to cash out, dumping their coins onto other pump participants, would almost be

guaranteed to make high returns from each pump. Most participants, up to 99 per cent in some cases, would lose their money.

Many of the cryptocurrencies that ended up getting pumped
and dumped were already dead projects, ones that had gone
bankrupt or their anonymous founders or developers had left
the teams; often there had been no work going on the project for
months or even years, but people still kept trading them.

Pump and dumps unfortunately weren't limited to the closed
groups created for this purpose. Organized pump and dump
market manipulations that were carried out by closed groups by
knowing participants were the tip of the iceberg. The majority of
the pump and dumps in crypto happened openly in the public
eye, promoted by influencers across social media, with their
participants tricked into being a part. Social media influencers
and celebrities played a key role. Several have now been fined or
even arrested for their roles in manipulating the crypto markets.

## Bringing celebrities into the mix

The crypto world worked out very quickly how to use influencers, influencers worked out very quickly how to profit from
crypto, and some early crypto followers worked out very quickly
how to become influencers.

YouTube channels cropped up hosted by salesy men or young,
generally vaguely attractive women wearing less clothing than
was arguably necessary to promote crypto projects. They would
share positive news and interviews about these cryptocurrencies,
all the while making sure their followers would buy up the cryptocurrencies they were promoting and reassuring them that the
price would soon increase.

Some of these new YouTubers were motivated by their own
gain; they had bought into that particular cryptocurrency early
and wanted it to go up in price. Many of the smaller cryptocurrencies had low enough volumes and were volatile enough that

one YouTuber's follower base was enough on its own to pump up the price of their chosen project. These YouTubers and influencers knew this and used their followers to this exact end.

They would often tell their followers how many of the coins they had and how much they had invested, trying to instil trust as they pumped up the price of their chosen cryptocurrency. The more followers they gained, the more the followers bought of that cryptocurrency, so the more the price went up and the more people trusted them.

It was a cycle that would serve to only make the YouTubers and their first followers rich. What they didn't tell their thousands of followers was that the higher the price of their chosen cryptocurrency went and the more followers they gained, the more of their own coins they sold out on to them, dumping their worthless but heavily inflated coins onto their fans. These YouTubers would keep pumping the price up until they'd sold the last of their coins of that cryptocurrency out into bitcoin or fiat, and then would move on, no one the wiser that it was their leader who had just pumped up and crashed the price of their chosen cryptocurrency, making millions, sometimes hundreds of millions, of dollars profit for themselves, often leaving their followers worse off than when they started.

Others were just paid to promote by the projects, and none gained more renown for doing so than John McAfee.

## John McAfee

Of all the celebrities that manipulated the crypto markets, one stood out, building an infamous name for himself amongst the crypto community. John McAfee founded the now-global McAfee anti-virus software in 1989, making himself $100 million almost overnight when he sold his company shares just a few years later. Since then, he has built up rather a colourful reputation for himself, as much centred around his penchant for hedonistic living as his subsequent business ventures.

McAfee moved to Belize. He said this was due to the 2008 economic crash wiping out 96 per cent of his wealth. Or it could have been to avoid tax problems from the USA. Or it could have been to avoid the legal and financial fallout of a crash of an ultralight aircraft in an Aerotrekking business he started, which killed his nephew and a paying customer. Rumours abound, but with McAfee one can never be sure. He likes telling stories for stories' sake, especially, as reporters like to reveal, when the stories can confuse reporters.[1] In Belize, McAfee did a lot of drugs, spent a lot of time with a harem of young women a fraction of his age,[2] drank a bit, smoked a lot more, went around with some body guards[3] and developed a habit for bath salts, a synthetic hallucinogenic and legal product he turned into a drug and used to get high.[4] Depending on his mood on the day, and presumably on how much he liked the reporter asking the questions, he spent the rest of his time in Belize trying to create natural antibiotics out of plants, making a female Viagra,[5] or making the bath salts he was addicted to, claims which all may or may not be true. One can never be quite sure if he's lying or telling the truth, or what parts of the story are designed purely to pull the leg of reporters.[6]

McAfee had his share of run-ins with law enforcement. In 2012, a Belizean Swat team suspected he was running a meth lab,[7] tracked him down and killed his dog. In November that year, his American neighbour in Belize was found dead from a bullet to his head, and McAfee was named a person of interest in the investigation. Faull, the now-dead neighbour, and McAfee had had their disagreements over their dogs and their security guards, but there's still no clear reason why he was killed.[8] McAfee says that maybe the killer was looking for him, but authorities seemed to think McAfee was behind it. McAfee fled to Guatemala by boat, where he invited a Vice team of reporters to follow him. Vice made one mistake – they shared a photo that contained some geo-data they'd omitted to take out, giving away his location.[9] He was arrested for illegally entering the country, managing to get himself out of the situation through a well-connected Guatemalan girlfriend, faked a heart attack to avoid extradition back to Belize and buy his lawyers some time, and eventually managed to go back to the USA.[10]

The night he got back to America, and whilst still accused of the murder of his neighbour in Belize, McAfee went to a café in Miami. At the café he met and started a whirlwind relationship with a prostitute, Janice.[11] They were married in 2013 and had their shares of drama but travelled a lot, staying between a mix of cheap motels and McAfee's yacht before ending up in Spain, unbeknownst to the media.[12] McAfee ran two presidential bids, coming second for the Libertarian party in 2016, and made a bigger name for himself outside of just tech, learning how to play up to the media. But by this time, in 2016, after years of running from the law and his fortune almost diminished, McAfee needed money.

## Learning how to manipulate markets

In 2016, McAfee was put in touch with a penny stock company called MGT Capital. MGT Capital traded the shares of small public companies that trade for less than a dollar per share, known as penny stocks. MGT Capital, by this point, was effectively a shell company. It had sold off its assets and had no worth except that it had one relatively rare advantage – it was listed on the New York Stock Exchange. This gave access to investors and a degree of respectability, but the company, like McAfee, needed to make money. They thought McAfee, with his reputation as a cyber tech genius and his name dominating the media for more than one reason, might be able to lend it a degree of credibility in its rebrand as a cybersecurity company as well as making some much-needed noise for the brand. The company paid him a handsome salary, $250,000 a year plus a $250,000 bonus to put his name to the new cybersecurity rebrand. MGT now had McAfee's name and renown, but they needed investment.[13]

MGT got that investment from Florida speculator Barry Honig, who put in $850,000 in exchange for a bunch of shares. Honig was described in subsequent trials as specializing in manipulating the prices of low-volume penny stocks to make them look like a more appealing investment to investors, effectively pump and dumps for the penny stock market.[14] He has since been charged by the SEC for his involvement in various market manipulations.[15] Honig's efforts worked; the new stock jumped from 37 cents to $4.15 per share,[16] leading the press to run headlines along the lines of 'John McAfee's mysterious new company is the hottest stock in America right now'.[17] By now, Honig's shares would have been worth $80 million, had McAfee paid out. But the company was now under McAfee's management, which meant his rules.[18] McAfee decided the existing share structure was too generous to investors. He changed the share structure, meaning Honig wouldn't get paid unless he invested another $11,655 million. Honig didn't really have time to even react, the stock pump soon dumped and the overinflated stock lost its value.[19] The SEC cracked down on it soon after in a flurry of lawsuits. By mid-2016, MGT Capital had pumped and dumped.

Soon after taking the reins at MGT Capital in 2016, McAfee had appointed Bruce Fenton, the Executive Director of the Bitcoin Foundation, to a new cryptocurrency advisory board he had created at the company. Bitcoin was the next big thing, he was told, and McAfee bought into it. MGT Capital became a Bitcoin mining company. The more mining rigs they bought, the less mention was made of cybersecurity. In the end, they never released any cyber security products.[20] MGT mined its bitcoin, which did well financially, but crypto mining isn't glamourous, it's hot and slow and predictable. For someone with McAfee's addiction to excitement and drama, this wasn't enough. The real money was in trading on the volatility of the crypto markets.

McAfee had learnt well from Honig how to manipulate low-volume volatile markets to your advantage. And low-volume volatile markets are easy to manipulate. Penny stocks are regulated, and, as McAfee had discovered, the SEC would swoop in. Cryptocurrency, however, was new and, at the time, unregulated. Crypto is more anonymous and law enforcement simply hadn't yet caught up. Crypto, McAfee soon realized, would be easier and lower risk to manipulate than any other market. Around this time, crypto was hotting up. Bitcoin had gone from being worth almost nothing to around $500 per coin, and roughly doubled again by the end of that year. Cryptocurrency was starting to get mainstream attention. A year later, in the early summer of 2017, there were over 2,000 cryptocurrencies and the price of bitcoin was beginning to shoot through the roof, as was awareness and trading in altcoins, the thousands of other, smaller cryptocurrencies.

By late 2017 crypto had shot up, everyone was talking about it, lots of coins had pumped and a lot of people had made a lot of speculative money. Everyone was looking for the next trend to invest in, impatient for the next round of riches.

## The next big investment

Crypto followers, and particularly YouTubers and influencers, started to place a lot of hype on a type of cryptocurrency known as privacy coins; private digital currencies where no part of their transaction can be traced and particularly popular on dark web marketplaces where they were used for drug and other illegal transactions. Not everyone who bought privacy coins used them for illegal purposes. Some people see privacy coins as an essential technology for maintaining some degree of privacy or self-governance in a world where human rights are being eroded and trust in governments is decreasing every day. Others just bought in speculatively, thinking that for these exact reasons their value would go up. Monero, the most known and popular and most frequently used privacy coin, already had gone up substantially in value by this point, but there were other privacy cryptocurrencies that until then had barely been noticed.

It is commonly thought to be easier to make something worth very little go up 10 or 100 times in value than something that's already worth a lot go up by the same multiple, and so many in the crypto community started looking to find the next privacy coin that could become the next big thing. One little-known privacy coin was a cryptocurrency called Verge, that went by the trading symbol XVG.

## The $2 billion tweet

In 2013, a Japanese meme of a Shiba Inu dog became popular across the country. Later that year, a joke cryptocurrency was formed using this meme of a cartoon dog as their logo. Dogecoin was never intended to be serious, and has no use cases, but has gone viral in crypto, popularized mostly by Japanese people seemingly into the dog, and by people who presumably thought it was a bit of fun. Verge was initially built as a privacy-based copy of Dogecoin known as a 'fork' of Doge, a practice of replicating cryptocurrencies that had become popularized. Verge hadn't yet shot to the same inexplicable highs of Dogecoin. But it was a cheap privacy coin, which a few crypto hopefuls saw as the next one with the potential to be pumped in the next pump or in the next crypto bull run, either due to its likeness to the popular dog-friendly Dogecoin or because of its privacy features.

An investor called Peter Galanko had bought a whole bunch of Verge cheap. Then almost immediately he watched the price shoot up, making him four times his investment. He was now rich and was hooked, wanting more. Peter set up a Twitter handle XVGWhale – whale being the term given to large crypto holders – and built up a following of 60,000 Verge fans. But Verge was only one out of thousands of cryptocurrencies and Peter needed help to make it stand out. Peter had heard about McAfee's renown in tech, his huge international following and his ability to pump up the value of companies and decided one thing: he needed McAfee's help if Verge was to pump to its peak and make him a truly rich man.[21]

John McAfee had by now acquired quite the reputation in crypto to go alongside his colourful and chequered past. He had made one tweet that cemented his place in crypto. On 17 July 2017 he promised on Twitter that if the price of one bitcoin didn't reach $500,000 in three years he would eat a certain crucial part of his anatomy on national television.[22] To nobody's surprise, three years later, he reneged on his promise and no body parts were eaten.[23] Nevertheless, the tweet got him the media attention and crypto fame he desired. That tweet can still be widely found in mentions all over the internet, and if anyone wants an example of the attention this one tweet gained in the crypto community, check out the fan site built around it at the aptly named www.dickening.com

By this point, McAfee had over 700,000 followers on Twitter, the main social platform used to drive crypto noise, and he was maybe the best man to make an impact. Peter Galanko just had to persuade him to tweet for Verge. A phone call through to John turned into a week-long stay at McAfee's house. No formal contract was exchanged, but not long after McAfee tweeted praise in favour of Verge, saying that the project 'couldn't lose'. The market cap of Verge shot up. By $2 billion. That one tweet shot up the price of Verge by 1,800 per cent. From its total growth, a dollar invested at the start of the year was now worth over $10,000.[24]

As with MGT Capital, where McAfee had felt his investor had got too good a deal, he now again felt cheated. He wanted his part of these $2 billion of speculative fortune he had tweeted out of thin air. He demanded from Peter the equivalent of $2 million in crypto for his tweet. Peter didn't want to pay this. He was only one investor – he wasn't the founder or a Verge team member, and he didn't represent the other investors who had all benefited from the pump. Peter spoke to the Verge team, who didn't want to or couldn't pay this either. They countered with $70,000. McAfee countered with $100,000, or, if they didn't agree, he said in their private exchange, he could do more damage than the good he had caused for the project.[25] Sure enough, the next tweet from him on Verge seems intended to crash its market. In it, he said he had made a huge miscalculation, asked for apology for his unpardonable error and said the coin was never worth anything near as much as its newfound value.[26] Sure enough, the market in Verge crashed. McAfee denies this, but this is crypto, there are many possibilities, and we'll probably never know.[27]

But, by now, McAfee had learnt the art of the pump and dump, and had learnt one even more crucial thing – he had seen how easily, with his following and with his influence, he could manipulate the crypto markets. For crypto, this is where the pump and dump rollercoaster begins. Too many people got caught up in what happened next, some making small fortunes, most losing their money, and others just sitting on the sidelines watching the crypto disaster that was about to ensue from their screens, some literally with popcorn at the ready for the ride.

## Lots of tweets

His Verge tweet gave McAfee a taste of how easy it was to make money in crypto. If he could manipulate the markets by $2 billion with just one tweet, then he could do this again. And he seemed the right man to do so. McAfee was known for being a tech genius; he founded an anti-virus company before the world knew they needed an anti-virus, before computer viruses even became a real, known thing. Whatever anyone can say about him, he is smart. And he clearly decided that the hype and money around crypto suited his anti-authoritarian, libertarian ethos. It helped that his predictions about crypto had so far turned out to be right. He tweeted about Bitcoin, Bitcoin rose. He tweeted about Bitcoin again, Bitcoin rose some more. His tweet about Verge had created $2 billion of value for the otherwise largely unknown cryptocurrency out of thin air, and his next, negative tweet, knocked it back down. People didn't necessarily know that it was his influence alone that had manipulated the price of Verge both ways, and enough people were beginning to think that maybe McAfee had the same type of foresight into crypto as he'd had into computer viruses and cybersecurity.

It was time for McAfee to capitalize on this. In December 2017 he started tweeting what he called his 'coin reports', recommending a different cryptocurrency with each tweet. He wouldn't go into much detail on why one should buy that particular crypto that day, citing reasons including one of the founders of the first project he pumped probably not being stupid.[28]

Less than a month later, in the new year of 2018, he made a declaration on Twitter, that 'Since there are over 100 new ICOs each week, and since you cannot pump and dump them (longer term investment) it makes no sense to do only one per week. Many of them are gems. I will do at least three per week on a random basis'.[29] Soon after, he moved to a coin a day. And then he started charging. $105,000 per tweet.[30] The cryptocurrency projects McAfee promoted went from bad to worse. There seemed to be nothing behind his choice of tweets except for, seemingly, who paid him. Some were scams, most were what the Securities Exchange Commission described as 'essentially worthless'.[31] Generally the projects McAfee promoted had no long-term use or value and weren't a safe play, but were rather the projects that would pay him for his promotions.[32] However, enough people liked the chance to make money and waited every day or every week for 'PumpAfee's[33] tweets, as he became known. By the end of December, there was enough backlash against these overt pump and dumps for McAfee to move back to just doing a coin of the week pump.

The influence of his tweets was indeed huge, initially. The McAfee tweets, as they became known, spiked the whole market for the coins he tweeted, causing immediate pumps of 50 to 350 or even more per cent gains[34] in value in minutes, with the pump starting within seconds of his tweet. Thousands upon thousands of individual crypto traders would sit at their screens each day at the time the McAfee tweet was expected, waiting with their bitcoin ready on multiple exchanges to act on his pump as quickly as possible, often panic buying into the coin as quickly as they could in the frenzied hope that it would keep on going up after they had managed to buy in. Some people did well, most lost money. The problem in crypto in these frenzied pump and dumps is that you're not just competing against the speed of people. In crypto, a lot of the trading on exchanges is done by bots. These bots aren't even reacting to human commands, they react to social media mentions, to increases of volume, as well as to other people and bots buying. These bots would buy fast, but even they wouldn't always be able to buy low enough or sell out fast enough to make profits given the huge surges of people wanting to buy in to coins with otherwise low liquidity and low volumes all at the same instance of the tweet. Some traders created special bots designed to read the names of the coins mentioned in McAfee's tweets and buy those automatically. Bots fared better than humans reacting to his tweets. But only those who had bought in the coin long before the tweet, at a low price, and who were lightning fast to sell out at the right time tended to make money. Even using trading bots, most people lost money.

On 27 December, either McAfee wanted a newsworthy way out of doing the tweets, or the cybersecurity genius' Twitter account really was hacked, but that day his account spewed out five tweets recommending different low-cap crypto projects.[35] All pumped, and dumped, the bots buying all on auto, but people started to doubt.

## Over and out

McAfee had learnt his lessons, and reading between the lines it seems he'd had enough threats – he was now out of promoting dodgy ICOs and low cap crypto projects. A year later, he sent a less than reassuring or sympathetic tweet to those who he'd tricked or talked into buying into all the scam and worthless coins his tweets had promoted, most of which by now had lost almost all of their valuations from their 2017 peaks. He said one thing: 'Due to SEC threats, I am no longer working with ICOs nor am I recommending them, and those doing ICOs can all look forward to arrest.'[36]

McAfee had arguably been the most famous crypto pumper and dumper and wielded the most influence, at least over many of the small cap crypto coins. Not long after his pump tweets ended, the ICO rush slowed down and the crypto markets started to crash. The pump and dump groups that operated out of the closed social chat rooms still ran, and still continue to, but a lot of the new and hopeful crypto investors had left the crypto markets and a lot of the hype around pumping worthless coins had, more or less, thankfully died.

Law enforcement did catch up with John McAfee. Despite social media claims and video interviews and conferences held from his yacht, it turned out that for the recent period of time that he'd been saying he'd been living on said yacht, he and his wife had apparently been hiding out in Spain. McAfee was found, arrested and charged with making $23.1 million profit for what the SEC describes as 'fraudulently touting ICOs'.[37]

CHAPTER TEN

# Crypto for the people

## Venezuela: A chicken and egg problem

Do a Google image search for 'buy a chicken in Venezuela'.

Google will show you rows of photos of how high the piles of banknotes are needed to buy certain foods. At the time these now viral photos were taken, it cost 14.6 million bolivares, the local currency, to buy a chicken. The stack of banknotes was multiple times larger than the chicken. Since then, inflation has only gone up; the stack of banknotes needed to buy a chicken now would be even larger.

Perhaps the most demonstrative photo in the collection is of the size of the piles of banknotes needed to buy a toilet roll. The banknotes dwarf the toilet roll, which would cost 2.6 million of the local currency for one roll.[1] In Venezuela, many use bank notes as toilet roll because bank notes are worth less.

Some workers are forced to collect their wages in suitcases. To go to a supermarket can mean wheeling in suitcases or wheelbarrows of cash. The biggest bill in Venezuela is for 100,000 bolivares but it's worth just $0.23,[2] maybe less now. You would need around 25 of these to buy a kilogram of pasta. The problem of physically having to transport large stacks of near-worthless cash are getting less as more people get access to digital banking, but the numbers on the banknotes are getting worse.

In Venezuela, hyperinflation has run rampant. The national currency has become devalued to the point that the minimum wage fluctuates in millions of bolivares but in international money is as little as $1 a month at the black-market exchange rate.[3] The government stopped quoting inflation rates years ago[4] but it's up to 10 million per cent depending on which source you ask.[5] Anyhow, exchange rates to the dollar vary enormously depending on where you can exchange your money. In one year, the currency devalued 97.5 per cent against the dollar.

Inflation goes up so fast that people don't know how much they will have to pay when they go to the supermarket; prices change, sometimes drastically, from when they enter a shop to the point they pick up their goods and go to the checkout. Food or ingredients might go up in price by hundreds of per cent in weeks. The national currency is so devalued that basic food essentials are set at government-controlled prices but are still totally out of reach and unaffordable for anyone who doesn't have family abroad sending back international currency. Many Venezuelans literally rely on friends and family sending home money from abroad; the average family needs over 100 times the official minimum wage just to meet its basic needs.[6] Skilled workers such as a university professor might earn enough in a month to buy the choice of some meat or some eggs,[7] but that's it, a standard salary in local currency can buy nothing more.

Government price controls aren't much help to anyone dependent on the local currency for buying all their food. Depending on ever-increasing interest rates, one month's pay on minimum wage gets you roughly your choice of any of the following: 24 eggs or 2.6 kg of tomatoes or 6.5 kg of sugar or half a kg of oats or 1.7 kg of potatoes or 2.8 litres of orange juice or 300 grams of coffee or three-quarters of a pizza or half a burger.[8]

Some companies in Venezuela have given up trying to pay their citizens in just money. To get good workers and encourage them to turn up on time and do their jobs, they have resorted to paying bonuses in food. Every week, you'll see workers walking home with cartons stacked high with foods such as eggs,[9] making up their weekly bonus. The eggs are worth as much as their salary, but provide more certainty.

Shops are only open to citizens on certain days, food is rationed, supermarket shelves are often empty, and queues might be hours long; it can sometimes take a whole day just to get some basics in one of the government price-controlled shops. Venezuela has one of the biggest oil reserves in the world but doesn't have the money to process it. Petrol is so cheap that they basically give it away for free. If you can't afford to pay when you fill up your tank, you can pay with an egg or a cigarette. The tip many people will give to petrol station workers will far exceed the cost of filling up one's tank. To give a sense of how cheap petrol really is, you can fill a tank for an average sized car for 200 bolivares. A fair tip to the attendant would be at least 500 bolivares. A cup of coffee, in contrast, can now cost 2 million bolivares[10] or 10,000 times the cost of a tank of petrol.


## Free fall to crypto

Since 2017, Venezuela's economy has been in free fall. Hyperinflation has driven the once prosperous nation into poverty. Venezuela, whilst extreme, is sadly far from unique in this situation; it is just one of many examples around the world of what can happen to an economy and to a national currency in the hands of corruption, mismanagement or repeated poor decisions.

It's no coincidence that Venezuela ranks third in the world for national cryptocurrency adoption, ahead of the USA, China and every other major country. In Venezuela, crypto adoption is not really by choice. People discovered crypto out of necessity. The national currency in Venezuela is so volatile, with such drastic increases in inflation, that it is almost literally worthless. Unless one can hold money in a more stable currency, savings disintegrate overnight and families aren't able to get enough food to survive, it really is that simple. Use of the dollar was forbidden until 2018, and black-market exchange rates were unfavourable to the bolivar, so people had to find alternatives to sending money home. Remittance companies such as Western Union enable people working abroad to send money home to Venezuela but, as we will see, charge extortionate rates, immediately taking away 14 per cent or more. Cryptocurrencies, despite their volatility, have been a natural safe haven for Venezuelans who as a nation hold $8 billion in crypto, a huge amount for a struggling country.

The Venezuelan government have tried to launch their own cryptocurrency, the supposedly oil-backed 'petro', for what is thought to be an attempt to avoid US sanctions and to provide an alternative to the country's hyperinflation. However, it isn't widely trusted, with much of external sentiment classing it as a failed project,[11] mostly due to inherent distrust in the government that issued it. Instead, traditional cryptocurrency such as Bitcoin has, for all its volatility, been a lifeline for many in Venezuela. It is almost the only way for citizens to hold money in a more stable way, and to send and store money internationally without government-imposed restrictions. Venezuela is sadly far from alone in printing money. Countries including the US have been printing money at extreme and worrying rates with the coronavirus lockdown in some places spiraling money printing out of control. Many have lost, or are losing faith in, the former stronghold of government and central bank controlled currency. Many see Bitcoin, and the potential of decentralized currency, as a true lifeline and source of economic freedom. And this is really what crypto was designed to be all about.

## In the beginning

In the early 1990s a small group of men started gathering in the San Francisco bay area. Their priority: to defend privacy. They talked about cryptography, a tool until then only used in secret by the military and spy agencies, and started calling themselves the Cypherpunks. Their actions were ahead of their time. Governments now are doing whatever they can to erode privacy in all of our lives – in regards to our data, our movements and our money. In the hands of the wrong government, with the surveillance tools and technology now available, this is scary. The future of money, when considering surveillance tech and how certain world governments already can control our money, is beyond scary. It's frankly terrifying. Governments can now limit your every movement through blocking your access to money if they want to; some already do so. They're now looking at bringing in advanced facial recognition to help with this. It's probably fair to say that 'terrifying' is an understatement.

The Cypherpunk movement evolved over the decades until one day, on 31 October 2008, the message appeared in an online forum from a mysterious figure posting an outline for a new digital currency called Bitcoin.

To this day, no one knows who Satoshi Nakamoto, the pseudonymous person or perhaps group of people who created Bitcoin, is, or where Bitcoin truly came from. But, despite the volatility and the hype-fuelled bubble and the scams that we've seen that have surrounded the crypto ecosystem, Bitcoin has held strong and has gone on to change how the world looks at money as we know it. The scams that we've seen are unfortunate but they mask the potential of what is an incredible technology.

## A financial revolution

Cryptocurrency is an incredible revolution in technology. Crypto, for the first time ever, makes it possible for anyone in the world to send and receive money from anyone else without needing to rely on any third party, bank, payment company or government, cutting out high fees, delays and avoiding blocks and sanctions. This shouldn't be understated. The potential of crypto is life-changing for billions of people around the world. Not everyone lives in a state of political or economic freedom; the ability to send money cheaply, digitally and freely, until the creation of Bitcoin, was the privilege of the few. Banks and third-party remittance and payment companies charge enormously high fees to transact money, and the less you earn, the more you have to pay.

Two and a half billion people around the world – roughly a third of the world's population – don't have access to banking. Banks simply don't deem it economically viable to serve them, leaving the world's poorest – who are often forced far away from home to find work – to pay huge chunks of their earnings just to send money home for their families to eat. The average fee to send remittances – the only real way many people have of sending money digitally– is 6.9 per cent, but can be as high as 30 per cent per transaction. That's a lot of money when those few daily cents can make the difference whether your family eats or not.

The advent of crypto brought the ability to send digital money – depending on the cryptocurrency you're sending – almost for free, and virtually instantly. Crypto brings financial freedom already to millions, and we're only just beginning.

## The road to mainstream adoption

Crypto is now going mainstream.

PayPal have just announced they are starting to accept bitcoin and other cryptocurrencies.[12] This is the latest in the line of big news for crypto adoption. PayPal's 26 million merchants and 346 million users will now be able to accept, buy, store and send crypto.

Traditional incumbent banks are struggling. The reality is that the user experience and customer service from challenger banks is just so much better. Challenger banks are friendlier, incomparably easier to use and more efficient. They don't have the overheads such as huge now-empty (due to coronavirus lockdown and remote working) office blocks to maintain, and so can offer better service for lower fees. What's more, they're targeted at millennials, young workers, and the tech savvy – the fastest adopters and those the most likely to promote. Ask anyone working in tech or any field of innovation what bank card they use; it will likely be in a bright colour representative of neobanks and won't be from a traditional, incumbent bank. And challenger banks now accept crypto. They let you store it and pay in crypto from their latest debit cards and are fast making crypto seem as regular a method of payment as anything else.

## Facebook

Facebook has 2.7 billion monthly users and 1.79 billion daily users.[13] Its reach is bigger than any bank or central government worldwide, it has more users, and, as films such as *The Great Hack* have made clear, has as great an influence, if not far greater. *The Great Hack* is just one of many sources to point out Facebook's ability to influence election results, affect politics and store so much data on their users that it can influence what they buy.

A few years ago, Facebook started a secretive side project. Employees either didn't know about it or couldn't talk about it and it was apparently housed in a totally separate building to their normal offices. That project is now out in the public domain. Whilst their newly rebranded Diem cryptocurrency project hasn't launched yet, Facebook has already made huge global waves across governments, central banks and payment conglomerates with the threat of its potential. Arguably, Facebook was overly ambitious and didn't contend with the amount of opposition and challenges it would face from global government legislation. But Diem, just as Bitcoin did, has shaken how the world looks at money. And one benefit that Facebook's Diem could offer to the world is that of shaking up remittances.

The global remittance industry is huge. Billions of people around the world rely on remittances to get money home to their families, or for basic survival. There may be some exceptions, but, as a generalization, the way that remittance companies operate is barbaric. They largely do what they can to squeeze as much as possible out of the poorest billions of people around the world.[14] These are people who earn less than a few dollars a day. Often those few dollars have to feed an entire family and remittance companies can get what they can from them because those people have no other choice but to use them to get money home to their families. According to the World Bank, 'Remittances are on track to become the largest source of external financing in developing countries.'[15] People are dependent on them and remittance companies, by large, abuse the position this puts them in.

Crypto is perfect for micropayments. In small corner shops you will often see signs asking for minimum card payments of £5 or £10. For any payment less than that they simply lose too much of the transaction to the payment processor to make it viable for them, they run on such low margins. With government-issued fiat currency there is a charge to send money, making it uneconomical to send less than around 50p digitally and still relatively expensive for merchants to accept. Crypto can remove a lot of these costs. For smaller transactions, such as sending daily wages home in the developing world, and for a myriad of other use cases for micro-transactions, crypto is now seen by a fast- and ever-growing number as the only way forward. Cryptocurrencies don't have to be volatile and central banks around the world are now looking at or are already issuing stable cryptocurrencies to be digital replacements or alternatives to national currencies.

## Plastic and oceans: A happy story

Wherever you live in the world, the plastic you throw away may quite likely end up in the ocean. Only a pitiful 9 per cent of plastic produced is ever recycled. Eighty per cent of plastic in the oceans is from land sources, and every day is killing turtles, whales, dolphins, seals and seabirds, by the millions every year. By 2050, there is expected to be more plastic in the oceans than fish. A large proportion of the plastic littering the oceans comes from poor coastal communities lacking waste management infrastructure.

Waste plastic has until now been considered worthless. It is cheaper to make new virgin plastic than to make or buy recycled plastic, and there has been no incentive for anyone to pick up waste plastic that is discarded on land or in the ocean other than a desire to keep the world clean. For communities where ends don't always meet, with people worried about day-to-day finances, taking the time out from providing for one's family to pick up waste plastic is a luxury many don't have. There has also been no incentive to prevent plastic from being thrown away in the first place.

In many of the communities where waste plastic is a particular issue, wages are low and people live in poverty. As with a third of the world's population, people have never been able to get bank accounts, and saving what little physical cash they can earn is hard. Various initiatives have tried to pay people to collect plastic but they paid in cash, which isn't a safe method of payment. Cash is stolen far too easily.

A Canadian fast-growing start-up called Plastic Bank has created a way to monetise waste plastic in communities around the world and provide an income for collecting this waste plastic. Plastic Bank recycles the plastic that collectors bring to their 'plastic banks' where they can exchange it for digital money.

Plastic Bank has created digital wallets for the plastic collectors to safely store money, easily accessible via an app on any cheap smartphone. Even if the phone is lost or stolen, their money is still safe. For the first time ever these people can save and budget ahead. Plastic Bank also gives its plastic collectors a digital identity and the equivalent of a credit score – thousands of people can now borrow money and get loans to buy their house or pay for education, basic things they never had access to before. If their plastic collectors don't want to exchange the plastic for money, they can get food, or cleaning products, or pay for their kids' school fees instead. This infrastructure has brought a lifeline of hope to communities all around the world, bringing economic freedom whilst clearing up the environment and the oceans.

All this has been made possible because of the technology that cryptocurrency is built on. Crypto means that micro-payments can be transferred instantly and almost for free, and digital wallets mean that people can hold, send and receive money digitally without needing a bank account. They provide a cashless method for financial inclusion for entire communities that have been left behind by traditional banks and finance. This is what crypto is about. We hope that you can overlook the scams and find a love for this amazing, life-changing technology.

# Endnotes

## Introduction

1  Lee, C (2017) I've been asked what I think about Bitconnect. From the surface, seems like a classic ponzi scheme. I wouldn't invest in it and wouldn't recommend anyone else to. I follow this rule of thumb: 'If it looks like a (duck emoji), walks like a (duck emoji), and quacks like a (duck emoji) then it's a ponzi' (laugh emoji), Twitter, 30 November, https://twitter.com/satoshilite/status/9363069658604011 52?lang=en (archived at https://perma.cc/3YNP-8XLK)

2  Seth, S (2018) 80 per cent of ICOs are scams: Report, Investopedia, 2 April, https://www.investopedia.com/news/80-icos-are-scams-report/ (archived at https://perma.cc/9Z2Y-6UWM)

## Chapter 1

1  CoinMarketCap (live) Bitcoin, CoinMarketCap, https://coinmarketcap.com/currencies/bitcoin/ (archived at https://perma.cc/R893-ZNEF)

2  Coinist (nd) Poor returns, failed technology and outright scams make ICO investors leery, https://www.coinist.io/6-worst-icos-of-all-time/ (archived at https://perma.cc/6M6P-PV9F)

3  Hester, J (2017) Internet browser company Brave raised $35m from its initial coin offering (ICO) in less than 30 seconds, Capital.com, 1 June, https://capital.com/internet-company-brave-raises-35m-in-less-than-30-seconds (archived at https://perma.cc/W3GG-JDEC)

4  Rogers, S (2017) 6 months on, Bancor explains what happened after its $153 million ICO, VentureBeat, 12 December, https://venturebeat.com/2017/12/12/6-months-on-bancor-explains-what-happened-after-its-153-million-ico/ (archived at https://perma.cc/R5KW-JPBP)

5  Stroe, L (2021) EOS price hangs by a thread as the $4 billion ICO that failed, FXStreet, https://www.fxstreet.com/cryptocurrencies/news/eos-price-hangs-by-a-thread-as-the-4-billion-ico-that-failed-202101271851 (archived at https://perma.cc/FL6E-WNKQ)

6 CoinMarketCap (live) Veritaseum, CoinMarketCap, https://coinmarketcap.com/currencies/veritaseum/ (archived at https://perma.cc/8PZW-FLSL)

7 US Securities and Exchange Commission (2019) United States District Court, Eastern District of New York, Case 1:19-cv-04625-CBR-RER US Securities and Exchange Commission, 12 August, https://www.sec.gov/litigation/complaints/2019/comp-pr2019-150.pdf (archived at https://perma.cc/BRM2-T4ZL)

8 Seth, S (2018) 80 per cent of ICOs are scams: Report, Investopedia, 2 April, https://www.investopedia.com/news/80-icos-are-scams-report (archived at https://perma.cc/6YRR-AV6S)

9 Mix (2018) Cryptocurrency startup Prodeum pulls an exit scam, leaves a penis behind, TNW, 29 January, https://thenextweb.com/hardfork/2018/01/29/cryptocurrency-prodeum-scam-exit-penis/ (archived at https://perma.cc/Q8QB-JU8C)

10 Mix (2018) Shady cryptocurrency touting Ryan Gosling as their designer raises $830K in ICO, TNW, 5 March, https://thenextweb.com/hardfork/2018/03/05/ryan-gosling-cryptocurrency-ico/ (archived at https://perma.cc/E8JM-P3VW)

11 Financial Times (2018) The ICO whose team members are literally cartoon characters, Financial Times, 18 July, https://www.ft.com/content/57805b32-0bbe-34cb-940c-66cdd1aec5e2 (archived at https://perma.cc/RE7D-USTR)

12 ScamcoinICO (nd) The only ICO you can be certain of! Get 0 per cent return from 100 per cent of your investments, guaranteed! Reddit, https://www.reddit.com/r/BitcoinScamCoins/comments/7tzcoz/the_only_ico_you_can_be_certain_of_get_0_return/ (archived at https://perma.cc/HRD8-58GS)

13 Useless Ethereum Token (2017) The world's first 100 per cent honest Ethereum ICO, Useless Ethereum Token, https://uetoken.com/ (archived at https://perma.cc/DB37-SW2F)

14 Volpicelli, G (2017) The $3.8bn cryptocurrency bubble is a huge deal. But it could break the blockchain, Wired, 14 July, https://www.wired.co.uk/article/what-is-initial-coin-offering-ico-token-sale (archived at https://perma.cc/ZZ7E-MHBJ)

15  Zhao, W (2018) Tea tokenizers arrested in China for alleged
    $47 million crypto fraud, Coindesk, 18 May, https://www.coindesk.
    com/tea-tokenizers-arrested-china-alleged-47-million-crypto-fraud
    (archived at https://perma.cc/NQ7F-BSFB)

16  Shome, A (2018) Benebit ICO scammed investors for at least 2.7
    million: The scam was well orchestrated – the team spent almost
    $500,000 on marketing, Finance Magnates, 24 January, https://www.
    financemagnates.com/cryptocurrency/news/benebit-ico-scammed-
    investors-least-2-7-million/ (archived at https://perma.cc/RGQ6-LCZC)

17  Deign, J (2018) The ICO scams hurting energy blockchain's credibility,
    GTM, 10 July, https://www.greentechmedia.com/articles/read/the-ico-
    scams-hurting-energy-blockchains-credibility (archived at https://perma.
    cc/AM6B-SKMV)

18  Shapira, A and Leinz, K (2017) Long Island Iced Tea soars after
    changing its name to Long Blockchain, Bloomberg, 21 December,
    https://www.bloomberg.com/news/articles/2017-12-21/crypto-craze-
    sees-long-island-iced-tea-rename-as-long-blockchain (archived at
    https://perma.cc/5789-HCMK)

19  Klein, J (2018) From SpankChain to Bigboobscoin, startups keep trying
    to get people to pay for sex on the blockchain, Vice, 3 April, https://www.
    vice.com/en/article/3k7ek8/spankchain-bigboobscoin-cryptocurrency-for-
    porn-startups (archived at https://perma.cc/5RJ8-MJ9M)

20  Sedgwick, K (2017) The most pointless cryptocurrency tokens ever
    invented, Bitcoin.com, 17 December, https://news.bitcoin.com/
    the-most-pointless-cryptocurrency-tokens-ever-invented/ (archived at
    https://perma.cc/ZYG2-3QU4)

21  Powell, D (2018) Sex industry blockchain startup intimate raises
    $4.5 million in pre-sale ahead of full ICO next month, SmartCompany,
    12 February, https://www.smartcompany.com.au/startupsmart/news/
    sex-industry-blockchain-startup-intimate-4-5-million-ico-pre-sale/
    (archived at https://perma.cc/64RW-96PP)

22  Hay, M (2018) Cryptocurrency finally takes off in the porn
    industry, Forbes, 31 October, https://www.forbes.com/sites/
    markhay/2018/10/31/cryptocurrency-finally-takes-off-in-the-porn-
    industry/?sh=11b41c71629e (archived at https://perma.cc/
    5FRC-GB6X) and Team, E (2018) Sex industry poised to
    penetrate cryptocurrency, CryptoBriefing, 4 March,

https://cryptobriefing.com/sex-industry-penetrate-cryptocurrency/ (archived at https://perma.cc/9DW6-TE3L)

23  Zetter, K (2018) Hackers finally post stolen Ashley Madison data, Wired, 8 August, https://www.wired.com/2015/08/happened-hackers-posted-stolen-ashley-madison-data/ (archived at https://perma.cc/4352-YA39)

24  Sedgwick, K (2017) The most pointless cryptocurrency tokens ever invented, Bitcoin.com, 17 December, https://news.bitcoin.com/the-most-pointless-cryptocurrency-tokens-ever-invented/ (archived at https://perma.cc/ZYG2-3QU4)

25  Bitcointalk (2018) [ANN] [NO ICO] The Wine Project (WINE)· Buy your wine with crypto! [AIRDROP], Bitcointalk, 12 March, https://bitcointalk.org/index.php?topic=3113664.0 (archived at https://perma.cc/SX6C-DUST)

26  Bitcointalk (2017) [ANN] [FUNDROP] Trash cash [TRASH] ERC20 token I No ICO I, Bitcointalk, 15 November, https://bitcointalk.org/index.php?topic=2410056.0 (archived at https://perma.cc/6ATC-7PUG)

27  Seth, S (2018) 80 per cent of ICOs are scams: Report, Investopedia, 2 April, https://www.investopedia.com/news/80-icos-are-scams-report/ (archived at https://perma.cc/9Z2Y-6UWM)

28  Financial Times (2018) The baroness, the ICO fiasco, and enter Steve Wozniak, Financial Times, 2 September, https://www.ft.com/content/fc9d3b82-de7b-3e67-bd3c-835575172608 (archived at https://perma.cc/L94R-FCP8)

29  Haan, C (2019) Post-disaster clean up: ICO class-action portal goes online, Crowdfund Insider, https://www.crowdfundinsider.com/2019/03/145420-post-disaster-clean-up-ico-class-action-portal-goes-online/ (archived at https://perma.cc/H89E-PF7B)

30  Bitcointalk (2018) [ANN] [ICO] Gems protocol – decentralized mechanical turk, Bitcointalk, 6 January, https://bitcointalk.org/index.php?topic=2700804.0 (archived at https://perma.cc/F3ZH-SQA9)

31  Popper, N (2018) Floyd Mayweather and DJ Khaled are fined in ICO crackdown, The New York Times, 29 November, https://www.nytimes.com/2018/11/29/technology/floyd-mayweather-dj-khaled-sec-fine-initial-coin-offering.html (archived at https://perma.cc/LS88-ZQFP)

32 Popper, N (2018) Floyd Mayweather and DJ Khaled are fined in ICO crackdown, *The New York Times*, 29 November, https://www.nytimes.com/2018/11/29/technology/floyd-mayweather-dj-khaled-sec-fine-initial-coin-offering.html (archived at https://perma.cc/LS88-ZQFP)

33 US Securities and Exchange Commission (2020) SEC charges John McAfee with fraudulently touting ICOs, Sec.gov, press release, https://www.sec.gov/news/press-release/2020-246 (archived at https://perma.cc/7NYC-YAX8)

34 Dodds, S (2018) Cryptocurrency markets are wide open to insider trading, say US regulators, *Telegraph*, 19 September, https://www.telegraph.co.uk/technology/2018/09/19/cryptocurrency-markets-wide-open-insider-trading-us-regulators/ (archived at https://perma.cc/9G7Q-VGZ4)

35 Seth, S (2018) 80 per cent of ICOs are scams: Report, Investopedia, 2 April, https://www.investopedia.com/news/80-icos-are-scams-report/ (archived at https://perma.cc/9Z2Y-6UWM)

36 Seth, S (2018) 80 per cent of ICOs are scams: Report, Investopedia, 2 April, https://www.investopedia.com/news/80-icos-are-scams-report/ (archived at https://perma.cc/9Z2Y-6UWM)

37 99Bitcoins (2021) DeadCoins, 99Bitcoins, https://99bitcoins.com/deadcoins/ (archived at https://perma.cc/ACR2-E4GZ)

## Chapter 2

1 Hankir, Y (2018) Thanks guys! Over and out... #savedroidICO, Twitter, 18 April, https://twitter.com/YassinHankir/status/986551967932735488? (archived at https://perma.cc/FWQ6-ZHTW)

2 Qader, A (2018) German ICO Savedroid pulls exit scam after raising $50 million, Finance Magnates, 18 April, https://www.financemagnates.com/cryptocurrency/news/german-ico-savedroid-pulls-exit-scam-raising-50-million/ (archived at https://perma.cc/EVJ5-MFKZ)

3 Zuckerman, M (2018) In apparent exit scam CEO of German startup is 'over and out' after $50 mln ICO, Cointelegraph, 18 April, https://cointelegraph.com/news/in-apparent-exit-scam-ceo-of-german-startup-is-over-and-out-after-50-mln-ico (archived at https://perma.cc/TR3Y-758D)

4   Varshney, N (2018) Savedroid ICO's exit scam was actually a very
    dumb PR stunt, The Next Web, 26 November, https://thenextweb.
    com/hardfork/2018/04/19/savedroid-ico-not-gone/ (archived at
    https://perma.cc/4B24-ABTB) and Golovtchenko, V (2018)
    Savedroid: Worst prank in crypto history or a reckless publicity
    stunt? Finance Magnates, 19 April, https://www.financemagnates.
    com/cryptocurrency/news/savedroid-worst-prank-crypto-history-
    reckless-publicity-stunt/ (archived at https://perma.cc/K75L-5Z63)
5   Rice, J (2018) Yassin Hankir of Savedroid on exit scams and ICO
    sustainability, Crypto Briefing, 26 May, https://cryptobriefing.com/
    yassin-hankir-savedroid-exit-scams-ico/ (archived at https://perma.cc/
    RH24-XZDB)
6   Coingecko (live) Savedroid, https://www.coingecko.com/en/coins/
    savedroid (archived at https://perma.cc/C47U-722T)
7   u/ICOClassAction (2020) Savedroid class action is accepting class
    members, Reddit, https://www.reddit.com/r/ico/comments/b3r5z7/
    savedroid_class_action_is_accepting_class_members/ (archived at
    https://perma.cc/3PYP-P6ZE)
8   Rice, J (2018) Yassin Hankir of Savedroid on exit scams and ICO
    sustainability, Crypto Briefing, 26 May, https://cryptobriefing.com/
    yassin-hankir-savedroid-exit-scams-ico/ (archived at https://perma.cc/
    RH24-XZDB)
9   Pearson, J (2018) Ethereum startup vanishes after seemingly making
    $11, leaves message: 'penis', Vice, 29 January, https://www.vice.com/en/
    article/yw5ygw/ethereum-startup-prodeum-vanishes-after-seemingly-
    making-11-leaves-message-penis (archived at https://perma.cc/2C2V-
    RR8R)
10  Mix (nd) Cryptocurrency startup Prodeum pulls an exit scam, leaves
    a penis behind, The Next Web, https://thenextweb.com/
    hardfork/2018/01/29/cryptocurrency-prodeum-scam-exit-penis/
    (archived at https://perma.cc/Q8QB-JU8C)
11  Alexander, D (2020) Quadriga downfall stemmed from founder's fraud,
    regulators find, Bloomberg, 11 June, https://www.bloomberg.com/news/
    articles/2020-06-11/quadriga-downfall-stemmed-from-founder-s-fraud-
    regulators-find (archived at https://perma.cc/LF4N-CDSZ)

12  Kim, C (2017) South Korea bans raising money through initial coin offerings, Reuters, 29 September, https://www.reuters.com/article/us-southkorea-bitcoin-idUSKCN1C408N (archived at https://perma.cc/EV74-GJZT)

13  Manning, L (2018) Fraudulent South Korean exchange Pure Bit nabs $2.8m in ICO exit scam, Bitcoin Magazine, 9 November, https://bitcoinmagazine.com/articles/fraudulent-south-korean-exchange-pure-bit-nabs-28m-ico-exit-scam (archived at https://perma.cc/XCP3-A5CX)

14  Manning, L (2018) Fraudulent South Korean exchange Pure Bit nabs $2.8m in ICO exit scam, Bitcoin Magazine, 9 November, https://bitcoinmagazine.com/articles/fraudulent-south-korean-exchange-pure-bit-nabs-28m-ico-exit-scam (archived at https://perma.cc/XCP3-A5CX)

15  Angelreyes (2018) Pure Bit ICO returns investor funds after exit scam, Crypto.iq, 20 November, https://www.cryptoiqtrading.com/pure-bit-ico-returns-investor-funds-after-exit-scam/ (archived at https://perma.cc/DVQ8-ZJEP)

16  Shome, A (2019) Coinroom exchange disappeared overnight with customers' funds, Finance Magnates, 3 June, https://www.financemagnates.com/cryptocurrency/news/coinroom-exchange-disappeared-overnight-with-customers-funds/ (archived at https://perma.cc/P9ND-YAHG)

17  Vitáris, B (2019) Polish cryptocurrency exchange coinroom exit scams with customer funds, CCN, 23 September, https://www.ccn.com/polish-cryptocurrency-exchange-coinroom-exit-scams-with-customer-funds/ (archived at https://perma.cc/WM4F-T3GU)

18  US Securities and Exchange Commission (2020) Report of the Provisional Administrator concerning the request to obtain a declaratory judgment, Case No: 358421-0001, US Securities and Exchange Commission, 26 February, https://www.sec.gov/divisions/enforce/claims/docs/plexcorp-receiver-report-2-26-2020.pdf (archived at https://perma.cc/7R23-4M4F) and PlexCoin (2017) PlexCoin: The next cryptocurrency, Whitepaper version 2.71, https://assets.bwbx.io/documents/users/iqjWHBFdfxIU/rwzk2_HjYOjw/v0 (archived at https://perma.cc/ZQA9-GN3T)

19  Coinisseur.com (2018) PlexCoin: The anatomy of an ICO scam,
    12 September, https://www.coinisseur.com/the-anatomy-of-an-ico-
    scam/ (archived at https://perma.cc/9Q7T-U7TS)
20  Bitcointalk (2017) What do you think about PlexCoin? Bitcointalk,
    8 July, https://bitcointalk.org/index.php?topic=2010097.0 (archived
    at https://perma.cc/435P-JTZ4)
21  PlexCoin (2017) PlexCoin: The next cryptocurrency, PlexCoin,
    August, https://assets.bwbx.io/documents/users/iqjWHBFdfxIU/
    rwzk2_HjYOjw/v0 (archived at https://perma.cc/ZQA9-GN3T)
22  US Securities and Exchange Commission (2020) Report of the
    Provisional Administrator concerning the request to obtain a
    declaratory judgment, Case No: 358421-0001, US Securities and
    Exchange Commission, 26 February, https://www.sec.gov/divisions/
    enforce/claims/docs/plexcorp-receiver-report-2-26-2020.pdf (archived
    at https://perma.cc/7R23-4M4F)
23  PlexCoin (2017) PlexCoin: The next cryptocurrency, PlexCoin,
    August, https://assets.bwbx.io/documents/users/iqjWHBFdfxIU/
    rwzk2_HjYOjw/v0 (archived at https://perma.cc/ZQA9-GN3T)
24  PlexCoin (2017) PlexCoin: The next cryptocurrency, PlexCoin,
    August, https://assets.bwbx.io/documents/users/iqjWHBFdfxIU/
    rwzk2_HjYOjw/v0 (archived at https://perma.cc/ZQA9-GN3T)
25  PlexCoin (2017) PlexCoin: The next cryptocurrency, PlexCoin,
    August, https://assets.bwbx.io/documents/users/iqjWHBFdfxIU/
    rwzk2_HjYOjw/v0 (archived at https://perma.cc/ZQA9-GN3T)
26  PlexCoin (2017) PlexCoin: The next cryptocurrency, PlexCoin,
    August, https://assets.bwbx.io/documents/users/iqjWHBFdfxIU/
    rwzk2_HjYOjw/v0 (archived at https://perma.cc/ZQA9-GN3T)
27  PlexCoin (2017) PlexCoin: The next cryptocurrency, PlexCoin,
    August, https://assets.bwbx.io/documents/users/iqjWHBFdfxIU/
    rwzk2_HjYOjw/v0 (archived at https://perma.cc/ZQA9-GN3T)
28  US Securities and Exchange Commission (2020) Report of the
    Provisional Administrator concerning the request to obtain a
    declaratory judgment, Case No: 358421-0001, US Securities and
    Exchange Commission, 26 February, https://www.sec.gov/divisions/
    enforce/claims/docs/plexcorp-receiver-report-2-26-2020.pdf (archived
    at https://perma.cc/7R23-4M4F)

29  United States Department of Justice (2020) Quebec trio charged with running fraudulent cryptocurrency, 24 July, https://www.justice.gov/usao-ndoh/pr/quebec-trio-charged-running-fraudulent-cryptocurrency (archived at https://perma.cc/N9LZ-Q44R)

30  Qader, A (2017) SEC freezes assets of PlexCoin ICO organizer, halts $15 million scam, Finance Magnates, 12 April, https://www.financemagnates.com/cryptocurrency/news/sec-freezes-assets-plexcoin-ico-organizer-halts-15-million-scam/ (archived at https://perma.cc/KB3J-U4K2)

31  Neironix.io (2018) Shopin whitepaper 3.3, English 010818, https://neironix.io/documents/whitepaper/1e88063f4a7625640100102d4a810eab.pdf (archived at https://perma.cc/7D43-YBHF)

32  US Securities and Exchange Commission (2019) SEC charges founder, digital-asset issuer with fraudulent ICO, US Securities and Exchange Commission, 11 December, https://www.sec.gov/news/press-release/2019-259 (archived at https://perma.cc/VJN9-PEV5)

33  Canellis, D (2019) SEC: Crypto 'entrepreneur' illegally raised $42m, spent funds on dating and rent, TNW, 12 December, https://thenextweb.com/hardfork/2019/12/12/cryptocurrency-ico-blockchain-shopin-sec-coin-offering-fraud/ (archived at https://perma.cc/9RCC-RV56)

34  US Securities and Exchange Commission (2019) SEC charges founder, digital-asset issuer with fraudulent ICO, US Securities and Exchange Commission, 11 December, https://www.sec.gov/news/press-release/2019-259 (archived at https://perma.cc/VJN9-PEV5)

35  Vu, K (2018) Vietnam calls for tougher measures on cryptocurrency deals amid alleged scam, Reuters, 11 April, https://www.reuters.com/article/us-vietnam-cryptocurrency-idUSKBN1HI1YV (archived at https://perma.cc/3FED-XQQJ)

36  Biggs, J (2018) Exit scammers run off with $660 million in ICO earnings, TC, 13 April, https://techcrunch.com/2018/04/13/exit-scammers-run-off-with-660-million-in-ico-earnings/ (archived at https://perma.cc/8WT8-BUCD)

37  Biggs, J (2018) Exit scammers run off with $660 million in ICO earnings, TC, 13 April, https://techcrunch.com/2018/04/13/exit-scammers-run-off-with-660-million-in-ico-earnings/ (archived at https://perma.cc/8WT8-BUCD)

38  Suberg, W (2018) Vietnam: PinCoin, Ifan ICOs exposed as scams that allegedly stole $660 million, Cointelegraph, 10 April, https://cointelegraph.com/news/vietnam-pincoin-ifan-icos-exposed-as-scams-that-allegedly-stole-660-million (archived at https://perma.cc/9HY8-LHTS)

39  Biggs, J (2018) Exit scammers run off with $660 million in ICO earnings, TC, 13 April, https://techcrunch.com/2018/04/13/exit-scammers-run-off-with-660-million-in-ico-earnings/ (archived at https://perma.cc/8WT8-BUCD)

## Chapter 3

1  BBC (2019) Cryptoqueen: How this woman scammed the world, then vanished, BBC, 24 November, https://www.bbc.com/news/stories-50435014 (archived at https://perma.cc/U4LW-FQQE)

2  Trading Education (2021) OneCoin: The biggest on-going cryptocurrency scam ever, Trading Education, 17 February, https://trading-education.com/onecoin-the-biggest-on-going-cryptocurrency-scam-ever (archived at https://perma.cc/4BH4-NN6Z)

3  Justice.gov (2019) *United States of America v Konstantin Ignatov*, https://www.justice.gov/usao-sdny/press-release/file/1141986/download (archived at https://perma.cc/T3D4-DGZV) (page 21)

4  Marson, J (2020) OneCoin took in billions. Then its leader vanished, *Wall Street Journal*, 27 August, https://www.wsj.com/articles/onecoin-took-in-billions-then-its-leader-vanished-11598520601 (archived at https://perma.cc/DE55-AHVT)

5  Bartlett, J (2019) The £4bn OneCoin scam: How crypto-queen Dr Ruja Ignatova duped ordinary people out of billions – then went missing, *The Times*, 15 December, https://www.thetimes.co.uk/article/the-4bn-onecoin-scam-how-crypto-queen-dr-ruja-ignatova-duped-ordinary-people-out-of-billions-then-went-missing-trqpr52pq (archived at https://perma.cc/GW8A-TBJL)

6  BBC (2019) Cryptoqueen: How this woman scammed the world, then vanished, BBC, 24 November, https://www.bbc.com/news/stories-50435014 (archived at https://perma.cc/U4LW-FQQE)

7   Penman, A (2016) Who wants to be a OneCoin millionaire? YOU
    don't – here's why hyped-up web currency is virtually worthless,
    *Mirror*, 10 February, https://www.mirror.co.uk/news/uk-news/
    who-wants-onecoin-millionaire-you-7346558 (archived at https://
    perma.cc/TZ3X-ZVJB)

8   Benji (2020) The complete story behind the OneCoin cryptocurrency
    scam, Hackernoon, 12 January, https://hackernoon.com/onecoin-
    scam-that-became-a-religion-3zr3xds (archived at https://perma.
    cc/4RNA-VXJY)

9   BBC (2019) 'Cryptoqueen' brother admits role in OneCoin fraud, BBC,
    14 November, https://www.bbc.co.uk/news/technology-50417908
    (archived at https://perma.cc/C8TS-KBDA)

10  BBC (2019) Cryptoqueen: How this woman scammed the world, then
    vanished, BBC, 24 November, https://www.bbc.com/news/
    stories-50435014 (archived at https://perma.cc/U4LW-FQQE)

11  BBC (2020) The missing cryptoqueen, BBC, 6 August, https://www.
    bbc.co.uk/programmes/p07nkd84 (archived at https://perma.cc/
    JCU5-NN7U)

12  Behind MLM (2019) New DealShaker abandoned. Is this OneCoin's
    final collapse? Behind MLM, 24 May, https://behindmlm.com/
    companies/onecoin/new-dealshaker-abandoned-is-this-onecoins-final-
    collapse/ (archived at https://perma.cc/EQK5-5EZT)

13  BBC (2020) The missing cryptoqueen, BBC, 6 August, https://www.
    bbc.co.uk/programmes/p07nkd84 (archived at https://perma.cc/
    JCU5-NN7U)

14  Behind MLM (2017) OneLife suspend OneCoin withdrawals,
    affiliates can't cash out, Behind MLM, 15 January, https://behindmlm.
    com/companies/OneCoin/OneLife-suspend-OneCoin-withdrawls-
    affiliates-cant-cash-out/ (archived at https://perma.cc/6ZSM-5YBW)

15  BBC (2020) The missing cryptoqueen, BBC, 6 August, https://www.
    bbc.co.uk/programmes/p07nkd84 (archived at https://perma.cc/
    JCU5-NN7U)

16  Marson, J (2020) OneCoin took in billions. Then its leader vanished,
    *Wall Street Journal*, 27 August, https://www.wsj.com/articles/
    onecoin-took-in-billions-then-its-leader-vanished-11598520601
    (archived at https://perma.cc/DE55-AHVT)

17  Justice (2019) *United States of America V Konstantin Ignatov*, US Department of Justice, 9 March, https://www.justice.gov/usao-sdny/press-release/file/1141986/download (archived at https://perma.cc/T3D4-DGZV) and BBC (2019) Cryptoqueen: How this woman scammed the world, then vanished, BBC, 24 November, https://www.bbc.com/news/stories-50435014 (archived at https://perma.cc/U4LW-FQQE)

18  Carter, A (2020) The notorious Igor E Alberts. #AntiMLM. Hey hun, you woke up! (Podcast) https://podcasts.apple.com/us/podcast/the-notorious-igor-e-alberts-antimlm/id1439473213?i=1000493805775 (archived at https://perma.cc/8XEN-A55X)

19  Business for Home (2017) Top 200 worldwide earners in MLM – April 2017, Business for Home, 3 April, https://www.businessforhome.org/2017/04/top-200-worldwide-earners-in-mlm-april-2017/ (archived at https://perma.cc/KWV4-FQRC)

20  Forklog (2020) Scam of the decade: The story of a doctor of law who organized the OneCoin Ponzi scheme and vanished with billions of euros, Forklog, 10 January, https://forklog.media/scam-of-the-decade-the-story-of-a-doctor-of-law-who-organized-the-onecoin-ponzi-scheme-and-vanished-with-billions-of-euros/ (archived at https://perma.cc/XK8U-AVSV)

21  BBC (2019) Cryptoqueen: How this woman scammed the world, then vanished, BBC, 24 November, https://www.bbc.com/news/stories-50435014 (archived at https://perma.cc/U4LW-FQQE)

22  BBC (2020) The missing cryptoqueen, BBC, 6 August, https://www.bbc.co.uk/programmes/p07nkd84 (archived at https://perma.cc/JCU5-NN7U)

23  Behind MLM (2018) To promote DagCoin, Igor Alberts slams Ponzi he earned millions in, Behind MLM, 13 January, https://behindmlm.com/companies/to-promote-dagcoin-igor-alberts-slams-ponzi-he-earned-millions-in/ (archived at https://perma.cc/UZM4-3N23)

24  Justice (2019) *United States of America V Konstantin Ignatov*, US Department of Justice, 9 March, https://www.justice.gov/usao-sdny/press-release/file/1141986/download (archived at https://perma.cc/T3D4-DGZV) (page 6)

25  BBC (2019) The missing cryptoqueen, BBC, 4 November, https://www.bbc.co.uk/programmes/p07sz990 (archived at https://perma.cc/T8GL-C66B)

26  BBC (2019) The missing cryptoqueen, BBC, https://www.bbc.co.uk/sounds/brand/p07nkd84 (archived at https://perma.cc/GS28-5ZTL)

and Tyson, E (1994) *Personal Finance For Dummies*, John Wiley & Sons Inc and Happyscribe (2019) Episode 7: In plain sight, Happyscribe, 28 October, https://www.happyscribe.com/public/ the-missing-cryptoqueen/episode-7-in-plain-sight-5c5ba8c8-d571- 4b71-8634-f0475b866765 (archived at https://perma.cc/ERL6-LEN2)

27  Lamando, M (2016) Dr Ruja Ignatova's introducing the Tycoon+ and Ultimate Packages, YouTube, 25 July, https://www.youtube.com/ watch?v=WBiqEJc1IRo (archived at https://perma.cc/Z3N3-VMA4)

28  BBC (2019) Cryptoqueen: How this woman scammed the world, then vanished, BBC, 24 November, https://www.bbc.com/news/ stories-50435014 (archived at https://perma.cc/U4LW-FQQE)

29  D'Anconia, F (2016) Keep money in the game: OneCoin moves on to new fantasy blockchain, Cointelegraph, 6 October, https://cointelegraph. com/news/keep-money-in-the-game-onecoin-moves-on-to-new-fantasy- blockchain (archived at https://perma.cc/3QU4-SREX)

30  Redman, J (2016) Buyer beware! The definitive OneCoin Ponzi exposé, News.bitcoin.com, 27 June, https://news.bitcoin.com/beware-definitive- onecoin-ponzi/ (archived at https://perma.cc/8EQ9-PWVM)

31  Lamando, M (2016) OneCoin split strategies and doubling of coins, explained by Dr Ruja Ignatov, YouTube, 26 July, https://www.youtube. com/watch?v=ft3FtWoP04s (archived at https://perma.cc/X8HN-BA4H)

32  Business for Home (2016) OneCoin Launches New Blockchain Appoints Pablo Munoz As CEO, Business for Home, 1 October, https://www.businessforhome.org/2016/10/onecoin-launches-new- blockchain/ (archived at https://perma.cc/DV7L-EHCN)

33  D'Anconia, F (2016) Keep money in the game: OneCoin moves on to new fantasy blockchain, Cointelegraph, 6 October, https://cointelegraph. com/news/keep-money-in-the-game-onecoin-moves-on-to-new-fantasy- blockchain (archived at https://perma.cc/3QU4-SREX)

34  DealShaker (nd) Miss Onelife – bronze sponsor advertising package 100 per cent OneCoin, DealShaker, https://dealshaker.com/en/deal/ miss-onelife-bronze-sponsor-advertising-package-100-onecoin/XY782 DJ2hP0sc0nCeWiqncwxO073mFp*BL8-nV5uT6k~ (archived at https://perma.cc/TB2Q-LS6L)

35  kusetukset.blogspot.com (2019) OneCoin members are idiots, 28 March, http://kusetukset.blogspot.com/2019/03/onecoin-members- are-idiots.html (archived at https://perma.cc/9VCM-EB4X)

36  BBC (2019) The missing cryptoqueen, BBC, https://www.bbc.co.uk/ sounds/brand/p07nkd84 (archived at https://perma.cc/GS28-5ZTL)

37  Redman, J (2019) OneCoin websites suspended as the $4 billion Ponzi crumbles, Bitcoin.com, 4 December, https://news.bitcoin.com/ multiple-onecoin-websites-suspended-as-the-4-billion-dollar-ponzi-crumbles/ (archived at https://perma.cc/6HK6-RQWY)

38  BBC (2019) The missing cryptoqueen, BBC, https://www.bbc.co.uk/ sounds/brand/p07nkd84 (archived at https://perma.cc/GS28-5ZTL)

39  Behind MLM (2019) Ruja Ignatova's warning underscores OneCoin mafia ties, Behind MLM, 18 November, https://behindmlm.com/ companies/onecoin/ruja-ignatovas-warning-underscores-onecoin-mafia-ties/ (archived at https://perma.cc/NR3Z-M7FS)

40  Soundcloud (2020) Inner City OneCoin's Ruja Ignatova tells Armenta to watch out for Russian guys, Soundcloud, https://soundcloud.com/ innercitypress/onecoins-ruja-ignatova-tells-armenta-to-watch-out-for-russian-guys (archived at https://perma.cc/7XDK-N5ZK)

41  BBC (2019) Cryptoqueen: How this woman scammed the world, then vanished, BBC, 24 November, https://www.bbc.com/news/ stories-50435014 (archived at https://perma.cc/U4LW-FQQE)

42  BBC (2019) Cryptoqueen: How this woman scammed the world, then vanished, BBC, 24 November, https://www.bbc.com/news/ stories-50435014 (archived at https://perma.cc/U4LW-FQQE)

43  BBC (2019) The missing cryptoqueen, BBC, https://www.bbc.co.uk/ sounds/brand/p07nkd84 (archived at https://perma.cc/GS28-5ZTL)

44  Behind MLM (2017) Ruja Ignatova arrested in Germany, report Bulgarian media, Behind MLM, 3 November, https://behindmlm.com/ companies/onecoin/ruja-ignatova-arrested-in-germany-report-bulgarian-media/ (archived at https://perma.cc/BE8S-WGA9)

45  Justice (2020) Manhattan US attorney announces charges against leaders of 'OneCoin,' a multibillion-dollar pyramid scheme involving the sale of a fraudulent cryptocurrency, US Department of Justice, 30 April, https://www.justice.gov/usao-sdny/pr/manhattan-us-attorney-announces-charges-against-leaders-onecoin-multibillion-dollar (archived at https://perma.cc/6NBA-CVX5)

46  Englund, P (2020) Dagcoin the next scam from Ponzi schemers OneCoin, Go Cryptowise, 18 June, https://gocryptowise.com/blog/ dagcoin-the-next-scam-from-ponzi-schemers-onecoin/ (archived at

https://perma.cc/DQ3X-K4A9) and Behind MLM (2017) Dagcoin
review: OneCoin affiliate launches Ponzi points clone, Behind MLM,
19 July, https://behindmlm.com/mlm-reviews/dagcoin-review-onecoin-
affiliate-launches-ponzi-points-clone/ (archived at https://perma.
cc/4YRM-6T7J)

47  Behind MLM (2017) Dagcoin review: OneCoin affiliate launches
Ponzi points clone, Behind MLM, 19 July, https://behindmlm.com/
mlm-reviews/dagcoin-review-onecoin-affiliate-launches-ponzi-points-
clone/ (archived at https://perma.cc/4YRM-6T7J)

48  Business for Home (2019) Igor Alberts and Andreea Cimbala achieve
$1.6 million per month with success factory – Dagcoin, Business for
Home, 15 April, https://www.businessforhome.org/2019/04/igor-
alberts-and-andreea-cimbala-achieve-1-6-million-per-month-with-
success-factory-dagcoin/ (archived at https://perma.cc/SBN9-LMHD)

## Chapter 4

1  GitHub (nd) Bitconnectcoin, GitHub, https://github.com/Bitconnectcoin/
Bitconnectcoin (archived at https://perma.cc/855X-8LPB)

2  Mix (2018) How Bitconnect pulled the biggest exit scheme in
cryptocurrency, TNW The Next Web, 17 January, https://thenextweb.
com/hardfork/2018/01/17/bitconnect-bitcoin-scam-cryptocurrency/
(archived at https://perma.cc/J2C8-VXXD)

3  Tepper, F (2018) Bitconnect, which has been accused of running a
Ponzi scheme, shuts down, TC, 17 January, https://techcrunch.
com/2018/01/16/Bitconnect-which-has-been-accused-of-running-a-
ponzi-scheme-shuts-down/ (archived at https://perma.cc/D7JU-CM9F)

4  Mix (2018) How Bitconnect pulled the biggest exit scheme in
cryptocurrency, The Next Web, 17 January, https://thenextweb.com/
hardfork/2018/01/17/bitconnect-bitcoin-scam-cryptocurrency/
(archived at https://perma.cc/J2C8-VXXD)

5  The Calculator Site (nd) Compound Interest Calculator, The
Calculator Site, https://www.thecalculatorsite.com/finance/
calculators/compoundinterestcalculator.php (archived at
https://perma.cc/36QS-PBNT)

6  Ponciano, J (2020) Jeff Bezos becomes the first person ever worth $200 billion, 26 August, Forbes, https://www.forbes.com/sites/jonathanponciano/2020/08/26/worlds-richest-billionaire-jeff-bezos-first-200-billion/?sh=48e98f8f4db7 (archived at https://perma.cc/PU6U-JTDR)

7  Morris, D (2018) New leaked chats reveal alleged Bitconnect scammers in action, 28 September, BreakerMag, https://breakermag.com/new-leaked-chats-reveal-alleged-bitconnect-scammers-in-action/ (archived at https://perma.cc/UA6K-R44U)

8  Mix (nd) How Bitconnect pulled the biggest exit scam in cryptocurrency, The Next Web, https://thenextweb.com/hardfork/2018/01/17/bitconnect-bitcoin-scam-cryptocurrency/ (archived at https://perma.cc/J2C8-VXXD)

9  Sedis, T (2018) The most bizarre Ponzi marketing event you'll ever see, 17 January, Behind MLM, https://behindmlm.com/companies/bitconnect/the-most-bizarre-ponzi-marketing-event-youll-ever-see/ (archived at https://perma.cc/X265-MPL8)

10  Matos, C (2018) Bitconnect, Genius, 23 January, https://genius.com/Carlos-matos-bitconnect-annotated (archived at https://perma.cc/ZC3Q-36N7) and Chronosceptor (2018) Bitconnect annual ceremony high lights (Carlos Matos from NY), YouTube, 17 January, https://www.youtube.com/watch?v=vabXXkZjKiw (archived at https://perma.cc/ED5D-PKMP)

11  Fitzgerald, B (2017) Bitconnect official music video we've got a good thing, YouTube, https://www.youtube.com/watch?v=q1ezZ7pBtrA (archived at https://perma.cc/9QBE-VANM)

12  MyCryptoCoin (2017) Blockchain expo North America and private yacht party with bitconnect promoters, Bitconnect, 28 October, https://bitconnectcash.wordpress.com/2017/10/28/blockchain-expo-north-america-and-private-yacht-party-with-bitconnect-promoters/ (archived at https://perma.cc/RE49-W7XQ)

13  Companies House (nd) Bitconnect Ltd, company number 10278342, https://find-and-update.company-information.service.gov.uk/company/10278342/filing-history (archived at https://perma.cc/JMY9-VSTW)

14  Mix (2017) UK threatens to shut down popular Bitcoin investment site Bitconnect, The Next Web, 13 November, https://thenextweb. com/hardfork/2017/11/13/bitcoin-bitconnect-uk-ponzi-investment/ (archived at https://perma.cc/5G6V-6LQE)

15  Mix (2018) How Bitconnect pulled the biggest exit scheme in cryptocurrency, 17 January, The Next Web, https://thenextweb.com/ hardfork/2018/01/17/bitconnect-bitcoin-scam-cryptocurrency/ (archived at https://perma.cc/J2C8-VXXD)

16  Mix (2018) How Bitconnect pulled the biggest exit scheme in cryptocurrency, 17 January, The Next Web, https://thenextweb.com/ hardfork/2018/01/17/bitconnect-bitcoin-scam-cryptocurrency/ (archived at https://perma.cc/J2C8-VXXD)

17  Trading Education (2020) The Bitconnect scam: The biggest price plunge in crypto history, Trading Education, 15 June, https://trading-education.com/the-bitconnect-scam-the-biggest-price-plunge-in-crypto-history (archived at https://perma.cc/8738-AKLZ) and Mix (2018) How Bitconnect pulled the biggest exit scheme in cryptocurrency, 17 January, The Next Web, https://thenextweb.com/ hardfork/2018/01/17/bitconnect-bitcoin-scam-cryptocurrency/ (archived at https://perma.cc/J2C8-VXXD)

18  Texas State Securities Board (2018) Emergency cease and desist order no ENF-18-CDO-1754, 4 January, Texas State Securities Board, https://www.ssb.texas.gov/sites/default/files/BitConnect_ENF-18-CDO-1754.pdf (archived at https://perma.cc/W8UR-52BF)

19  Mix (2018) Bitconnect handed yet another cease and desist letter – this time in North Carolina, The Next Web, 11 January, https://thenextweb. com/hardfork/2018/01/11/bitconnect-served-yet-another-cease-desist-order/ (archived at https://perma.cc/7F6Y-H8AH)

20  Mix (2018) How Bitconnect pulled the biggest exit scheme in cryptocurrency, 17 January, The Next Web, https://thenextweb.com/ hardfork/2018/01/17/bitconnect-bitcoin-scam-cryptocurrency/ (archived at https://perma.cc/J2C8-VXXD)

21  McKay, T (2018) Bitconnect, anonymously-run crypto exchange, crashes after states issue cease and desists, Gizmodo, 17 January, https://gizmodo.com/bitconnect-anonymously-run-crypto-exchange-crashes-af-1822144652 (archived at https://perma.cc/6USZ-SLNH)

22  CoinMarketCap (live) Bitconnect, CoinMarketCap, https://coinmarketcap.com/currencies/bitconnect/ (archived at https://perma.cc/P9G2-A774)

23  Osborne, C (2018) Alleged head of Bitconnect cryptocurrency scam arrested in Dubai, 20 August, ZDNet, https://www.zdnet.com/article/alleged-bitconnect-head-arrested-in-dubai/ (archived at https://perma.cc/Z66D-2TYW) and newsbtc (2018) The Bitconnect Ponzi scheme finally collapsed – scam becomes evident, newsbtc, https://www.newsbtc.com/news/bitconnect-ponzi-scheme-finally-collapsed-exit-scam-becomes-evident/ (archived at https://perma.cc/8W3R-V65E)

24  Sedgwick, K (2018) Not content scamming $1.5 billion, Bitconnect wants another $500 million for ICO, Bitcoin.com, 20 January, https://news.bitcoin.com/not-content-with-scamming-1-5-billion-bitconnect-wants-another-500-million-for-its-ico/ (archived at https://perma.cc/4NLN-K7FG)

25  u/Quinchonez (nd) Bitconnect X ICO price switched from $5 to $50!! Reddit, https://www.reddit.com/r/Bitconnect/comments/7pd1m5/bitconnect_x_ico_price_switched_from_5_to_50/ (archived at https://perma.cc/6CVE-RJZ8) and Bitcoin Forum (2021) What you think of BitconnectX? Bitcointalk, https://bitcointalk.org/index.php?topic=2751009.0 (archived at https://perma.cc/WC2T-RAMJ)

26  Sedgwick, K (2018) Not content scamming $1.5 billion, Bitconnect wants another $500 million for ICO, Bitcoin.com, 20 January, https://news.bitcoin.com/not-content-with-scamming-1-5-billion-bitconnect-wants-another-500-million-for-its-ico/ (archived at https://perma.cc/4NLN-K7FG)

27  Alford, T (2020) Bitconnect scam: The $2.6 BN Ponzi scheme (2020 update), Totalcrypto, 5 March, https://totalcrypto.io/bitconnect-scam/ (archived at https://perma.cc/VE42-MZYL)

28  Varshney, N (2018) Arrested Bitconnect kingpin is connected to yet another cryptocurrency scam, TNW, 20 August, https://thenextweb.com/hardfork/2018/08/20/bitconnect-cryptocurrency-scam-india/ (archived at https://perma.cc/QGF5-XT35)

29  Cuthbertson, A (2019) Bitcoin millionaire 'on the run' after second cryptocurrency scam, Independent, 5 June, https://www.independent.co.uk/life-style/gadgets-and-tech/news/bitcoin-scam-bitconnect-cryptocurrency-regal-coin-a8945291.html (archived at https://perma.cc/6TWC-5TP4)

30  Dean (2020) What is Regalcoin? Another crypto Ponzi scheme (2020), Quick Penguin, 15 April, https://quickpenguin.net/regalcoin-scam/ (archived at https://perma.cc/6FCF-2VRY)

31  Rodrigues, J (2018) Cryptokidnapping, or how to lose $3 billion of Bitcoin in India, *Hindustan Times*, 10 August, https://www.hindustantimes.com/india-news/cryptokidnapping-or-how-to-lose-3-billion-of-bitcoin-in-india/story-D82N2NAbgheQl7dPJIYs1K.html (archived at https://perma.cc/MV87-CFY3)

32  Rodrigues, J (2018) Cryptokidnapping, or how to lose $3 billion of Bitcoin in India, *Hindustan Times*, 10 August, https://www.hindustantimes.com/india-news/cryptokidnapping-or-how-to-lose-3-billion-of-bitcoin-in-india/story-D82N2NAbgheQl7dPJIYs1K.html (archived at https://perma.cc/MV87-CFY3)

33  Huillet, M (2018) Police arrest alleged India head of now-defunct Bitconnect scam, Cointelegraph, 20 August, https://cointelegraph.com/news/police-arrest-alleged-india-head-of-now-defunct-bitconnect-scam (archived at https://perma.cc/JA4A-TUE6)

34  Varshney, N (2018) Arrested Bitconnect kingpin is connected to yet another cryptocurrency scam, TNW, 20 August, https://thenextweb.com/hardfork/2018/08/20/bitconnect-cryptocurrency-scam-india/ (archived at https://perma.cc/QGF5-XT35)

35  Rodrigues, J (2018) Cryptokidnapping, or how to lose $3 billion of Bitcoin in India, *Hindustan Times*, 10 August, https://www.hindustantimes.com/india-news/cryptokidnapping-or-how-to-lose-3-billion-of-bitcoin-in-india/story-D82N2NAbgheQl7dPJIYs1K.html (archived at https://perma.cc/MV87-CFY3)

## Chapter 5

1  Silkjaer, T (2020) Is this $3 billion crypto Ponzi still alive? Forbes, 6 July, https://www.forbes.com/sites/thomassilkjaer/2020/07/06/is-this-3-billion-crypto-ponzi-still-alive/?sh=56eaf53d4d42 (archived at https://perma.cc/73SH-REW7)

2  Harper, C (2019) How the PlusToken scam absconded with over 1 percent of the Bitcoin supply, Bitcoin Magazine, 19 August,

https://bitcoinmagazine.com/articles/how-the-plustoken-scam-absconded-with-over-1-percent-of-the-bitcoin-supply (archived at https://perma.cc/9ZWG-SQ8R)

3   Harper, C (2019) How the PlusToken scam absconded with over 1 percent of the Bitcoin supply, Bitcoin Magazine, 19 August, https://bitcoinmagazine.com/articles/how-the-plustoken-scam-absconded-with-over-1-percent-of-the-bitcoin-supply (archived at https://perma.cc/9ZWG-SQ8R)

4   Tech Telegraph (2020) PlusToken guide: The scam that brought cryptocurrency prices down, Tech Telegraph, 16 January, https://www.techtelegraph.co.uk/plus-token-guide-the-scam-that-brought-cryptocurrency-prices-down/ (archived at https://perma.cc/9HGR-A68R)

5   McIntosh, R (2019) PlusToken scam could be much larger than $2.9 billion, Finance Magnates, 3 September, https://www.financemagnates.com/cryptocurrency/news/plustoken-scam-could-be-much-larger-than-2-9-billion/ (archived at https://perma.cc/V3RS-3DVD)

6   Gash, L (2020) China arrests PlusToken primary suspects, currency.com, 30 July, https://currency.com/china-arrests-plustoken-primary-suspects (archived at https://perma.cc/W23Q-ZDZV)

7   PlusToken Wallet (nd) Plus Token Wallet make your dream come true, Plus Token Wallet, https://plustokenwallet.biz/ (archived at https://perma.cc/TZP3-DUPL)

8   Chainalysis (2020) *The 2020 State of Crypto Crime*, Chainalysis, January, https://go.chainalysis.com/rs/503-FAP-074/images/2020-Crypto-Crime-Report.pdf (archived at https://perma.cc/YWF7-QC8W)

9   Plus Token Wallet (nd) Plus Token: How to open AI Dog robot, add fund, withdrawal in details, Plus Token Wallet, https://plustokenwallet.com/plus-token-how-to-open-ai-dog-robot-add-fund-withdrawal-in-details/ (archived at https://perma.cc/57TC-QYTE)

10  McIntosh, R (2019) PlusToken scam could be much larger than $2.9 billion, Finance Magnates, 3 September, https://www.financemagnates.com/cryptocurrency/news/plustoken-scam-could-be-much-larger-than-2-9-billion/ (archived at https://perma.cc/V3RS-3DVD)

11  Chainalysis (2020) *The 2020 State of Crypto Crime*, Chainalysis, January, https://go.chainalysis.com/rs/503-FAP-074/images/2020-Crypto-Crime-Report.pdf (archived at https://perma.cc/YWF7-QC8W)

12  Plus Token Wallet (nd) Plus Token Wallet make your dream come true, Plus Token Wallet, https://plustokenwallet.biz/ (archived at https://perma.cc/TZP3-DUPL)

13  Jit (2018) PlusToken marketing plan – active user, PlusToken Wallet, 18 October, https://plustokenwallet.com/plus-token-marketing-plan-active-user/ (archived at https://perma.cc/MY62-8THC)

14  Harper, C (2019) How the PlusToken scam absconded with over 1 percent of the Bitcoin supply, Bitcoin Magazine, 19 August, https://bitcoinmagazine.com/articles/how-the-plustoken-scam-absconded-with-over-1-percent-of-the-bitcoin-supply (archived at https://perma.cc/9ZWG-SQ8R)

15  Huillet, M (2019) $3b Ponzi scheme is now allegedly dumping Bitcoin by the hundreds, Cointelegraph, 15 August, https://cointelegraph.com/news/3b-ponzi-scheme-is-now-allegedly-dumping-bitcoin-by-the-hundreds (archived at https://perma.cc/M8PA-T3N5)

16  Jit (2018) PlusToken marketing plan – active user, PlusToken Wallet, 18 October, https://plustokenwallet.com/plus-token-marketing-plan-active-user/ (archived at https://perma.cc/MY62-8THC)

17  Jit (2018) PlusToken marketing plan – active user, PlusToken Wallet, 18 October, https://plustokenwallet.com/plus-token-marketing-plan-active-user/ (archived at https://perma.cc/MY62-8THC)

18  Roots, S (2020) Plustoken exit scam – tales from the Crypt – chapter two, Changelly, 27 October, https://changelly.com/blog/plustoken-exit-scam/ (archived at https://perma.cc/QD6C-CGKR)

19  Harper, C (2019) How the PlusToken scam absconded with over 1 percent of the Bitcoin supply, Bitcoin Magazine, 19 August, https://bitcoinmagazine.com/articles/how-the-plustoken-scam-absconded-with-over-1-percent-of-the-bitcoin-supply (archived at https://perma.cc/9ZWG-SQ8R)

20  Harper, C (2019) How the PlusToken scam absconded with over 1 percent of the Bitcoin supply, Bitcoin Magazine, 19 August, https://bitcoinmagazine.com/articles/how-the-plustoken-scam-absconded-with-over-1-percent-of-the-bitcoin-supply (archived at https://perma.cc/9ZWG-SQ8R)

21  Michael (2020) PlusToken (PLUS) scam – anatomy of a Ponzi, Boxmining, 27 November, https://boxmining.com/plus-token-ponzi/ (archived at https://perma.cc/KX8T-F9P2)

22  Blocking (nd) Media: PlusToken is suspected of crashing, the current wallet can not withdraw coins, Blocking, https://blocking.net/8802/media-plustoken-is-suspected-of-crashing-the-current-wallet-can-not-withdraw-coins/ (archived at https://perma.cc/8ZSL-QC3P)

23  Michael (2020) PlusToken (PLUS) scam – anatomy of a Ponzi, Boxmining, 27 November, https://boxmining.com/plus-token-ponzi/ (archived at https://perma.cc/KX8T-F9P2)

24  Pick, L (2016) Bitcoin celebrates 7th birthday, Finance Magnates, 3 January, https://www.financemagnates.com/cryptocurrency/education-centre/bitcoin-celebrates-7th-birthday/ (archived at https://perma.cc/MZU3-RCTZ)

25  Silkjær, T (2020) Is this $3 billion crypto Ponzi still alive? Forbes, 6 July, https://www.forbes.com/sites/thomassilkjaer/2020/07/06/is-this-3-billion-crypto-ponzi-still-alive/?sh=a07235d4d42 (archived at https://perma.cc/2RQR-VURP)

26  PlusToken Wallet (nd) PlusToken: How to open AI dog robot, add fund, withdrawal in details, PlusToken Wallet, https://plustokenwallet.com/plus-token-how-to-open-ai-dog-robot-add-fund-withdrawal-in-details/ (archived at https://perma.cc/57TC-QYTE)

27  Vigna, P (2020) Cryptocurrency scams took in more than $4 billion in 2019, *The Wall Street Journal*, 8 February, https://www.wsj.com/articles/cryptocurrency-scams-took-in-more-than-4-billion-in-2019-11581184800 (archived at https://perma.cc/K9YS-MN7J)

28  Osborne, C (2020) China arrests over 100 people suspected of involvement in PlusToken cryptocurrency scam, ZDnet, 31 July, https://www.zdnet.com/article/china-arrests-over-100-people-suspected-of-involvement-in-plustoken-cryptocurrency-scam/ (archived at https://perma.cc/Q3G6-WBNU)

29  Harper, C (2019) How the PlusToken scam absconded with over 1 percent of the Bitcoin supply, Bitcoin Magazine, 19 August, https://bitcoinmagazine.com/articles/how-the-plustoken-scam-absconded-with-over-1-percent-of-the-bitcoin-supply (archived at https://perma.cc/9ZWG-SQ8R)

30  Power, J (2019) Is Vanuatu's deportation of six Chinese nationals an erosion of its democratic rights at Beijing's bidding? *This Week in Asia*, 10 July, https://www.scmp.com/week-asia/geopolitics/article/3018076/vanuatus-deportation-six-chinese-nationals-erosion-its (archived at https://perma.cc/5FGV-LS94)

31 Harper, C (2019) How the PlusToken scam absconded with over
1 percent of the Bitcoin supply, Bitcoin Magazine, 19 August,
https://bitcoinmagazine.com/articles/how-the-plustoken-scam-
absconded-with-over-1-percent-of-the-bitcoin-supply (archived at
https://perma.cc/9ZWG-SQ8R)

32 Qader, A (2019) Crypto wallet PlusToken pulls off alleged exit scam,
Finance Magnates, 1 July, https://www.financemagnates.com/
cryptocurrency/news/crypto-wallet-plustoken-pulls-off-alleged-exit-
scam/ (archived at https://perma.cc/T7J8-HXNS)

33 Harper, C (2019) How the PlusToken scam absconded with over
1 percent of the Bitcoin supply, Bitcoin Magazine, 19 August, https://
bitcoinmagazine.com/articles/how-the-plustoken-scam-absconded-
with-over-1-percent-of-the-bitcoin-supply (archived at https://perma.
cc/9ZWG-SQ8R)

34 Team, C (2019) PlusToken scammers didn't just steal $2+ billion
worth of cryptocurrency. They may also be driving down the price of
Bitcoin [updated 3/12/2020], Insights, 16 December, https://blog.
chainalysis.com/reports/plustoken-scam-bitcoin-price (archived at
https://perma.cc/46WT-6ZGJ)

35 Ciphertrace (2020) *Cryptocurrency Crime and Anti-Money
Laundering Report, Spring 2020*, Ciphertrace, https://ciphertrace.com/
wp-content/uploads/2020/06/spring-2020-cryptocurrency-anti-money-
laundering-report.pdf (archived at https://perma.cc/UYM3-YH3A)

36 Wo Token World Team (nd), https://wotokenworldteam.com/
(archived at https://perma.cc/ZZ2P-ECJT)

37 Haig, S (2020) PlusToken scammer implicated in China's second
ten-figure crypto Ponzi, Cointelegraph, 16 May, https://cointelegraph.
com/news/plustoken-scammer-implicated-in-chinas-second-ten-figure-
crypto-ponzi (archived at https://perma.cc/9S7L-MNVZ)

38 Haig, S (2020) PlusToken scammer implicated in China's second
ten-figure crypto Ponzi, Cointelegraph, 16 May, https://cointelegraph.
com/news/plustoken-scammer-implicated-in-chinas-second-ten-figure-
crypto-ponzi (archived at https://perma.cc/9S7L-MNVZ)

39 Redman, J (2020) 6 members of the multi-billion dollar PlusToken
scam charged with fraud in China, Bitcoin.com, 9 September, https://
news.bitcoin.com/6-members-of-the-multi-billion-dollar-plustoken-
scam-charged-with-fraud-in-china/ (archived at https://perma.cc/
JYZ7-KVNK)

40 Gash, L (2020) China arrests PlusToken primary suspects, currency. com, 30 July, https://currency.com/china-arrests-plustoken-primary-suspects (archived at https://perma.cc/W23Q-ZDZV)

## Chapter 6

1 Saminather, N (2020) Canadian cryptocurrency firm collapsed due to Ponzi scheme by late founder, regulator says, Reuters, 11 June, https://www.reuters.com/article/us-crypto-currencies-quadriga/canadian-cryptocurrency-firm-collapsed-due-to-ponzi-scheme-by-late-founder-regulator-says-idINKBN23I3AF?edition-redirect=in (archived at https://perma.cc/3KJN-YFKR)

2 Rushe, D (2019) Cryptocurrency investors locked out of $190m after exchange founder dies, *Guardian*, 4 February, https://www.theguardian.com/technology/2019/feb/04/quadrigacx-canada-cryptocurrency-exchange-locked-gerald-cotten (archived at https://perma.cc/B3FW-Z9GH)

3 Rich, N (2019) Ponzi schemes, private yachts, and a missing $250 million in crypto: The strange tale of Quadriga, Vanity Fair, 22 November, https://www.vanityfair.com/news/2019/11/the-strange-tale-of-quadriga-gerald-cotten (archived at https://perma.cc/K6C9-RWU2)

4 Rich, N (2019) Ponzi schemes, private yachts, and a missing $250 million in crypto: The strange tale of Quadriga, Vanity Fair, 22 November, https://www.vanityfair.com/news/2019/11/the-strange-tale-of-quadriga-gerald-cotten (archived at https://perma.cc/K6C9-RWU2)

5 Rich, N (2019) Ponzi schemes, private yachts, and a missing $250 million in crypto: The strange tale of Quadriga, Vanity Fair, 22 November, https://www.vanityfair.com/news/2019/11/the-strange-tale-of-quadriga-gerald-cotten (archived at https://perma.cc/K6C9-RWU2)

6 Castaldo, J (2019) Before Quadriga: How shady ventures in Gerald Cotten's youth led to the creation of his ill-fated cryptocurrency exchange, *The Globe and Mail*, 24 November, https://www.theglobeandmail.com/business/article-before-quadriga-how-shady-ventures-in-gerald-cottens-youth-led-to/ (archived at https://perma.cc/U5DF-GNNP)

7   Rich, N (2019) Ponzi schemes, private yachts, and a missing $250 million in crypto: The strange tale of Quadriga, Vanity Fair, 22 November, https://www.vanityfair.com/news/2019/11/the-strange-tale-of-quadriga-gerald-cotten (archived at https://perma.cc/K6C9-RWU2)

8   Castaldo, J (2019) Before Quadriga: How shady ventures in Gerald Cotten's youth led to the creation of his ill-fated cryptocurrency exchange, The Globe and Mail, 24 November, https://www.theglobeandmail.com/business/article-before-quadriga-how-shady-ventures-in-gerald-cottens-youth-led-to/ (archived at https://perma.cc/U5DF-GNNP)

9   Vanderklippe, N (2019) How did Gerald Cotten die? A Quadriga mystery, from India to Canada and back, The Globe and Mail, 1 March, https://www.theglobeandmail.com/world/article-how-did-gerald-cotten-die-a-quadriga-mystery-from-india-to-canada/ (archived at https://perma.cc/9Y39-H6EW)

10  BBC (2019) Quadriga: Lawyers for users of bankrupt crypto firm seek exhumation of founder 13 December, https://www.bbc.co.uk/news/world-us-canada-50751899 (archived at https://perma.cc/W385-4B99)

11  Vanderklippe, N (2019) How did Gerald Cotten die? A Quadriga mystery, from India to Canada and back, The Globe and Mail, 1 March, https://www.theglobeandmail.com/world/article-how-did-gerald-cotten-die-a-quadriga-mystery-from-india-to-canada/ (archived at https://perma.cc/9Y39-H6EW)

12  Beauregard, M (2019) Show us the money! Quadriga investors demand answers over Gerald Cotten's mystery death, The Times, 8 February, https://www.thetimes.co.uk/article/show-us-the-money-quadriga-investors-demand-answers-over-gerald-cottens-mystery-death-kzxk06z6m (archived at https://perma.cc/N3QB-HD6T)

13  Rich, N (2019) Ponzi schemes, private yachts, and a missing $250 million in crypto: The strange tale of Quadriga, Vanity Fair, 22 November, https://www.vanityfair.com/news/2019/11/the-strange-tale-of-quadriga-gerald-cotten (archived at https://perma.cc/K6C9-RWU2)

14  OSC (2020) QuadrigaCX: A review by staff of the Ontario Securities Commission, Ontario Securities Commission, 14 April,

https://www.osc.gov.on.ca/quadrigacxreport/web/files/QuadrigaCX-A-Review-by-Staff-of-the-Ontario-Securities-Commission.pdf (archived at https://perma.cc/F92R-9FKN)

15 Moskvitch, K (2019) How a tragic death (and paranoia) wiped out £145m of crypto wealth, Wired, 6 February, https://www.wired.co.uk/article/quadrigacx-cryptocurrency-exchange-canada (archived at https://perma.cc/6TUY-XNUR)

16 Webb, S (2019) 'It's like burning cash': QuadrigaCX's Gerald Cotten spoke about losing keys in 2014, Coin Rivet, 18 February, https://coinrivet.com/its-like-burning-cash-quadrigacxs-gerald-cotten-spoke-about-losing-keys-in-2014/ (archived at https://perma.cc/36DZ-GCJX)

17 Rich, N (2019) Ponzi schemes, private yachts, and a missing $250 million in crypto: The strange tale of Quadriga, Vanity Fair, 22 November, https://www.vanityfair.com/news/2019/11/the-strange-tale-of-quadriga-gerald-cotten (archived at https://perma.cc/K6C9-RWU2)

18 OSC (2020) *QuadrigaCX: A review by staff of the Ontario Securities Commission, Ontario Securities Commission*, 14 April, https://www.osc.gov.on.ca/quadrigacxreport/web/files/QuadrigaCX-A-Review-by-Staff-of-the-Ontario-Securities-Commission.pdf (archived at https://perma.cc/F92R-9FKN)

19 De, N (2019) Mystery Man, Coin Desk, https://www.coindesk.com/most-influential/2019/gerald-cotten (archived at https://perma.cc/3CR9-DERS)

20 De, N (2019) A big four audit firm lost $1 million in Bitcoin. Victims are losing patience, Coin Desk, 16 August, https://www.coindesk.com/a-big-four-audit-firm-lost-1-million-in-bitcoin-victims-are-losing-patience (archived at https://perma.cc/A8AY-Z64G)

21 Rich, N (2019) Ponzi schemes, private yachts, and a missing $250 million in crypto: The strange tale of Quadriga, Vanity Fair, 22 November, https://www.vanityfair.com/news/2019/11/the-strange-tale-of-quadriga-gerald-cotten (archived at https://perma.cc/K6C9-RWU2)

22 Bloomberg (2019) After Singh brothers' alleged fraud, new Fortis CEO plans fixes, *The Economic Times*, 20 August, https://economictimes.indiatimes.com/industry/healthcare/biotech/healthcare/after-singh-brothers-alleged-fraud-new-fortis-ceo-plans-fixes/articleshow/70747663.cms?from=mdr (archived at https://perma.cc/WS3U-VS5M)

23 Murphy, M (2015) Revealed: London bank accounts could hold key dead crypto tycoons, *Telegraph*, 15 March, https://www.telegraph.co.uk/technology/2020/03/15/revealed-london-bank-accounts-could-hold-key-dead-crypto-tycoons/ (archived at https://perma.cc/LU2G-Q4EP)

24 Leeder, J (2019) A laptop, a sudden death and $180-million gone missing: Quadriga investors search for their cryptocurrency, *The Globe and Mail*, 7 February, https://www.theglobeandmail.com/business/article-nova-scotia-judge-plans-to-grant-stay-of-proceedings-for-embattled/ (archived at https://perma.cc/4SJH-PKZJ)

25 Rich, N (2019) Ponzi schemes, private yachts, and a missing $250 million in crypto: The strange tale of Quadriga, Vanity Fair, 22 November, https://www.vanityfair.com/news/2019/11/the-strange-tale-of-quadriga-gerald-cotten (archived at https://perma.cc/K6C9-RWU2)

26 Rich, N (2019) Ponzi schemes, private yachts, and a missing $250 million in crypto: The strange tale of Quadriga, Vanity Fair, 22 November, https://www.vanityfair.com/news/2019/11/the-strange-tale-of-quadriga-gerald-cotten (archived at https://perma.cc/K6C9-RWU2)

27 Rich, N (2019) Ponzi schemes, private yachts, and a missing $250 million in crypto: The strange tale of Quadriga, Vanity Fair, 22 November, https://www.vanityfair.com/news/2019/11/the-strange-tale-of-quadriga-gerald-cotten (archived at https://perma.cc/K6C9-RWU2)

28 Rich, N (2019) Ponzi schemes, private yachts, and a missing $250 million in crypto: The strange tale of Quadriga, Vanity Fair, 22 November, https://www.vanityfair.com/news/2019/11/the-strange-tale-of-quadriga-gerald-cotten (archived at https://perma.cc/K6C9-RWU2)

29 Markay, L (2018) Feds seized a fortune from #Resistance icons accused of boosting online Ponzi schemes, The Daily Beast, May 22, https://www.thedailybeast.com/feds-seized-a-fortune-from-resistance-icons-accused-of-boosting-online-ponzi-schemes (archived at https://perma.cc/D7T8-EGNX)

30 Castaldo, J (2019) Before Quadriga: How shady ventures in Gerald Cotten's youth led to the creation of his ill-fated cryptocurrency

exchange, *The Globe and Mail*, 24 November, https://www.
theglobeandmail.com/business/article-before-quadriga-how-shady-
ventures-in-gerald-cottens-youth-led-to/ (archived at https://perma.cc/
U5DF-GNNP)

31 Castaldo, J (2019) Before Quadriga: How shady ventures in Gerald
Cotten's youth led to the creation of his ill-fated cryptocurrency
exchange, *The Globe and Mail*, 24 November, https://www.
theglobeandmail.com/business/article-before-quadriga-how-shady-
ventures-in-gerald-cottens-youth-led-to/ (archived at https://perma.cc/
U5DF-GNNP)

32 Castaldo, J (2019) Before Quadriga: How shady ventures in Gerald
Cotten's youth led to the creation of his ill-fated cryptocurrency
exchange, *The Globe and Mail*, 24 November, https://www.
theglobeandmail.com/business/article-before-quadriga-how-shady-
ventures-in-gerald-cottens-youth-led-to/ (archived at https://perma.cc/
U5DF-GNNP)

33 Castaldo, J (2019) Before Quadriga: How shady ventures in Gerald
Cotten's youth led to the creation of his ill-fated cryptocurrency
exchange, *The Globe and Mail*, 24 November, https://www.
theglobeandmail.com/business/article-before-quadriga-how-shady-
ventures-in-gerald-cottens-youth-led-to/ (archived at https://perma.cc/
U5DF-GNNP)

34 Castaldo, J (2019) Before Quadriga: How shady ventures in Gerald
Cotten's youth led to the creation of his ill-fated cryptocurrency
exchange, *The Globe and Mail*, 24 November, https://www.
theglobeandmail.com/business/article-before-quadriga-how-shady-
ventures-in-gerald-cottens-youth-led-to/ (archived at https://perma.cc/
U5DF-GNNP)

35 Alexander, D (2019) Criminal past haunts surviving founder of
troubled crypto exchange, Bloomberg, 19 March, https://www.
bloomberg.com/news/articles/2019-03-19/from-fraud-to-fintech-
quadriga-co-founder-s-past-crimes-emerge (archived at https://perma.
cc/A9HD-8FDS)

36 Kumar, N (2013) Founders of 'PayPal for criminals' Liberty Reserve
are charged with money laundering, *Independent*, 29 May,
https://www.independent.co.uk/news/world/americas/founders-
paypal-criminals-liberty-reserve-are-charged-money-
laundering-8635248.html (archived at https://perma.cc/9TEQ-JU8S)

37  Castaldo, J (2019) Before Quadriga: How shady ventures in Gerald
    Cotten's youth led to the creation of his ill-fated cryptocurrency
    exchange, *The Globe and Mail*, 24 November, https://www.
    theglobeandmail.com/business/article-before-quadriga-how-shady-
    ventures-in-gerald-cottens-youth-led-to/ (archived at https://perma.cc/
    U5DF-GNNP)

38  Castaldo, J (2019) Before Quadriga: How shady ventures in Gerald
    Cotten's youth led to the creation of his ill-fated cryptocurrency
    exchange, *The Globe and Mail*, 24 November, https://www.
    theglobeandmail.com/business/article-before-quadriga-how-shady-
    ventures-in-gerald-cottens-youth-led-to/ (archived at https://perma.cc/
    U5DF-GNNP)

39  Dhanani, O (2019) TalkGold – the Ponzi forum where Quadriga's
    Patryn and Cotten first met, Amy Caster, 12 February, https://amycastor.
    com/tag/omar-dhanani/ (archived at https://perma.cc/ZVT4-UFLU) and
    Rich, N (2019) Ponzi schemes, private yachts, and a missing $250
    million in crypto: The strange tale of Quadriga, Vanity Fair, 22
    November, https://www.vanityfair.com/news/2019/11/the-strange-tale-
    of-quadriga-gerald-cotten (archived at https://perma.cc/K6C9-RWU2)

40  Rich, N (2019) Ponzi schemes, private yachts, and a missing
    $250 million in crypto: The strange tale of Quadriga, Vanity Fair,
    22 November, https://www.vanityfair.com/news/2019/11/the-strange-
    tale-of-quadriga-gerld-cotten (archived at https://perma.cc/K6C9-
    RWU2)

41  Rich, N (2019) Ponzi schemes, private yachts, and a missing
    $250 million in crypto: The strange tale of Quadriga, Vanity Fair,
    22 November, https://www.vanityfair.com/news/2019/11/the-strange-
    tale-of-quadriga-gerald-cotten (archived at https://perma.cc/K6C9-
    RWU2)

42  Posadzki, A (2019) Quadriga monitor's report offers strongest
    evidence yet of fraud, experts say, *The Globe and Mail*, 20 June,
    https://www.theglobeandmail.com/business/article-deceased-
    quadrigacx-ceo-gerald-cotten-moved-customer-funds-to-personal/
    (archived at https://perma.cc/D6J5-TH4T)

43  Macdonald, M (2019) FBI reaching out to Quadriga users as it steps
    up investigation, *The Globe and Mail*, 4 June, https://www.
    theglobeandmail.com/business/article-fbi-reaching-out-to-quadriga-
    users-as-it-steps-up-investigation/ (archived at https://perma.cc/
    Q4N9-YTHN)

44  De, N (2020) QuadrigaCX users' law firm launches blockchain analytics investigation, Yahoo News, 8 September, https://uk.news. yahoo.com/quadrigacx-users-law-firm-launches-080104467. html?guccounter=1 (archived at https://perma.cc/X9K4-UH3Z)

45  Rich, N (2019) Ponzi schemes, private yachts, and a missing $250 million in crypto: The strange tale of Quadriga, Vanity Fair, 22 November, https:// www.vanityfair.com/news/2019/11/the-strange-tale-of-quadriga-gerald-cotten (archived at https://perma.cc/K6C9-RWU2)

46  Rich, N (2019) Ponzi schemes, private yachts, and a missing $250 million in crypto: The strange tale of Quadriga, Vanity Fair, 22 November, https://www.vanityfair.com/news/2019/11/the-strange-tale-of-quadriga-gerald-cotten (archived at https://perma.cc/K6C9-RWU2)

47  Rich, N (2019) Ponzi schemes, private yachts, and a missing $250 million in crypto: The strange tale of Quadriga, Vanity Fair, 22 November, https://www.vanityfair.com/news/2019/11/the-strange-tale-of-quadriga-gerald-cotten (archived at https://perma.cc/K6C9-RWU2)

48  OSC (2020) *QuadrigaCX: A review by staff of the Ontario Securities Commission, Ontario Securities Commission,* 14 April, https://www. osc.gov.on.ca/quadrigacxreport/web/files/QuadrigaCX-A-Review-by-Staff-of-the-Ontario-Securities-Commission.pdf (archived at https:// perma.cc/F92R-9FKN)

49  Murphy, M (2015) Revealed: London bank accounts could hold key dead crypto tycoons, *Telegraph*, 15 March, https://www.telegraph.co. uk/technology/2020/03/15/revealed-london-bank-accounts-could-hold-key-dead-crypto-tycoons/ (archived at https://perma.cc/LU2G-Q4EP)

50  Posadzki, A (2019) Quadriga monitor's report offers strongest evidence yet of fraud, experts say, *The Globe and Mail*, 20 June, https://www.theglobeandmail.com/business/article-deceased-quadrigacx-ceo-gerald-cotten-moved-customer-funds-to-personal/ (archived at https://perma.cc/D6J5-TH4T)

51  Hochstein, M and De, N (2019) QuadrigaCX CEO set up fake crypto exchange accounts with customer funds, Coindesk, 20 June, https://www. coindesk.com/quadrigacx-ceo-set-up-fake-crypto-exchange-accounts-with-customer-funds (archived at https://perma.cc/B6MF-LFH5)

52  Rich, N (2019) Ponzi schemes, private yachts, and a missing
$250 million in crypto: The strange tale of Quadriga, Vanity Fair,
22 November, https://www.vanityfair.com/news/2019/11/the-strange-
tale-of-quadriga-gerald-cotten (archived at https://perma.cc/K6C9-
RWU2)

53  Beedham, M (2019) Report: QuadrigaCX CEO used fake
trades to misappropriate users' cryptocurrency, TNW, 20 June,
https://thenextweb.com/hardfork/2019/06/20/quadrigacx-fraudulent-
cryptocurrency-exchange/ (archived at https://perma.cc/A7FF-BMDA)

54  Rich, N (2019) Ponzi schemes, private yachts, and a missing
$250 million in crypto: The strange tale of Quadriga, Vanity Fair,
22 November, https://www.vanityfair.com/news/2019/11/the-strange-
tale-of-quadriga-gerald-cotten (archived at https://perma.cc/K6C9-
RWU2)

55  Kimberley, D (2019) QuadrigaCX CEO made 67,000 trades with
client funds, Finance Magnates, https://www.financemagnates.com/
cryptocurrency/exchange/quadrigacx-ceo-made-67000-trades-with-
client-funds/ (archived at https://perma.cc/T47N-KB44)

56  Kimberley, D (2019) QuadrigaCX CEO made 67,000 trades with
client funds, Finance Magnates, https://www.financemagnates.com/
cryptocurrency/exchange/quadrigacx-ceo-made-67000-trades-with-
client-funds/ (archived at https://perma.cc/T47N-KB44)

57  OSC (2020) *QuadrigaCX: A review by staff of the Ontario Securities
Commission, Ontario Securities Commission*, 14 April, https://www.
osc.gov.on.ca/quadrigacxreport/web/files/QuadrigaCX-A-Review-by-
Staff-of-the-Ontario-Securities-Commission.pdf (archived at
https://perma.cc/F92R-9FKN)

58  Rich, N (2019) Ponzi schemes, private yachts, and a missing
$250 million in crypto: The strange tale of Quadriga, Vanity Fair,
22 November, https://www.vanityfair.com/news/2019/11/the-strange-
tale-of-quadriga-gerald-cotten (archived at https://perma.cc/K6C9-
RWU2)

59  Castaldo, J (2019) Before Quadriga: How shady ventures in Gerald
Cotten's youth led to the creation of his ill-fated cryptocurrency
exchange, *The Globe and Mail*, 24 November, https://www.
theglobeandmail.com/business/article-before-quadriga-how-shady-
ventures-in-gerald-cottens-youth-led-to/ (archived at https://perma.cc/
U5DF-GNNP)

60 Castaldo, J (2019) Before Quadriga: How shady ventures in Gerald Cotten's youth led to the creation of his ill-fated cryptocurrency exchange, *The Globe and Mail*, 24 November, https://www.theglobeandmail.com/business/article-before-quadriga-how-shady-ventures-in-gerald-cottens-youth-led-to/ (archived at https://perma.cc/U5DF-GNNP)

61 Rich, N (2019) Ponzi schemes, private yachts, and a missing $250 million in crypto: The strange tale of Quadriga, Vanity Fair, 22 November, https://www.vanityfair.com/news/2019/11/the-strange-tale-of-quadriga-gerald-cotten (archived at https://perma.cc/K6C9-RWU2)

62 Vanderklippe, N (2019) How did Gerald Cotten die? A Quadriga mystery, from India to Canada and back, *The Globe and Mail*, 1 March, https://www.theglobeandmail.com/world/article-how-did-gerald-cotten-die-a-quadriga-mystery-from-india-to-canada/ (archived at https://perma.cc/9Y39-H6EW)

63 BBC (2019) Quadriga: Lawyers for users of bankrupt crypto firm seek exhumation of founder, BBC, 13 December, https://www.bbc.com/news/world-us-canada-50751899 (archived at https://perma.cc/4NTL-ULWC)

64 OSC (2020) *QuadrigaCX: A review by staff of the Ontario Securities Commission, Ontario Securities Commission*, 14 April, https://www.osc.gov.on.ca/quadrigacxreport/web/files/QuadrigaCX-A-Review-by-Staff-of-the-Ontario-Securities-Commission.pdf (archived at https://perma.cc/F92R-9FKN)

65 OSC (2020) *QuadrigaCX: A review by staff of the Ontario Securities Commission, Ontario Securities Commission*, 14 April, https://www.osc.gov.on.ca/quadrigacxreport/web/files/QuadrigaCX-A-Review-by-Staff-of-the-Ontario-Securities-Commission.pdf (archived at https://perma.cc/F92R-9FKN)

66 OSC (2020) *QuadrigaCX: A review by staff of the Ontario Securities Commission, Ontario Securities Commission*, 14 April, https://www.osc.gov.on.ca/quadrigacxreport/web/files/QuadrigaCX-A-Review-by-Staff-of-the-Ontario-Securities-Commission.pdf (archived at https://perma.cc/F92R-9FKN)

## Chapter 7

1    Gibbs, S (2017) Head of Mt. Gox Bitcoin exchange on trial for embezzlement and loss of millions, *Guardian*, 11 July, https://www. theguardian.com/technology/2017/jul/11/gox-bitcoin-exchange-mark-karpeles-on-trial-japan-embezzlement-loss-of-millions (archived at https://perma.cc/5QGM-JS44)

2    Cook, J (2018) The CEO of Bitcoin exchange Mt. Gox described what it was like to discover he had been hacked: 'It felt like I was about to die', Business Insider, 7 March, https://www.businessinsider. com/mt-gox-ceo-mark-karpeles-hacked-i-was-about-to-die-2018-3?r=US&IR=T (archived at https://perma.cc/AW6Q-CARE)

3    McMillan, M (2014) The inside story of Mt. Gox, Bitcoin's $460 million disaster, Wired, 3 March, https://www.wired.com/2014/03/bitcoin-exchange/ (archived at https://perma.cc/KSV2-QJ58)

4    Hajdarbegovic, N (2014) Mt. Gox founder claims he lost $50k in exchange's collapse, Coindesk, 2 May, https://www.coindesk.com/mt-gox-founder-claims-lost-50000-exchanges-collapse (archived at https://perma.cc/JVV8-LQ87)

5    Beedham, M (2019) A brief history of Mt. Gox, the $3B Bitcoin tragedy that just won't end, TNW, 9 December, https://thenextweb.com/hardfork/2019/03/14/a-brief-history-of-mt-gox-the-3b-bitcoin-tragedy-that-just-wont-end/ (archived at https://perma.cc/G9YS-UZR5)

6    McMillan, M (2014) The inside story of Mt. Gox, Bitcoin's $460 million disaster, Wired, 3 March, https://www.wired.com/2014/03/bitcoin-exchange/ (archived at https://perma.cc/KSV2-QJ58)

7    Magazine, B (2020) Infographic: An overview of compromised Bitcoin exchange events, Merian Ventures, 24 February, https://www. merianventures.com/perspectives/infographic-an-overview-of-compromised-bitcoin-exchange-events (archived at https://perma.cc/N28G-QLLA)

8    Magazine, B (2020) Infographic: An overview of compromised Bitcoin exchange events, Merian Ventures, 24 February, https://www. merianventures.com/perspectives/infographic-an-overview-of-compromised-bitcoin-exchange-events (archived at https://perma.cc/N28G-QLLA)

9   Schwartz, M (2014) Mt. Gox Bitcoin meltdown: What went wrong, Darkreading, 3 March, https://www.darkreading.com/attacks-and-breaches/mt-gox-bitcoin-meltdown-what-went-wrong/d/d-id/1114091 (archived at https://perma.cc/Q88V-6R7L) and Cybereason (nd) The fall of Mt. Gox: Part 1, https://malicious.life/episode/ep-40-the-fall-of-mt-gox-part-1/ (archived at https://perma.cc/DL3C-9SZC)

10  Cybereason (nd) The fall of Mt. Gox: Part 1, https://malicious.life/episode/ep-40-the-fall-of-mt-gox-part-1/ (archived at https://perma.cc/DL3C-9SZC)

11  Sedgwick, K (2019) Bitcoin history part 17: That time Mt. Gox destroyed 2,609 BTC, Bitcoin.com, 20 September, https://news.bitcoin.com/bitcoin-history-part-17-that-time-mt-gox-destroyed-2609-btc/ (archived at https://perma.cc/BGB6-9J8Q)

12  Smolaks, M (2013) CoinLab sues Mt. Gox Bitcoin exchange for $75 million, Silicon, 3 May, https://www.silicon.co.uk/workspace/coinlab-sues-mt-gox-bitcoin-exchange-for-75-million-115238?cmpredirect (archived at https://perma.cc/TL8E-7DN8)

13  Dillet, R (2013) Feds seize another $2.1 million from Mt. Gox, adding up to $5 million. TC, 23 August, https://techcrunch.com/2013/08/23/feds-seize-another-2-1-million-from-mt-gox-adding-up-to-5-million/ (archived at https://perma.cc/2GZ6-Y8SG)

14  Associated Press (2017) Mt. Gox CEO facing trial in Japan as Bitcoin gains traction, Business Insider, 10 July, https://www.businessinsider.com/ap-mt-gox-ceo-facing-trial-in-japan-as-bitcoin-gains-traction-2017-7?r=US&IR=T (archived at https://perma.cc/U3N5-D8XK)

15  AGP Law Firm/AG Paphitis & Co LLC (2019) Cyprus: Defending reputation is priceless... €38 million compensation for our clients Mayzus being the victims of BTC-E, Mondaq, 30 October, https://www.mondaq.com/cyprus/white-collar-crime-anti-corruption-fraud/858376/defending-reputation-is-priceless-38-million-compensation-for-our-clients-mayzus-being-the-victims-of-btc-e (archived at https://perma.cc/G9EX-DTLG)

16  Wong, J (2014) 68 per cent of Mt. Gox users still awaiting their funds, survey reveals, Coindesk, 25 July, https://www.coindesk.com/mt-gox-users-awaiting-funds-survey-reveals (archived at https://perma.cc/U7CC-T728)

17  BBC (2014) MtGox gives bankruptcy details, BBC, 4 March,
    https://www.bbc.co.uk/news/technology-26420932 (archived at
    https://perma.cc/BTC4-K3C6)

18  Hornyak, T (2014) FAQ: What happened to Mt. Gox, Computerworld,
    6 March, https://www.computerworld.com/article/2488322/faq--what-
    happened-to-mt--gox.html (archived at https://perma.cc/BX7D-W65Q)

19  Nilsson, K (2020) The 80,000 stolen MtGox Bitcoins, Wizsec,
    19 June, https://blog.wizsec.jp/2020/06/mtgox-march-2011-theft.html
    (archived at https://perma.cc/NC2U-JHGA)

20  Tuwiner, J (2020) What was the Mt. Gox hack? Buy Bitcoin
    Worldwide, 22 March, https://www.buybitcoinworldwide.com/
    mt-gox-hack/ (archived at https://perma.cc/WF49-YGKS)

21  Wieczner, J (2018) Mt. Gox and the surprising redemption of Bitcoin's
    biggest villain, Fortune, 19 April, https://fortune.com/longform/bitcoin-
    mt-gox-hack-karpeles/ (archived at https://perma.cc/KC6D-4F8C)

22  Byford, S (2014) 'Mt. Gox, where is our money?' The Verge,
    19 February, https://www.theverge.com/2014/2/19/5425220/protest-
    at-mt-gox-bitcoin-exchange-in-tokyo (archived at https://perma.
    cc/9BKW-DPE2)

23  Wieczner, J (2018) Mt. Gox and the surprising redemption of
    Bitcoin's biggest villain, Fortune, 19 April, https://fortune.com/
    longform/bitcoin-mt-gox-hack-karpeles/ (archived at https://perma.cc/
    KC6D-4F8C)

24  Wieczner, J (2018) Mt. Gox and the surprising redemption of
    Bitcoin's biggest villain, Fortune, 19 April, https://fortune.com/
    longform/bitcoin-mt-gox-hack-karpeles/ (archived at https://perma.cc/
    KC6D-4F8C)

25  Wieczner, J (2018) Mt. Gox and the surprising redemption of
    Bitcoin's biggest villain, Fortune, 19 April, https://fortune.com/
    longform/bitcoin-mt-gox-hack-karpeles/ (archived at https://perma.cc/
    KC6D-4F8C)

26  Wieczner, J (2018) Mt. Gox and the surprising redemption of
    Bitcoin's biggest villain, Fortune, 19 April, https://fortune.com/
    longform/bitcoin-mt-gox-hack-karpeles/ (archived at https://perma.cc/
    KC6D-4F8C)

27  Nilsson, K (2015) The missing MtGox Bitcoins, Wizsec, 19 April,
    https://blog.wizsec.jp/2015/04/the-missing-mtgox-bitcoins.html
    (archived at https://perma.cc/8AES-XM9U)

28  Nilsson, K (2017) Breaking open the MtGox case, part 1, Wizsec,
    27 July, https://blog.wizsec.jp/2017/07/breaking-open-mtgox-1.html
    (archived at https://perma.cc/P4RH-VZRZ)

29  Wieczner, J (2018) Mt. Gox and the surprising redemption of
    Bitcoin's biggest villain, Fortune, 19 April, https://fortune.com/
    longform/bitcoin-mt-gox-hack-karpeles/ (archived at https://perma.cc/
    KC6D-4F8C)

30  Patterson, J (2017) Recently arrested, Alexander Vinnik suspected of
    ties to MtGox theft, Finance Magnates, 26 July, https://www.
    financemagnates.com/cryptocurrency/news/recently-arrested-
    alexander-vinnik-suspected-ties-mtgox-theft/ (archived at
    https://perma.cc/4EF9-GJUY)

31  Patterson, J (2017) Recently arrested, Alexander Vinnik suspected of
    ties to MtGox theft, Finance Magnates, 26 July, https://www.
    financemagnates.com/cryptocurrency/news/recently-arrested-
    alexander-vinnik-suspected-ties-mtgox-theft/ (archived at https://
    perma.cc/4EF9-GJUY)

32  Brandom, R (2017) Why the feds took down one of Bitcoin's largest
    exchanges, The Verge, 29 July, https://www.theverge.
    com/2017/7/29/16060344/btce-bitcoin-exchange-takedown-mt-gox-
    theft-law-enforcement (archived at https://perma.cc/
    WC2R-XYBF)

33  Wieczner, J (2018) Mt. Gox and the surprising redemption of
    Bitcoin's biggest villain, Fortune, 19 April, https://fortune.com/
    longform/bitcoin-mt-gox-hack-karpeles/ (archived at https://perma.cc/
    KC6D-4F8C)

34  Wieczner, J (2018) Mt. Gox and the surprising redemption of
    Bitcoin's biggest villain, Fortune, 19 April, https://fortune.com/
    longform/bitcoin-mt-gox-hack-karpeles/ (archived at https://perma.cc/
    KC6D-4F8C)

35  Baydakova, A (2020) BTC-e operator Vinnik sentenced to 5 years
    in prison on money laundering charges, Coindesk, 7 December,
    https://www.coindesk.com/btc-e-operator-vinnik-sentenced-to-5-
    years-in-prison-on-money-laundering-charges (archived at
    https://perma.cc/U3AQ-T9TB)

36  The Willy Report (2014) The Willy Report: Proof of massive
    fraudulent trading activity at Mt. Gox, and how it has affected the

price of Bitcoin, 25 May, https://willyreport.wordpress.
com/2014/05/25/the-willy-report-proof-of-massive-fraudulent-
trading-activity-at-mt-gox-and-how-it-has-affected-the-price-of-
bitcoin/ (archived at https://perma.cc/KPZ2-PMBC)

37  The Willy Report (2014) The Willy Report: Proof of massive
    fraudulent trading activity at Mt. Gox, and how it has affected the
    price of Bitcoin, 25 May, https://willyreport.wordpress.
    com/2014/05/25/the-willy-report-proof-of-massive-fraudulent-
    trading-activity-at-mt-gox-and-how-it-has-affected-the-price-of-
    bitcoin/ (archived at https://perma.cc/KPZ2-PMBC)

38  Floyd, D (2019) Fraudulent trading drove Bitcoin's $150-to-$1,000
    rise in 2013: Paper, Investopedia, 25 June, https://www.investopedia.
    com/news/bots-drove-bitcoins-150to1000-rise-2013-paper/ (archived
    at https://perma.cc/WM6Z-MG99)

39  Floyd, D (2019) Fraudulent trading drove Bitcoin's $150-to-$1,000
    rise in 2013: Paper, Investopedia, 25 June, https://www.investopedia.
    com/news/bots-drove-bitcoins-150to1000-rise-2013-paper/ (archived
    at https://perma.cc/WM6Z-MG99)

40  Floyd, D (2019) Fraudulent trading drove Bitcoin's $150-to-$1,000
    rise in 2013: Paper, Investopedia, 25 June, https://www.investopedia.
    com/news/bots-drove-bitcoins-150to1000-rise-2013-paper/ (archived
    at https://perma.cc/WM6Z-MG99)

41  Leising, M (2021) Trillian dollar Mt. Gox demise as told by a Bitcoin
    insider, Bloomberg, 31 January, https://www.bloomberg.com/news/
    articles/2021-01-31/-trillion-dollar-mt-gox-demise-as-told-by-a-
    bitcoin-insider (archived at https://perma.cc/MWR8-GHNU)

42  Wieczner, J (2018) Mt. Gox and the surprising redemption of
    Bitcoin's biggest villain, Fortune, 19 April, https://fortune.com/
    longform/bitcoin-mt-gox-hack-karpeles/ (archived at https://perma.cc/
    KC6D-4F8C)

43  Pick, L (2015) Report: Karpeles rearrested again, allegedly spent
    Bitcoins on prostitutes, Finance Magnates, 2 November, https://www.
    financemagnates.com/cryptocurrency/news/report-karpeles-rearrested-
    again-allegedly-spent-bitcoins-on-prostitutes/ (archived at
    https://perma.cc/NS97-VEXY)

44 Moon, M (2019) Mt. Gox CEO Mark Karpeles cleared of embezzlement, Engadget, 15 March, https://www.engadget.com/2019-03-15-mt-gox-ceo-mark-karpeles-cleared-embezzlement.html (archived at https://perma.cc/7Z5T-KZNX)

45 Leising, M (2021) Trillian dollar Mt. Gox demise as told by a Bitcoin insider, Bloomberg, 31 January, https://www.bloomberg.com/news/articles/2021-01-31/-trillion-dollar-mt-gox-demise-as-told-by-a-bitcoin-insider (archived at https://perma.cc/MWR8-GHNU)

46 Moneyweek (2015) Mark Karpeles: The rise and fall of the cat-loving Baron of Bitcoin, Moneyweek, 12 August, https://moneyweek.com/403576/profile-of-mark-karpeles (archived at https://perma.cc/SL8J-Q3CD)

47 Moneyweek (2015) Mark Karpeles: The rise and fall of the cat-loving Baron of Bitcoin, Moneyweek, 12 August, https://moneyweek.com/403576/profile-of-mark-karpeles (archived at https://perma.cc/SL8J-Q3CD)

48 Dent, S (2021) Mt. Gox exchange users may finally get to recover some of their lost Bitcoin, Engadget, 18 January, https://www.engadget.com/mt-gox-bitcoin-users-recovery-153025831.html (archived at https://perma.cc/JHQ6-3MFN)

## Chapter 8

1 US Department of Justice (2019) Three men arrested in $722 million cryptocurrency fraud scheme, US Department of Justice, 10 December, https://www.justice.gov/usao-nj/pr/three-men-arrested-722-million-cryptocurrency-fraud-scheme (archived at https://perma.cc/8FTJ-KX49)

2 Morelli, B (2018) 50 states in 42 days: Baby Liberty becomes the youngest to travel the US, The Gazette, 7 December, https://www.thegazette.com/50-states-in-42-days-baby-liberty-becomes-the-youngest-to-travel-the-us-20181207 (archived at https://perma.cc/2Z6V-B6FY)

3 Instagram (nd) I'm the youngest person to visit all 50 states. I did it in 42 days at 43 days old! I've been to 45 countries and 4 continents. These are my adventures, Instagram, https://www.instagram.com/liberty.weeks/ (archived at https://perma.cc/AA36-BWKC)

4   Morelli, B (2018) 50 states in 42 days: Baby Liberty becomes the youngest to travel the US, The Gazette, 7 December, https://www.thegazette.com/50-states-in-42-days-baby-liberty-becomes-the-youngest-to-travel-the-us-20181207 (archived at https://perma.cc/2Z6V-B6FY)

5   Morelli, B (2018) 50 states in 42 days: Baby Liberty becomes the youngest to travel the US, The Gazette, 7 December, https://www.thegazette.com/50-states-in-42-days-baby-liberty-becomes-the-youngest-to-travel-the-us-20181207 (archived at https://perma.cc/2Z6V-B6FY)

6   Guthrie, A (2019) Anarchy, Bitcoin, and murder in Acapulco, Wired, 1 March, https://www.wired.com/story/anarchy-bitcoin-and-murder-in-mexico/ (archived at https://perma.cc/BB9L-2KAY)

7   Prendergast, A (2018) The rise and fall of a Bitcoin mining scheme that was 'too big to fail', Westword, 18 February, https://www.westword.com/news/bitclub-network-was-too-big-to-fail-but-cost-investors-722-million-11642618 (archived at https://perma.cc/68E2-8A2N)

8   Prendergast, A (2018) The rise and fall of a Bitcoin mining scheme that was 'too big to fail', Westword, 18 February, https://www.westword.com/news/bitclub-network-was-too-big-to-fail-but-cost-investors-722-million-11642618 (archived at https://perma.cc/68E2-8A2N)

9   Weill, K (2019) 'It needs to look real': The Bitcoin scam that took buyers for a $722 million ride, The Daily Beast, 16 December, https://www.thedailybeast.com/bitclub-network-and-the-bitcoin-scam-that-took-buyers-for-a-billion-dollar-ride (archived at https://perma.cc/8LA9-CWM2)

10  Prendergast, A (2018) The rise and fall of a Bitcoin mining scheme that was 'too big to fail', Westword, 18 February, https://www.westword.com/news/bitclub-network-was-too-big-to-fail-but-cost-investors-722-million-11642618 (archived at https://perma.cc/68E2-8A2N)

11  Nikolova, M (2020) Programmer admits helping create cryptocurrency scam BitClub Network, Finance Feeds, 10 July, https://financefeeds.com/programmer-admits-helping-create-cryptocurrency-scam-bitclub-network/ (archived at https://perma.cc/M273-XP93)

12 Prendergast, A (2018) The rise and fall of a Bitcoin mining scheme that was 'too big to fail', Westword, 18 February, https://www.westword.com/news/bitclub-network-was-too-big-to-fail-but-cost-investors-722-million-11642618 (archived at https://perma.cc/68E2-8A2N)

13 Prendergast, A (2018) The rise and fall of a Bitcoin mining scheme that was 'too big to fail', Westword, 18 February, https://www.westword.com/news/bitclub-network-was-too-big-to-fail-but-cost-investors-722-million-11642618 (archived at https://perma.cc/68E2-8A2N)

14 Barber, G (2019) This alleged bitcoin scam looked a lot like a pyramid scheme, Wired, 10 December, https://www.wired.com/story/alleged-bitcoin-scam-like-pyramid-scheme/ (archived at https://perma.cc/GSR6-56MP)

15 Barber, G (2019) This alleged bitcoin scam looked a lot like a pyramid scheme, Wired, 10 December, https://www.wired.com/story/alleged-bitcoin-scam-like-pyramid-scheme/ (archived at https://perma.cc/GSR6-56MP)

16 Levenson, M (2019) 5 charged in New Jersey in $722 million cryptocurrency Ponzi scheme, The New York Times, 11 December, https://www.nytimes.com/2019/12/11/us/cryptocurrency-ponzi-scheme-nj.html (archived at https://perma.cc/YJ9A-AZPB)

17 United States Attorneys Office District of New Jersey (2019) Three men arrested in $722 million cryptocurrency fraud scheme, United States Department of Justice, 10 December, https://www.justice.gov/usao-nj/pr/three-men-arrested-722-million-cryptocurrency-fraud-scheme (archived at https://perma.cc/8FTJ-KX49)

18 Prendergast, A (2018) The rise and fall of a Bitcoin mining scheme that was 'too big to fail', Westword, 18 February, https://www.westword.com/news/bitclub-network-was-too-big-to-fail-but-cost-investors-722-million-11642618 (archived at https://perma.cc/68E2-8A2N)

19 Prendergast, A (2018) The rise and fall of a Bitcoin mining scheme that was 'too big to fail', Westword, 18 February, https://www.westword.com/news/bitclub-network-was-too-big-to-fail-but-cost-investors-722-million-11642618 (archived at https://perma.cc/68E2-8A2N)

20  Prendergast, A (2018) The rise and fall of a Bitcoin mining scheme that was 'too big to fail', Westword, 18 February, https://www. westword.com/news/bitclub-network-was-too-big-to-fail-but-cost-investors-722-million-11642618 (archived at https://perma.cc/68E2-8A2N)

21  Nikolova, M (2020) Programmer admits helping create cryptocurrency scam BitClub Network, Finance Feeds, 10 July, https://financefeeds.com/programmer-admits-helping-create-cryptocurrency-scam-bitclub-network/ (archived at https://perma.cc/M273-XP93)

22  Prendergast, A (2018) The rise and fall of a Bitcoin mining scheme that was 'too big to fail', Westword, 18 February, https://www. westword.com/news/bitclub-network-was-too-big-to-fail-but-cost-investors-722-million-11642618 (archived at https://perma.cc/68E2-8A2N)

23  Prendergast, A (2018) The rise and fall of a Bitcoin mining scheme that was 'too big to fail', Westword, 18 February, https://www. westword.com/news/bitclub-network-was-too-big-to-fail-but-cost-investors-722-million-11642618 (archived at https://perma.cc/68E2-8A2N)

24  Levenson, M (2019) 5 charged in New Jersey in $722 million cryptocurrency Ponzi scheme, *The New York Times*, 11 December, https://www.nytimes.com/2019/12/11/us/cryptocurrency-ponzi-scheme-nj.html (archived at https://perma.cc/YJ9A-AZPB)

25  Bitcoin Revolution Philippines (2019) Joe Abel is no longer in BitClub find out why, Bitcoin Revolution Philippines, 1 June, https://www. youtube.com/watch?v=_0WnJOyvzxQ&t=3s (archived at https://perma. cc/RS5K-NZV3)

26  Prendergast, A (2018) The rise and fall of a Bitcoin mining scheme that was 'too big to fail', Westword, 18 February, https://www. westword.com/news/bitclub-network-was-too-big-to-fail-but-cost-investors-722-million-11642618 (archived at https://perma.cc/68E2-8A2N)

27  Prendergast, A (2018) The rise and fall of a Bitcoin mining scheme that was 'too big to fail', Westword, 18 February, https://www.westword. com/news/bitclub-network-was-too-big-to-fail-but-cost-investors-722-million-11642618 (archived at https://perma.cc/68E2-8A2N)

28  Network, B (2020) BitClub Network scammers plead not guilty, Weeks wants out, Behind MLM, 17 January, https://behindmlm.com/mlm/regulation/bitclub-network-scammers-plead-not-guilty-weeks-want-out/ (archived at https://perma.cc/C8DR-2GFA)

29  Levenson, M (2019) 5 charged in New Jersey in $722 million cryptocurrency Ponzi scheme, *The New York Times*, 11 December, https://www.nytimes.com/2019/12/11/us/cryptocurrency-ponzi-scheme-nj.html (archived at https://perma.cc/YJ9A-AZPB)

30  Prendergast, A (2018) The rise and fall of a Bitcoin mining scheme that was 'too big to fail', Westword, 18 February, https://www.westword.com/news/bitclub-network-was-too-big-to-fail-but-cost-investors-722-million-11642618 (archived at https://perma.cc/68E2-8A2N)

31  United States Attorneys Office District of New Jersey (2019) Three men arrested in $722 million cryptocurrency fraud scheme, United States Department of Justice, 10 December, https://www.justice.gov/usao-nj/pr/three-men-arrested-722-million-cryptocurrency-fraud-scheme (archived at https://perma.cc/8FTJ-KX49)

## Chapter 9

1  Barkham, P (2012) John McAfee: 'I don't see myself as paranoid', *Guardian*, 20 November, https://www.theguardian.com/world/2012/nov/20/john-mcafee-dont-see-myself-as-paranoid (archived at https://perma.cc/X7V5-5V6P)

2  Bates, D (2013) Exclusive: Meet the harem of seven women who lived with fugitive software tycoon John McAfee before he fled Belize, Mail Online, 14 January, https://www.dailymail.co.uk/news/article-2262413/John-McAfee-Meet-SEVEN-women-lived-eccentric-software-tycoon-fled-Belize.html (archived at https://perma.cc/4992-XSW2)

3  Althaus, D (2012) Girls, guns and yoga: John McAfee's odd life in 'pirate haven', Reuters, 16 November, https://uk.reuters.com/article/belize-mcafee-murder-yoga/girls-guns-and-yoga-john-mcafees-odd-life-in-pirate-haven-idINDEE8AF03B20121116 (archived at https://perma.cc/6RDF-YV49)

4  Wise, J (2018) 'My power to demolish is ten times greater than my power to promote': How John McAfee became the spokesman for the

crypto bubble, New York, 17 December, https://nymag.com/
intelligencer/2018/12/bath-salts-to-bitcoin-john-mcafees-bizarre-
crypto-hustle.html (archived at https://perma.cc/6FXZ-Y3NL)

5 Barkham, P (2012) John McAfee: 'I don't see myself as paranoid',
*Guardian*, 20 November, https://www.theguardian.com/world/2012/
nov/20/john-mcafee-dont-see-myself-as-paranoid (archived at
https://perma.cc/X7V5-5V6P)

6 Rodrick, S (2015) John McAfee: The prophet of paranoia, Men's Journal,
9 September, https://www.mensjournal.com/features/the-prophet-of-
paranoia-20150909/ (archived at https://perma.cc/SX8T-RYQS)

7 Yahoo (2017) John McAfee's lab in Belize raided on suspicions he
was making meth, Yahoo, 13 May, https://news.yahoo.com/john-
mcafees-lab-belize-raided-011637364.html (archived at https://perma.
cc/J8Y4-SVQG)

8 Musil, S (2012) Fugitive John McAfee arrested by police in
Guatemala, Cnet, 5 December, https://www.cnet.com/news/fugitive-
john-mcafee-arrested-by-police-in-guatemala/ (archived at
https://perma.cc/4AGU-DYWG)

9 Honan, M (2012) How trusting in vice led to John McAfee's
downfall, Wired, 12 June, https://www.wired.com/2012/12/how-vice-
got-john-mcafee-caught/ (archived at https://perma.cc/R5FZ-64RM)

10 Zarrella, J (2012) John McAfee says he faked heart attack to avoid
deportation to Belize, CNN, 13 December, https://edition.cnn.
com/2012/12/13/justice/florida-john-mcafee/index.html (archived at
https://perma.cc/6WRH-L4MC)

11 Griffith, K (2017) 'It was magical': Wife of eccentric cybersecurity
millionaire John McAfee opens up about their first meeting – when he
hired her as a prostitute while on the run from murder accusations,
Mail Online, 12 May, https://www.dailymail.co.uk/news/
article-4500686/John-McAfee-s-wife-opens-life-prostitute.html
(archived at https://perma.cc/P6ZZ-6CY6)

12 White, D (2019) Fugitive anti-virus guru John McAfee, 73, arrested
with cache of firearms in the Dominican Republic while fleeing rape
and murder allegations, *The Sun*, 26 July, https://www.thesun.co.uk/
news/9571247/fugitive-anti-virus-guru-john-mcafee-arrested-cache-
firearms-dominican-republic/ (archived at https://perma.cc/4JSA-FMB5)

13 Wise, J (2018) 'My power to demolish is ten times greater than my
power to promote': How John McAfee became the spokesman for the

crypto bubble, New York, 17 December, https://nymag.com/intelligencer/2018/12/bath-salts-to-bitcoin-john-mcafees-bizarre-crypto-hustle.html (archived at https://perma.cc/6FXZ-Y3NL)

14  Wise, J (2018) 'My power to demolish is ten times greater than my power to promote': How John McAfee became the spokesman for the crypto bubble, New York, 17 December, https://nymag.com/intelligencer/2018/12/bath-salts-to-bitcoin-john-mcafees-bizarre-crypto-hustle.html (archived at https://perma.cc/6FXZ-Y3NL)

15  SEC (2020) Case 1:18-cv-08175-ER document 233, SEC, 16 March, https://www.sec.gov/litigation/complaints/2020/comp24771.pdf (archived at https://perma.cc/5ABT-TCHU)

16  Wise, J (2018) 'My power to demolish is ten times greater than my power to promote': How John McAfee became the spokesman for the crypto bubble, New York, 17 December, https://nymag.com/intelligencer/2018/12/bath-salts-to-bitcoin-john-mcafees-bizarre-crypto-hustle.html (archived at https://perma.cc/6FXZ-Y3NL)

17  Bryan, B (2016) John McAfee's mysterious new company is the hottest stock in America right now, Yahoo Finance, 18 May, https://finance.yahoo.com/news/john-mcafees-mysterious-company-most-183103324.html (archived at https://perma.cc/8X2V-VFFE)

18  Wise, J (2018) 'My power to demolish is ten times greater than my power to promote': How John McAfee became the spokesman for the crypto bubble, New York, 17 December, https://nymag.com/intelligencer/2018/12/bath-salts-to-bitcoin-john-mcafees-bizarre-crypto-hustle.html (archived at https://perma.cc/6FXZ-Y3NL)

19  Wise, J (2018) 'My power to demolish is ten times greater than my power to promote': How John McAfee became the spokesman for the crypto bubble, New York, 17 December, https://nymag.com/intelligencer/2018/12/bath-salts-to-bitcoin-john-mcafees-bizarre-crypto-hustle.html (archived at https://perma.cc/6FXZ-Y3NL)

20  Wise, J (2018) 'My power to demolish is ten times greater than my power to promote': How John McAfee became the spokesman for the crypto bubble, New York, 17 December, https://nymag.com/intelligencer/2018/12/bath-salts-to-bitcoin-john-mcafees-bizarre-crypto-hustle.html (archived at https://perma.cc/6FXZ-Y3NL)

21  Wise, J (2018) 'My power to demolish is ten times greater than my power to promote': How John McAfee became the spokesman for the

crypto bubble, New York, 17 December, https://nymag.com/
intelligencer/2018/12/bath-salts-to-bitcoin-john-mcafees-bizarre-
crypto-hustle.html (archived at https://perma.cc/6FXZ-Y3NL)

22  McAfee, J (2017) Bitcoin bouncing back fast from it technical
correction, Twitter, 17 July, https://twitter.com/officialmcafee/status/8
87024683379544065?lang=en (archived at https://perma.cc/HP9V-
48WG)

23  Canellis, D (2019) [Best of 2019] Find out how long until John McAfee
must eat his own dick (cos Bitcoin), TNW, 17 July, https://thenextweb.
com/hardfork/2019/07/17/john-mcafee-bitcoin-bet-million-dick-eat-
twitter-cryptocurrency/ (archived at https://perma.cc/MJ7L-WNHK)

24  Wise, J (2018) 'My power to demolish is ten times greater than my
power to promote': How John McAfee became the spokesman for the
crypto bubble, New York, 17 December, https://nymag.com/
intelligencer/2018/12/bath-salts-to-bitcoin-john-mcafees-bizarre-
crypto-hustle.html (archived at https://perma.cc/6FXZ-Y3NL)

25  Wise, J (2018) 'My power to demolish is ten times greater than my
power to promote': How John McAfee became the spokesman for the
crypto bubble, New York, 17 December, https://nymag.com/
intelligencer/2018/12/bath-salts-to-bitcoin-john-mcafees-bizarre-
crypto-hustle.html (archived at https://perma.cc/6FXZ-Y3NL)

26  Stead, C (2018) Verge cryptocurrency reportedly blackmailed by John
McAfee ahead of Wraith launch, Finder, 1 January, https://www.
finder.com.au/verge-mcafee-blackmail (archived at https://perma.cc/
N2K9-R926)

27  Stead, C (2018) Verge cryptocurrency reportedly blackmailed by John
McAfee ahead of Wraith launch, Finder, 1 January, https://www.
finder.com.au/verge-mcafee-blackmail (archived at https://perma.cc/
N2K9-R926)

28  Pearson, J (2018) John McAfee appears to move cryptocurrency
markets with a single tweet, Vice, 1 October, https://www.vice.com/
en/article/9knnpz/john-mcafee-twitter-coin-of-the-day-cryptocurrency-
markets (archived at https://perma.cc/W9XK-4GJW)

29  McAfee, J (2017) Since there are over 100 new ICOs each week,
and since you cannot pump and dump them (longer term
investment) it makes no sense to do only one per week. Many of
them are gems. I will do at least three per week on a random basis,

Twitter, 4 January, https://twitter.com/officialmcafee/status/9486841 54174099461?lang=en (archived at https://perma.cc/FG6F-MG4D)

30  Liao, S (2018) John McAfee reveals he charges $105,000 per promotional cryptocurrency tweet, The Verge, 2 April, https://www. theverge.com/2018/4/2/17189880/john-mcafee-bitcoin-cryptocurrency-twitter-ico (archived at https://perma.cc/9QYP-QDZF)

31  US Securities and Exchange Commission (2020) SEC charges John McAfee With fraudulently touting ICOs, US Securities and Exchange Commission, 5 October, https://www.sec.gov/news/press-release/2020-246 (archived at https://perma.cc/9Y9Z-YGVV)

32  US Securities and Exchange Commission (2020) SEC charges John McAfee With fraudulently touting ICOs, US Securities and Exchange Commission, 5 October, https://www.sec.gov/news/press-release/2020-246 (archived at https://perma.cc/9Y9Z-YGVV)

33  Kelion, L (2017) John McAfee says his Twitter account was hacked, BBC, 28 December, https://www.bbc.co.uk/news/technology-42502770 (archived at https://perma.cc/BM5E-2T5R)

34  US Securities and Exchange Commission (2020) SEC charges John McAfee With fraudulently touting ICOs, US Securities and Exchange Commission, 5 October, https://www.sec.gov/news/press-release/2020-246 (archived at https://perma.cc/9Y9Z-YGVV)

35  Kelion, L (2017) John McAfee says his Twitter account was hacked, BBC, 28 December, https://www.bbc.com/news/technology-42502770 (archived at https://perma.cc/DL7G-C9BV)

36  McAfee, J (2018) Due to SEC threats, I am no longer working with ICOs nor am I recommending them, and those doing ICOs can all look forward to arrest. It is unjust but it is reality. I am writing an article on an equivalent alternative to ICOs which the SEC cannot touch. Please have patience, Twitter, 19 June, https://twitter.com/officialmcafee/status/1008957156819914752 (archived at https://perma.cc/28MY-WJ8V)

37  SEC (2020) Case 1:20-cv-08281 document 1, SEC, 5 October, https://www.sec.gov/litigation/complaints/2020/comp-pr2020-246.pdf (archived at https://perma.cc/B4LN-TQAK)

## Chapter 10

1 NBC News (2018) See how many bills it took to buy a chicken in Venezuela, NBC News, 22 August, https://www.nbcnews.com/slideshow/see-how-many-bills-it-took-buy-chicken-venezuela-n902491 (archived at https://perma.cc/9YJX-M8VG)

2 Maduro, N (2020) Venezuela mulls 100,000 bolivar bill. Guess how much it's worth? Aljazeera, 5 October, https://www.aljazeera.com/economy/2020/10/5/venezuela-mulls-100000-bolivar-bill-guess-how-much-its-worth (archived at https://perma.cc/EM3M-H2NW)

3 Martinez, A (2018) Salary + 144 eggs: Venezuelan firm offers unusual monthly compensation, Reuters, 16 February, https://www.reuters.com/article/us-venezuela-economy-eggs/salary-144-eggs-venezuelan-firm-offers-unusual-monthly-compensation-idUSKCN1G02B5 (archived at https://perma.cc/JR54-8V3E)

4 Martinez, A (2018) Salary + 144 eggs: Venezuelan firm offers unusual monthly compensation, Reuters, 16 February, https://www.reuters.com/article/us-venezuela-economy-eggs/salary-144-eggs-venezuelan-firm-offers-unusual-monthly-compensation-idUSKCN1G02B5 (archived at https://perma.cc/R3W7-GFXB)

5 Sanchez, V (2019) Venezuela hyperinflation hits 10 million percent. 'Shock therapy' may be only chance to undo the economic damage, CNBC, 3 August, https://www.cnbc.com/2019/08/02/venezuela-inflation-at-10-million-percent-its-time-for-shock-therapy.html (archived at https://perma.cc/9JG8-AFKV)

6 Maduro, N (2020) Venezuela mulls 100,000 bolivar bill. Guess how much it's worth? Aljazeera, 5 October, https://www.aljazeera.com/economy/2020/10/5/venezuela-mulls-100000-bolivar-bill-guess-how-much-its-worth (archived at https://perma.cc/YW4P-N4CR)

7 Araujo, F (2019) Bitcoin v bolivar: Can cryptos save Venezuela? Raconteur, 17 December, https://www.raconteur.net/finance/cryptocurrency/venezuela-cryptocurrencies/ (archived at https://perma.cc/H9B6-63WG)

8 Bello, C (2019) Half a burger? Here's what one month's pay will get you in Venezuela, Euronews, 15 January, https://www.euronews.com/2018/07/02/half-a-burger-here-s-what-one-month-s-pay-will-get-you-in-venezuela (archived at https://perma.cc/JA76-HSVS)

9   Martinez, A (2018) Salary + 144 eggs: Venezuelan firm offers unusual monthly compensation, Reuters, 16 February, https://www.reuters.com/article/us-venezuela-economy-eggs/salary-144-eggs-venezuelan-firm-offers-unusual-monthly-compensation-idUSKCN1G02B5 (archived at https://perma.cc/U4K8-G2J6)

10  Laya, P and Zerpa, F (2018) The cost of a cup of coffee in Caracas just hit 2,000,000 bolivars, BNN Bloomberg, 26 July, https://www.bnnbloomberg.ca/the-cost-of-a-cup-of-coffee-in-caracas-just-hit-2-000-000-bolivars-1.1114321 (archived at https://perma.cc/V9ZS-AJHP)

11  Laya, P and Yapur, N (2020) Venezuela's Maduro vows to revive petro coin in his annual address, Bloomberg, 15 January, https://www.bloomberg.com/news/articles/2020-01-14/venezuela-s-maduro-vows-to-revive-petro-in-his-annual-address (archived at https://perma.cc/7XF4-HSPS)

12  BBC (2020) PayPal allows Bitcoin and crypto spending, BBC, 21 October, https://www.bbc.co.uk/news/technology-54630283 (archived at https://perma.cc/QHU3-8SF4)

13  Statista (2021) Number of daily active Facebook users worldwide as of 3rd quarter 2020, Statista, 2 February, https://www.statista.com/statistics/346167/facebook-global-dau/ (archived at https://perma.cc/MT5N-KXR6)

14  Cecchetti, S and Schoenholtz, K (2018) The stubbornly high cost of remittances, Vox EU, 27 March, https://voxeu.org/article/stubbornly-high-cost-remittances (archived at https://perma.cc/K3ZZ-8E84)

15  World Bank (2019) Record high remittances sent globally in 2018, World Bank, 8 April, https://www.worldbank.org/en/news/press-release/2019/04/08/record-high-remittances-sent-globally-in-2018 (archived at https://perma.cc/R964-VEKM)

# Index

# Also by Kogan Page

Available at **koganpage.com**